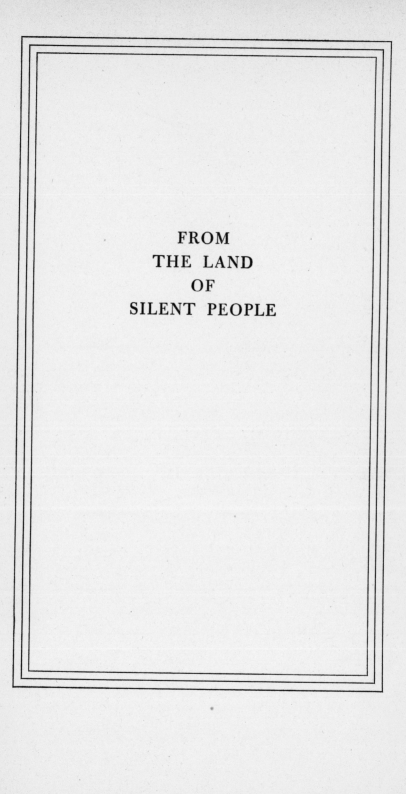

FROM
THE LAND
OF
SILENT PEOPLE

FROM
THE LAND
OF
SILENT PEOPLE

———◆◆◆———

Robert St. John

———◆◆◆———

DOUBLEDAY, DORAN & CO., INC.
GARDEN CITY 1942 NEW YORK

DEDICATION

*To Paul, Max, Sonia,
the Polish Playwright
with the Letter from
Mrs. Roosevelt, and
All the Other
Silent People
of Europe.*

Contents

vii

Contents

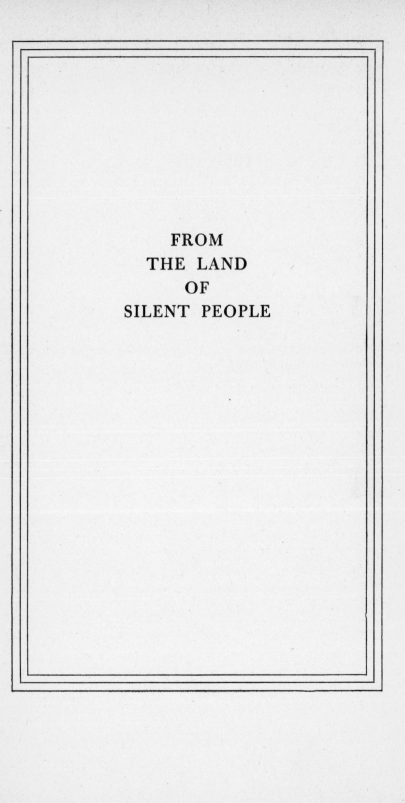

FROM
THE LAND
OF
SILENT PEOPLE

Foreword

———◄◆►———

WAR TODAY is that little curly-haired girl in the hospital in Argos, Greece, whimpering in the dark all night because her right arm hangs in blackened tatters and she wants her mother, who is dead.

War today is that man lying on the sidewalk with his guts sticking out of his belly and a hole through his skull and both hands blown off, screaming because he can't reach into his pocket to get a drachma to buy aspirin tablets to stop the funny feeling inside his head.

War today is that line of dead bodies in the doorways of little shops in Belgrade's Terrazia, killed when they rushed out to see what that crazy noise in the sky meant.

War today is that Serbian girl you promised to get out of Yugoslavia before the Germans or Italians caught her, and then didn't. War is what you think when you say "God-damned coward" to yourself and wonder what the Germans or Italians did to her when they found your name in her passport.

War today is thousands of Australian soldiers lying on the

deck of a boat taking them out of the hell of Greece and Crete, and reading books like *Propaganda for War* and trying to figure out what it's all about.

War today is smells. Smells from the red-hot motors of British lorries being run without oil on the quays of Greece so that the Nazis wouldn't be able to use them after the evacuation. Smells of chemicals dropped from the sky to set houses on fire. Smells from burning oil dumps. Smells of roasting human flesh.

War today is noises. Especially the noise that Stukas make when they scream down in a dive right at your head, with the wind making their sirens go round and round like mad. War is the noise the bomb makes when it drops. Thick, heavy noise. Then the noise when the glass breaks and the walls crumble. Then the noise of silence. That silence which holds all eternity in its grasp for a split second, and then lets go, quickly. More than anything else war today is the noise people make. Hopeless, scared, soul-seared people. When the split second of silence is over they scream and moan, or just whimper. War is the noise those seven hundred Greek soldiers made when the Messerschmitt came alongside their train and pumped death from machine guns into every car; and they ran up into the mountains and climbed trees or hid behind rocks and kept screaming for an hour after the Messerschmitt went away. Or the noise those other soldiers made when the Stukas dive-bombed the hospital train in which they were lying wounded and set all thirty cars on fire. Or the noise those thousands of Palestinian Jewish soldiers made when they were abandoned on the tip of Greece with two days' rations when the British finished evacuating the country.

You can forget what you see. And what you smell. But you can never forget noises. They beat through your head. They make you see Belgrade when you're in Cairo. They make you smell burning human flesh in Corinth when you're in New York. Noises won't let you sleep. You think you know about noises? Wait until you hear the noises of war, then you'll believe what I tell you. The noises war makes may soon drive the whole world mad.

I know about the little girl with the arm that hung in black shreds, because I lay beside her in a hospital all one night while she whimpered. I know about the rest, too, because I was there and saw things and smelled things and heard things. But I can't put it down so that it will make any sense to you. I don't know any of the answers, and so don't expect me to figure them out for you. I'm just an observer of the human comedy, only it begins to look like the human tragedy.

If I were on somebody's payroll in Berlin I could tell you things that would either make you hate the British, or make you say I was on somebody's payroll in Berlin. If I were on somebody's payroll in London I could tell you things that would either make you hate the Germans, or make you say I was on somebody's payroll in London. And it would all be the truth, either way. Part of the truth anyway. You can see what you want to see and think what you want to think when a war's on, and you can make it all fit into any pattern you wish, if you have a pattern already, but you can't change the noises and smells of war. It's easy to be a propaganda dispenser or a propaganda consumer. Everything fits in so perfectly. But I'm just telling you what I saw and smelled and heard. If it makes sense to you, all right. It makes no sense to me. If it fits in, fine. If it doesn't, just skip it. Then you will be able to forget. And that will be fine too—for you.

CHAPTER ONE

"Oi, Serbia!"

———◆———

It was a great day for us newspapermen when Yugoslavia's Prime Minister finally signed the Tri-Partite Pact one cold morning in March. Of course none of us approved this diplomatic defeat of another free country. It was simply that we wanted some sleep, and it looked now as if we could get it. Those of us who had already been through the same sort of thing in other countries like Rumania and Bulgaria were beginning to get worn out by this Hitler technique. I know that we correspondents lost more sleep and more weight than any of the kings or ministers or diplomats during the weeks of pressure politics and uncertainty, the flood of conflicting rumors, the war of nerves.

In every country the story had followed the same old pattern. When we got orders to buy plane tickets for Bucharest or Sofia or Belgrade because a new crisis had developed we knew exactly what it was going to mean. Weeks of "Will they? Won't they?" Weeks of dope stories based on the slimmest of chancellery gossip. Weeks of writing two or three long dispatches a day trying to keep the story alive while we waited for the inevitable to happen.

4

We felt most of the time as if we were pygmies, with our note-books in our hands, standing in the middle of an immense half-darkened stage (cf. *Emperor Jones*) while a hidden orchestra (strong on the drums) played a dreary dirge with a beat like the "Volga Boat Song" and two choruses, hidden in the wings, chanted across the stage alternate lines of something like this:

"Maybe they'll sign."
     "Never, never, never!"
"X says they will sign."
     "Y says they won't sign."
"Now they're weakening."
     "No, they're resisting!"
"Tomorrow they'll sign."
     "Yes, tomorrow they'll sign!"
"Wait, hold everything!"
     "Somebody's changed his mind!"
"Maybe they're just stalling."
     "No, they're resisting!"
"Maybe they'll sign."
     "Never, never, never!"

(Crash of drums and cymbals.)

"THEY'VE SIGNED!"

We had gone through that same sort of thing in Bucharest, waiting for the German troops to march into Rumania. And in Sofia, waiting for Bulgaria to knuckle under to Berlin and let the Nazi army sweep down across the Danube. Now we had gone through it all over again in Belgrade. But at last the jittery days were over. Yugoslavia had given Hitler the green light; sold out —body, soul, and railroad lines. We had written our capitulation stories, packed our bags, and argued over where the next crisis was likely to break out. Turkey was my choice. I was waiting only for an okay from the Associated Press to move on. But then something happened that forced us to unlimber our typewriters in a hurry, dig copy paper out of our suitcases, and get to work in Belgrade again. It was a completely screwball development. It wasn't at all according to the old pattern of Rumania, Bulgaria, and the other capitulation countries. That, of course, made it big news.

Despite public speeches, despite what the controlled radio said and what the weak-livered Yugoslav press told us, we all knew that Prime Minister Cvetkovich had at best only twenty per cent of the population behind him when he joined Yugoslavia to the Axis. But it had been the same in Rumania. There the eighty per cent had remained dumb. And we all expected the same pattern to be followed here in Yugoslavia. There was no reason to believe the eighty per cent would dare speak out in denunciation. But none of us had considered the possibility of a "Diaper Revolution." Yet that is just what it was, a Diaper Revolution. It all started with boys and girls ten, eleven, and twelve years old letting off steam with typical Balkan gusto. Sit-down strikes. Riots. A young revolution in the classrooms of the grammar schools. Hitler pictures torn to shreds. Cvetkovich denounced as a traitor. Slogans deriding the weakness of the government scrawled in childish writing on walls and doors. Thousands of hungry youngsters barricading themselves in their schoolhouses and refusing to obey orders from anyone.

Belgrade was never prouder of its young than that day in March when its young said the things the whole city wanted to say but didn't dare. Crowds of parents gathered around the schoolhouses and smiled silent encouragement up at the kid-packed windows. Police officials scratched their heads and wondered what to do about it. Riots and demonstrations by university students were old stuff to them. For generations they had been putting down outbursts like that with rubber hose and bayonets, but you can't use rubber hose and bayonets on ten-year-old boys and girls, especially if they are your own boys and girls, and more especially if they're saying things you believe yourself and just haven't the nerve to say.

One of the demonstration centers was a school across the

street from the Srpski Kralj Hotel, where most of the American press slept, ate, drank, and labored. At one point we watched boys and girls sitting at their desks working away with an eagerness seldom demonstrated before. We could see them through the windows with our field glasses. They were scribbling out inflammatory pamphlets. We watched them during the busy noon hour rush out onto the street and distribute them among the passing crowds. We also saw a furtive fellow in plain clothes slip one of the amateurish handbills in his pocket and duck into our hotel. I followed him to the telephone room, and when he went into a booth I eavesdropped from the next one. He called Secret Police Headquarters, identifying himself merely with a number. Then he read off the words on the leaflet slowly enough for someone at the other end to copy them down.

"Interesting handbills the kids put out," I said casually but with a wink as we bumped into each other coming out of the booths. He looked a bit startled; then he took me off into a corner of the lobby.

"You're an American, aren't you? All right. We're on the same side then. I tell you those kids out there may be making history today. Don't you see what this means?"

"What?" I asked dumbly.

"If this were just a few hundred kids writing a lot of nonsense it wouldn't mean anything, but these kids are only parrots. They're just repeating stuff they heard at home. That's why my office"—he looked around nervously—"that's why my office is watching this thing. This shows how the country feels. This is important. You newspaper boys better keep your pencils sharp. Things are going to happen in Yugoslavia yet!"

It was two-thirty the next morning when things did start happening. I was getting a little sleep, thanks to an arrangement with Ray Brock, of the New York *Times*. He had agreed to keep an eye on the city from midnight until dawn each morning while the post-crisis crisis lasted. I watched things from dawn until noon. We both worked during the afternoon and evening. It was a happy arrangement, because Brock had a weakness for rumba-dancing, which kept him, from midnight until dawn seven mornings a week, traveling from one to another of Belgrade's Serbian cafés, Russian basement dives, and cosmopolitan hot spots. And in those places it was always possible to pick up the latest news, fit to print or not.

At two-thirty on the morning of March twenty-seventh, between rumbas, Brock ran into a hot piece of news in one of his hangouts.

"They tell me," he shouted over the phone, "that fifty to a hundred army tanks are taking up positions around the city. Nobody knows what it all means. I'm going out now through Terrazia."

I agreed to look over the north end of the city and meet Brock in fifteen minutes at the Majestic Hotel.

I found that the streets were not only full of tanks but that thousands of soldiers, all in air force uniform, were taking up some sort of battle formation.

"Move on!" they barked when I tried to approach them. No one would give a hint of what it was all about.

I ordered my Serbian chauffeur to make for the Majestic. We were still two blocks away from the hotel when we were forced to a sudden stop. Soldiers with bayonets held at belly level made a circle around the car. The chauffeur and I were dragged from our seats and marched into a small park. What little Serbian I knew did me no good. We were prisoners, that was clear. Never mind why. Never mind what was happening. Never mind who I was. It made no difference. And never mind what all those soldiers with machine guns hidden in the bushes were there for. Just sit down on a bench and shut up. It was clear that those were the orders and no arguing.

The little park was filled with a select gathering. It was nearly three o'clock. The people who had been pulled in from the streets were a typical three o'clock in the morning crowd in any city. A few women who had been scrubbing office floors. A puzzled policeman. Two night club entertainers in backless dresses that swept along the ground. At least a dozen women of easy virtue, groggy from their night's work. A few girls of semipro status in various stages of intoxication. One man in spotless evening dress with a beautiful French girl who insisted: "You can't do this to us." Three old men loaded down with copies of *Politika*, the morning paper, full of stories designed to please Yugoslavia's new Axis partners, yet without a word about what had happened in the schoolhouses of Belgrade yesterday.

We gathered in little groups under the trees, away from the glare of street lights, and talked in whispers. Every few minutes a soldier came over and menaced us with a bayonet and told us in short Serb words to shut up. One man who had been an army captain said it looked like a military putsch to him. The crowd laughed him down. No one laughed when someone else guessed that the German army was probably coming down through Yugoslavia to attack Greece and that this was just a little precaution to see that the people didn't express their feelings too openly.

Just then I saw a squad of soldiers bringing in a familiar figure. Milan! Good old Milan, our favorite barman at the Srpski Kralj Hotel. Milan was one of my best sources of information. If anyone knew the answers, he did. We went off into the bushes and had a hooker or two out of a bottle of slivovich Milan always carried in his hip pocket for emergencies, and then he opened up.

Simovich, the commander of the air force, was behind it all. The retired captain was right. We were watching the unfolding of a first-class, full-dress *coup d'état*. On the stroke of two o'clock army units all over the country had been ordered out. At two-thirty they struck, surrounding the royal palace, the regent's palace, the home of every cabinet minister, all the police stations, the gendarmeries, city halls, and other public buildings. They had all their tanks, light artillery, and motorized equipment ready for action in case of opposition. Simovich was pro-British. He was convinced the country would be with him in his attempt to throw out the government that had sold Yugoslavia to Hitler and Mussolini. He was playing a dangerous game and he knew it. Prince Paul, who was ruling as regent for the boy king, Peter, was a "tough old bird," as Milan put it.

"Then there's the Gypsy," Milan said with a snarl of contempt. He was using the term of derision they all used when they talked in whispers about Cvetkovich, the Prime Minister, who had such a gypsy cast that the purity of his blood stream was often questioned. "The Gypsy'll fight like a cornered wildcat!"

"But they're taking no chances," Milan went on as he held out the slivovich bottle again. "That's why we're here." He grabbed the bottle back and took a big slug of the plum brandy himself. "See that building over there? That's the main police station. Everyone gets pulled in to the park here who approaches the place."

Milan said the coup was really being directed by the officers of the air force. Simovich trusted them down to the last man. Their plan called for the coup to be completed, for the country to be entirely in their hands, by dawn, which meant five o'clock.

The more Milan talked the more my blood pressure rose. This began to look like the biggest story in all of Yugoslavia's history. I remembered what the plain-clothes man had told me in the Srpski Kralj lobby. Out of the mouths of babes had come a call for the overthrow of the treacherous Cvetkovich government, and now Simovich and his air force boys were answering that call with tanks and cannon and machine guns. The Diaper Revolution! Whether Simovich won or lost, it was front page stuff. If he won, little Yugoslavia would be the first country in the Balkans to defy Hitler. Just last night Hitler had put on a big dinner party in Berlin for Matsuoka. The Yugoslav capitulation had been timed to impress the sly little Japanese Foreign Minister. Now, with the ink on the treaty hardly dry, it would be repudiated. Schoolchildren were going to make Hitler the laughingstock of the world. What would the German Führer say to the little Japanese Foreign Minister when they met at breakfast this morning? If Simovich had the nerve to go the whole way, this might just possibly be the turning point in the whole war. What a story!

I ran over to the light of a street lamp and looked at my watch. It was just four o'clock in the morning. That meant nine o'clock in the evening in New York. Eight o'clock in Chicago. Six o'clock in Los Angeles. Still plenty of time to make the morning papers, even allowing for the customary two or three hours for cables to get to America.

But the young air force officer guarding the entrance to the park wasn't impressed. He didn't know English, but he understood a little French and he listened patiently while I tried to tell him how important it was for me to get the news to America. As we talked he unwittingly confirmed all that Milan had told me, but that only made me the more eager to get out of this temporary concentration camp.

"Maybe in an hour," he finally said. "If at five o'clock all is quiet . . . If we have won without trouble, then you people . . ." And he made a gesture to indicate we would be set free.

Four-ten! Fifty minutes to wait! There was no sense trying to impress on the air force officer what those fifty minutes might mean to me. No one in the Balkans has any time sense. I finally was reconciled to that, after two years of futile arguing and pleading. There was no use trying to explain to him that Belgrade was full of other British and American newspapermen; that competition was keen; that a beat of a few minutes these days brought cables of congratulation for the man on top and "What-the-hell's-the-matter-with-you" cables for the rest. I had seen Leon Kay of the United Press and Michael Chinigo of the International News Service scooting out of the Srpski Kralj as I stumbled down the front steps at two-thirty. And Brock the Rumba Dancer! I was supposed to meet him at two forty-five! These men and a lot of others might be busy with telephone calls to Switzerland or New York right now, while I, trapped in a park with a lot of shivering prostitutes, drunks, and news vendors, was muffing the biggest story of the year.

I paced the park like a caged lion while a tough peasant soldier from the mountains, with long walrus mustaches, told two of the girls what he thought of them for breaking into an underground air-raid shelter in the center of the park and trying to set up business there. I tried to find a loophole in the bushes surrounding the park, but General Simovich had organized his coup, even to the guarding of his temporary concentration camps, with military thoroughness. There was a soldier with a machine gun or rifle every five feet, and no one was napping.

But finally at four forty-five the air force lieutenant, in a typically Balkan burst of softheartedness, called me aside, explained he was going to give me a break, and assigned a soldier to escort me through military lines in the direction of the Srpski Kralj. Near the hotel I ran into Kay and Chinigo. We walked along together doing that defensive parrying which rival reporters do so often when each wants to find out what the other knows and yet not disclose his own story. This time we finally agreed to trade information. They had a lot more details than I had about the extent of the military preparations. They knew how many pieces of light artillery had been set up in the streets, how many tanks had rolled into town, what regiments had entrenched themselves behind barbed-wire barricades. But they laughed at my version of what it was all about. Their story was that a peasant revolution had broken out. Mobs of Serbs from the mountain districts were marching on Belgrade to make some kind of demands on Cvetkovich. The army had been called out to defend the capital against the revolters.

By that time we had reached the hotel. All three of us broke formation and dashed up the steps and through the lobby. The telephone girl grinned as she saw "ze tres crazy Americans" diving toward her.

"You can keep your—what ees it you say?—chemises on," she blurted out in her broken English.

All three of us were shouting Berne, Zurich, Rome, Budapest numbers at her. She put her hands to her ears until we quieted down. Then she patiently explained that since exactly one minute past two all international lines had been cut; that the radio station was accepting no press messages, and that . . .

"I tink now ze breakfast ees good for ze tired journaleests."

Foolishly none of us took her suggestion. I went into the booth and called the American Legation. Maybe they could get word to New York somehow. But the ban on communications had now been extended to diplomats, an unusual procedure even in the Balkans, where we were growing accustomed to having every conceivable obstacle put in the way of sending news whenever there was any news worth sending. Then I studied a map. The Rumanian border was a matter of a hundred miles. It was a hundred and fifty miles to the Bulgarian frontier. It might even be possible to get up to Budapest or down into Greece before the phone lines were opened up again. But if this really was a military putsch, a dash in any direction would be futile. Frontiers would be closed and heavily guarded. And if a man did find some way to get out of the country it might be impossible to get back for days. By that time the story might have assumed even greater proportions: a bloody civil war or a clash with the Nazi troops who were already poised on the frontiers. Belgrade mustn't be left uncovered. Better stay here and take a chance on getting the first call out when the lines open.

While I was changing from the pajamas and overcoat in which I had been tramping the city, two local telephone calls came in. One was from a friend who said he had seen Kay and Chinigo in an automobile, apparently making for the frontier. The other call brought absolute confirmation that it was, after all, a *coup d'état,* which was succeeding beyond the wildest dreams of the plotters. That made the score even. If the two other press association men got out of the country with their stories about the military defending the capital against rebellious peasants, so much the better. They probably never would get back to report the real story.

It was light now, and I made another attempt to get to the Majestic Hotel and keep that two forty-five date with Brock. Traffic was moving freely through the streets. Early morning pedestrians blinked at the tanks, the barbed-wire barricades, the swarms of soldiers, but they kept moving. No one knew then whether to cheer or to curse under his breath. The city still didn't know what it was all about.

A cordon had been thrown around the Majestic. Those inside

the circle of soldiers couldn't get out. Those outside, like myself, couldn't get in. On the sidewalk in front of the hotel I suddenly spotted Dave Walker of Reuter's and the London *Daily Mirror*. For two years Dave and I together had covered every major crisis in the Balkans. Of the hundred or more Americans and Englishmen who had worked in these countries since the war began, Walker was without a doubt the best informed, no matter which country he happened to be in. We rushed toward each other. A good-natured soldier in the cordon let us talk a minute over his shoulder. It didn't take Dave long to unload what he knew. The facts were snapped across the soldier's shoulder in quick little sentences.

"Prince Paul has fled. Little King Peter will take over the country. Simovich will be Prime Minister. Cvetkovich, Cinco-Markovitch, and all the rest of the cabinet have been arrested. They caught some of them right here in the Majestic. They're still searching the hotel. That's why all these soldiers are guarding the place."

While we talked, the streets were filling up with people. They were dazed, bewildered people, still wondering what it all meant. Then faintly, far in the distance, we heard a feeble little cheer. It came closer, grew louder. You could sense the news spreading down Mihilova, the main street of Belgrade, and into the little avenues that crisscross Mihilova, like tongues of fire along gasoline-soaked bands of dry grass. The faint cheer became a roar, then an infernal din. No one could talk any more. No one wanted to talk. Everyone just opened his mouth and let out all the noise he could. Here were thousands of people who for months had been throttled, gagged, suppressed.

In the last few weeks they had wanted more than ever before to bellow out denunciation of their own leaders. They had wanted to sing their fiery old Serbian marching songs and carry flags in parades and tell the world how they felt. But they had been gagged. Now the gag was off. Simovich had done that. Simovich was a hero. Long live Simovich! Peter was going to be a king now in something more than name alone. Long live the boy king! Oi, Serbia! Someone started to sing that greatest of national anthems, "Oi, Serbia!" Thousands of lungs filled with air and roared out the words.

A little old shopkeeper ran into his back room and came out with a picture of Peter. Someone nailed it onto a stick, and the parade began. The day had started. A day Serbs will never forget, despite all the tragedy it eventually led to. Street hawkers began selling British emblems for the buttonhole. Where they got the thousands of little metal gadgets no one ever found out, but by night everyone wore one. Paraders carried Union Jacks of all sizes. Big American flags were pulled out of cedar chests and mothballs and hung on buildings.

But the pro-British, pro-Greek, pro-American part was incidental. A lot of people, a lot of sideline observers, missed that point. This riot of emotion was primarily a pro-Serbian party. Yugoslavia's new independence day. A celebration of the end of tyranny and suppression. Freedom had returned. Freedom to yell "Long live the British!" if you wanted to. Freedom to cheer for someone besides Hitler if you wanted to.

"How about the Nazis?" someone yelled. Ah yes, the Nazis. The crowd had almost forgotten the Nazis. A roar went through Terrazia. "Down with the Nazis!" I kept thinking, if Hitler could only hear them now! If Hitler could only hear how they said that word "Nazis" between their teeth, with all the hatred of a people betrayed and then liberated. If Hitler could only see how Yugoslavia really felt about him—Yugoslavia, which he had put down as his new ally—then maybe it would make him realize something about these other countries he had signed up, these other countries that were paying lip service to him. "Down with the Nazis!" The crowd kept roaring out its hatred, and then they started off with a great rush toward the north.

We were all swept along in the turbulent stream of the demonstrators. No one seemed to know where we were going except the leaders up ahead. Then we stopped and we saw we were in front of the German Travel Agency, with its invitingly large plate-glass windows and its big cotton swastikas on flagpoles over the sidewalk. If you're mad you have to hit something. That word "Nazis" had reminded the crowd it was mad. And when the crowd saw the big plate-glass windows they knew they had something to hit, a ready-made target. The only trouble was that there weren't enough windows. Everyone wanted to throw stones. The Serbs throw stones rather accurately. In a few seconds the plate-glass windows were in piles of ground glass on the sidewalk. The swastikas had been torn in shreds and burned. The interior of the German Travel Agency was a wreck.

I skipped off long enough to get my camera. When I came back I tried to take a few shots over the heads of the crowd, but the Serbs were too recently under Turkish domination not to be suspicious of cameras; and besides they were seeing Nazi agents everywhere that day. If I wanted to photograph this scene I must be a Nazi agent gathering evidence, trying to get onto a film the faces of those responsible, so that they could be punished in true Nazi style when and if Hitler got this country under his thumb again. That was the way they seemed to figure it.

It was a delicate situation. I hid the camera quickly and pulled out my American passport. But it was too late for that. Those on the edge of the crowd around me couldn't see the passport or hear me shouting: "Amerikanski! Amerikanski!" There weren't any more windows left to break, and they needed some new object of fury. It began to look as if I were it. Those close to me were growling short Serb words. Those in the middle of the crowd were roaring for action. Those on the fringe were crying for blood. Just then I remembered the foot-square American silk flag folded up inside my cigarette case. I had carried it for months, "in case of emergencies," as a soldier carries a roll of bandages. I yanked it out, waved it over the heads of those closing in tighter around me, and shouted: "Oi, Serbia! Oi, Amerikanski!" There was a split second of hesitation. My life might depend on whether this trick worked. Then the crowd roared back: "Oi, Serbia! Oi, Amerikanski!"

But the thing that really saved me was someone remembering the Italian Travel Agency, back in the heart of Terrazia. A new target. Another debt to be paid. And off surged the crowd. I ducked down a side street with my camera under my coat (thousands of other cameras were smashed or confiscated that day) and made for Nicky's apartment on the top floor of the Albania Building, Belgrade's one skyscraper, at the head of Terrazia.

Nicky was a handsome young Serb who had an important job in the State Senate. A private celebration was going on in his apartment. A dozen semihysterical friends were dividing their time between drinking strong slivovich from big water tumblers, leaning out the windows watching the people down in Terrazia, and slapping one another on the back. I stood there at the windows with them, watching the mob close in on the Italian Travel Agency. We laughed at the halfhearted attempts of the soldiers to hold them back. Then we saw someone throw a stone. The soldiers put down their rifles and bayonets and let the fun begin.

It went that way all day. From dawn until it was too dark to read the slogans people printed on pieces of cardboard and nailed to sticks and carried through the streets. From dawn until people were so tired they began to remember they hadn't eaten since yesterday.

Even the sky over Belgrade was happy. But once, about noon, a black cloud came across the sun. Thousands of people, only a generation or two removed from the soil, glanced nervously up over their shoulders at the sky. I knew what was going through their heads. The Serbs are a simple people and a superstitious people. It was a bad sign, that blot on the sun. Maybe some of them stopped singing and shouting long enough to wonder what this was all leading to anyway, this defiance of the steel and might of the Nazis. But then another brass band came along and they forgot—for the moment.

Periodically that day we tried to find some way of sending out the story of what was happening, but the phone lines were still cut and the radio station was still not accepting any messages. Late in the afternoon Kay and Chinigo suddenly showed up. I had been hoping all day they would succeed in getting across some frontier into Bulgaria or Rumania with their story of a peasant revolt. Instead they had been arrested not far from Belgrade and had spent the day trying to argue with soldiers who knew no English and spoke a language neither of them could understand. Finally they had been released. Now they were back and there was danger they would find some way to get the jump on the rest of us.

Just at dusk word spread that a new propaganda ministry had been set up. We all stormed the place, stories in hand. We waited in line for hours. A word was finally cut here and there, and our dispatches were stamped "Passed by Censor," and they said we were free to send them. No, we were told in answer to questions, we still could not use the telephone lines, but we could use the radio. A mad dash to the radio station. But there we learned a new rule had gone into effect. No dispatches could be sent by the usual collect method. That meant digging up great quantities of dinars, for our stories ran to thousands of words. Even by pooling all our dinars we didn't have enough to pay for even one dispatch. More valuable time wasted. And when we got back with big bundles of paper money everything had been changed again. Now the radio was closed down but the telephone lines had opened up. Only all calls had to be made from the three booths in the telephone exchange building, which was in complete charge of the military. And there were six or eight of us frantic to get stories off! In the sprint for the telephone building my long legs helped, and within five minutes I had the AP office in Berne, Switzerland, on the phone. The first call of the day out of Belgrade.

"St. John's 11928 Belgrade Direct. Yugoslavia tonight has more than a million soldiers massed on her frontiers in preparation for war, following a day of . . ."

That's as far as I got. Then the line suddenly went dead. I shouted to the operator in the big switchboard room. In a combination of French, Serbian, and English she told me, in effect, to keep my pants on; she'd get Berne back again in a minute. It wasn't a minute. It was twenty. In the meantime other men were dictating their stories. Finally I was talking with Berne again.

"St. John's 11928 Belgrade Direct. Yugoslavia tonight has more than a million soldiers massed . . ."

That's as far as I got the second time. By now it was beginning to be obvious that I was being cut intentionally by the military censor upstairs in this same building.

The third conversation, half an hour later, began something like this:

"Hey, Berne, skip the first paragraph. I don't think they like it. Let's start with the second. Ready? For twelve hours today a frenzied crowd . . ."

Then they cut me again.

Upstairs I found the chief military censor and tried to argue with him. I showed him how the civil censor at the propaganda ministry had read every word of the dispatch and had put his big rubber stamp on every page. It made no impression. I had discussed military matters in my first paragraph and they didn't like it. It would be useless for me to try to use the phone any more. They said, quite frankly, that they would cut me after a few words if I tried to telephone. My plea that none of us knew anything about a military censorship got me nowhere. They admitted they had no facilities for reading dispatches and cutting out what they didn't like. There was only one man available who understood English, and he was busy listening in and throwing a switch when he didn't like something. The switch had been thrown for me permanently.

It was a hard blow, because just the night before, the old Cvetkovich Minister of Propaganda had given me forty-eight hours to get out of the country on the ground that Berlin had objected to my stories about the schoolhouse demonstrations and had demanded my expulsion. I had chuckled to myself all day over my good luck. The *coup d'état* hadn't come a day too soon to save me. Now, cut from the use of telephone lines, I was in just as bad a fix.

It was midnight before I finished my futile argument and went out of the building to find that the military had taken over all taxicabs. I started to tramp the two miles to the Srpski Kralj. No food for the last twenty-four hours. Now all restaurants were closed. No AP story from Yugoslavia in any papers in America tomorrow morning except those twenty-odd words I got across before they threw the switch.

But at the Srpski Kralj I found that Eda had saved the day for me. Eda, who had wandered all over the Balkans with me, translating, getting arrested as a foreign spy, arguing with officials, and backstopping me in emergencies. I found Eda, with perspiration running from her in great rivulets, sitting at a telephone just phoning the last paragraph of my three-thousand-word dispatch from a copy which by some freak of luck I had left with her. A call had come in for me from Berne about eleven o'clock in the evening. Eda had grabbed it and saved me. But it wasn't a complete victory, because Kay had also received an incoming call, only his came through at ten-thirty, half an hour before mine. The military boys, in their confusion, had forgotten that newspapermen can send stories on incoming calls as well as outgoing ones.

While we had been fuming about communications Simovich and his new ministers had been busy. They realized what a dangerous step they had taken. They knew what Hitler in Berlin and Mussolini in Rome would be saying by now. They knew, as we all knew, that a necklace of steel had already been placed gently around Yugoslavia's neck. If Berlin and Rome gave the word, the noose might be yanked quickly and Yugoslavia might be strangled. Italian troops on the northwest. Italian troops in Albania. Nazi troops, Nazi planes, Nazi tanks lined up along the Rumanian, Bulgarian, and Hungarian frontiers and along the old line between Yugoslavia and what used to be Austria.

There was only one gap in the necklace of steel. That was to the south. The border with Greece. The narrow Vardar Valley. That was the hope. The Vardar Valley. They said there were three hundred thousand British troops in Greece waiting to back up the rebellious Yugoslavs. Three hundred thousand British troops with plenty of tanks, planes, and munitions. Who said so? Well . . . of course it wasn't exactly official. Not exactly. But for three weeks a tall, slim young Greek journalist, Pappas by name, had been shuttling back and forth from Athens to Belgrade. He carried a diplomatic passport and he whispered that he was on a "diplomatic mission."

While the Cvetkovich government was negotiating with the Axis about signing up, the ubiquitous figure of the Greek Pappas slithered here and there. He chose his confidants carefully. Foreign correspondents he felt he could trust. Serbian oppositionists, like the Simovich crowd. A few selected diplomats. It was dangerous business. He was dealing in dynamite. Not the kind of dynamite you use to blow up bridges but the kind of dynamite you use to blow up nations. He had just come from Athens. From "our friends down in Athens," he said, and he winked slyly. "You know, *our* friends!"

"Our friends" wanted Yugoslavia to know that a hundred thousand British troops had landed at half a dozen different ports in the south of Greece. He even gave us the names of the ports. The blue waters of the Mediterranean were black with ships. British ships. Ships carrying a mighty Balkan army that would help Greece and Yugoslavia defy the Axis, if Yugoslavia only had the nerve to do any defying.

I was one of the correspondents Pappas chose to confide in. I was introduced to him by a reputable, honest British newspaperman whom I knew and trusted. What Pappas said was hot news, because up until then there had been only vague rumors about British troop landings in Greece. He said I was welcome to use the figures and all the details he gave me if I swore not to disclose where they came from. "Of course," he explained, "I must warn you that the British will deny the story. They will deny it officially, but they will confirm it unofficially. They don't dare admit it for publication. You can understand why. It would give the Germans just the excuse they may want to attack us. But you can take my word for it that it's all true. The easiest way to check up on the story is to check up on me."

I did. It was too serious a story to put out without careful checking. All of us were bending over backward trying not to fall for anyone's propaganda. I asked some of the boys who had been in Athens all about Pappas. They gave me detailed reports. They were sure he was all right. Fine reputation. Important connections inside the Greek government. Very close to the British High Command. Often was given important diplomatic missions.

And then I went to the British Legation and asked them flatly how about these landings of British troops in Greece? Officially, they said, they were obliged to deny it. Categorically, in fact. But unofficially . . . well . . . and they hesitated and smiled. Who gave me the information? Pappas? Well, Pappas was a very reputable man, all right, and he had just come from Athens, and he ought to know what was going on down in Greece. So I sent the story about a hundred thousand British troops in Greece, with planes and tanks and munitions. Then I sent a story about the blue Mediterranean being black with British ships. Later I boosted the number to two hundred thousand and eventually to three hundred thousand, all on the say-so of the Greek Pappas and on the unofficial confirmation (but official denial) of the British Legation in Belgrade.

How seriously General Simovich himself took the Pappas reports and how much these reports inspired his *coup d'état* and his defiance of Hitler no one will ever know definitely, but weeks later some of his little circle of advisors, ministers, and army officers told me they had believed every word of the reports and had been convinced that at least fifteen British divisions and hundreds of British planes would rush to Yugoslavia's aid when the zero hour came.

So Simovich reformed the government and stalled for time while Hitler demanded to know what he was going to do about the Tri-Partite Pact and began preparing for the war all of us knew now was inevitable.

CHAPTER TWO

Waiting for War

———◆•◉•◆———

W<small>E SAT</small> in the open-faced dining room of the Srpski Kralj, watching endless columns of cavalry and artillery parade past the windows on their way to the frontiers. We were full of admiration of the horses as well as the men. Sturdy men and husky little horses, their harnesses decorated with the first flowers of spring and with branches of trees that had just sprouted finger-sized leaves. The men all seemed eager for action, and even the animals looked happy about it. They were going off to battle. They were going to show Hitler. A pint-sized nation was going to speak up. Look out, Berlin, here we come!

Most of these million or more soldiers who were mobilized during the last days of March and the first days of April really thought they were going places. They knew they had the reputation of being the grizzliest, fightingest bunch of soldiers in the Balkans, which really meant something, for fighting wars has always been to the Balkans what playing cricket is to the English or watching someone else play baseball is to the Americans. But often during that week some of us who had been up in Rumania and had lived with the three hundred thousand German soldiers camped there for months had some dark thoughts.

"Listen," someone would suddenly lean across the table and say in dead earnest, "you can't throw horses and peasant carts and mountain guns like that assortment out there in the street against the steel and stuff the Nazis have got all oiled up and ready for this show!"

"But Serbia's a mountainous place," someone would pipe back. "This is no blitz country. These babies will lose the plains, but wait until they get the Nazis into the mountains. The Serbs know their mountains. Remember the last war? They can retire to the mountains of southern Serbia and fight there for a year."

"And if the Germans cut their transportation lines how will they get food?"

Back came the answer: "Did you ever see what these peasants live on? Black bread and onions. They've got enough flour and onions back in those mountains to feed the entire army for at least a year. Besides they'll eat their shoe leather before they'll give in to the Germans."

"But will the Croats remain loyal? They hate the Serbs, you know."

The answer to that one never did sound completely convincing. Croat officers were scattered thinly throughout all six Yugoslav armies. They were expected to remain loyal, but even if some of them turned coat there was little danger, because few of them held posts of importance. As for the common soldiers, all of the Croats were stationed down in southern Serbia, whereas pure Serb soldiers were guarding the Croatian frontiers.

Despite all the arguing, the prospects looked pretty dark to many of us, even if there really were three hundred thousand British soldiers in Greece with plenty of British planes and even if the Croats didn't kick up any trouble. I remembered back a few months when I was living in Bucharest and saw division after division of those grim, gray-uniformed Nazis parading past my window. I remembered watching their twenty-ton, fifty-ton, hundred-ton monsters of steel snorting along Calei Victoriei. I remembered how they amazed Bucharest by never inquiring directions. Most of them, tens of thousands of them, had memorized the map of Bucharest, with its maze of winding streets, before they ever left Germany. And whenever there was any necessity for conversation they talked Rumanian. Maybe not perfectly, but a whole lot better than any of us who had lived in the country for a year or two.

I remembered seeing at the head of every motorized column huge vehicles that looked like moving vans. Before the wheels of the column had stopped, mechanics had unfolded the sides and were getting ready for work. Inside each of these vans there was a complete machine shop ready to do anything from fixing a flat to reboring a cylinder block. That was just one little example of the cold Nazi efficiency we saw everywhere. It was that kind of an army these poor Serbs would soon be fighting with the rifles they clutched so lovingly and the horses they patted so gently. No matter how much we might have disliked the Nazis, we were impressed by their army. No matter how much we sympathized with the Serbs, we knew theirs was a peasant-cart army.

One night that week in a cheap Belgrade *cafana* I met a Serb soldier from a remote mountain district. He spoke a little English. We got to talking about the approaching war. Someone mentioned tanks.

"Tanks? What are tanks?" he asked. It was obvious he wasn't trying to pull our legs.

We explained patiently, as you would to a man who had never heard of a telephone, just what this particular thing was. He listened in amazement.

"Those are the things you are going to fight," we told him. "And your job is going to be to stop them. But how are you going to do it?"

He just patted the rifle that lay across his knees. When we told him rifle bullets wouldn't make a dent on a tank, he went into a blue study for a brief minute, and then his face wrinkled up in thought.

"Are you sure there are men in those—those tanks?"

When we assured him there most certainly were, he brightened up. The problem was all solved.

"Then it's easy. If there are men inside, they've got to come out sometime, don't they? Well then, we wait until they come out, and then"—he patted his rifle again—"when they come out we shoot 'em!"

It was as simple as that! I shuddered. If this was the kind of an army Simovich was planning to throw against the Nazis, God help Serbia! Tomahawks against rifles. Rifles against machine guns. Machine guns against planes. But this was worse than any of them. Rifles against tanks!

One thing everyone agreed on was that Belgrade couldn't hold out long. Simovich issued a cagily worded proclamation announcing to the world, in effect, that there wasn't more than one chance in a million of Yugoslavia's becoming involved in war, but if anything like that did happen, "all governments concerned will be promptly notified that Belgrade is an undefended city."

Yes, Belgrade would fall quickly. The government would flee to a safe spot. Communications, if any, would be where the government was. And so my orders from Bureau Chief Robert Parker in Berne were to flee with the government. Meanwhile make any arrangements you think necessary.

Where would the government go? That was the big question. Naturally it was not a secret anyone was telling newspapermen. But we did know that Simovich had ordered a new short-wave radio station in Skoplje made ready for immediate use. It was the only other sending station in the country outside Belgrade. There were other hints that the government might flee to that south Serbian city. To the south of Skoplje was friendly Greece. To the west was the Adriatic. To the east Bulgaria, full of Germans; but the only way to get from Bulgaria to Skoplje was through one of the narrowest, steepest mountain passes in all Europe.

I can show you exactly what it was like. Put the palms of your hands together, pointing upward. Separate the fingers of one hand from the fingers of the other hand by one inch. The road is down where your palms touch each other. There you have that Skoplje pass. It was an old Serbian axiom that two men with rifles could hold that pass against anything. The invention of tanks, the military men said, hadn't changed the situation much. Two regiments or two battalions of properly equipped men up the sides of the pass could destroy anything that tried to get through. Yes, Skoplje was safe except from the north, and it would take months to push the entire Yugoslav army from the north down through the mountains to Skoplje.

It all made sense, and so I sent Paul Vajda to Skoplje to make contacts with the radio people, set up an office, and get ready for the big show. Paul Vajda was a Hungarian Jew, one of the most valuable men on the whole European staff. He had worked for the AP in Budapest for years. But a few weeks ago Berlin had been offended by a story the Germans mistakenly thought he had written. Vajda's friends in Hungary had whispered to him that he had better move quickly to a healthier climate, and so he was transferred by the Bureau Chief Parker down to Belgrade.

I was worried about Vajda's falling into German hands if war came, and we had to start scrambling in a hurry. Parker and I talked it over and agreed that Skoplje was the answer. Even if the Germans swept down from the north faster than we expected, Paul could always move on south into Greece.

Then I suggested that Max Harrelson, also of AP, go to Zagreb. His job was going to be to cover the capture of the old Croatian capital, which we figured would occur within the first few days of war. If it was impossible for him to get the story out of Zagreb he would make his way to Budapest as quickly as possible. The story in Croatia would all be pro-Nazi anyway, because no one expected that the Yugoslavs could hold back the invaders for long in that perfect blitz territory. Therefore we figured that it would make no difference even if Harrelson did have to submit to Hungarian or German censorship. He would at least have a colorful first-person story of the invasion.

As the week drew to a close we felt we had the situation well in hand. We were surely better prepared to cover the war than

Simovich was to fight it. That much was obvious. So we just hovered over Belgrade waiting for the kill to begin, like a flock of hungry vultures. Leigh White, of Columbia Broadcasting, and young Russell Hill, of the New York *Herald Tribune,* who had gone down to Greece late in March, thinking the Yugoslav story was all washed up, came rushing back. So did Cy Sulzberger, of the New York *Times,* who now decided that the Serbs would make mincemeat of the Italians in Albania the minute war was declared and left Belgrade to be on the scene in Albania for that show. Sam Brewer, of the Chicago *Tribune,* we were told, was also on his way up from Greece.

Toward the end of the week Vajda began phoning some beautiful color stories from Skoplje. Peasant women, their faces hidden by the traditional black veils, were pouring in from the hills, leading donkeys on which their warrior husbands rode, rifles in hand, ready to do battle for the fatherland. The south Serbian city echoed all night with the oriental wailing of the women as they saw their menfolk taken away on trains, and then they mounted the donkeys themselves and rode down the steps of the railroad depot and off into the hills again.

Some of the women sent a message to Simovich: "Take our men to fight the Germans, the Hungarians, the Bulgarians, and the Rumanians, but don't worry about the Italians. We'll take care of them ourselves."

Little Serbian boys made small fortunes exhibiting trained fleas that tried to jump from a chalked square marked "Germany" into a chalked square marked "Yugoslavia" and were driven off by other fleas, which the boys explained were the Serbs. Skoplje was in carnival mood. War was coming, and they looked forward to it down there. They looked forward to it with gusto. War made you strong. War made you brave. War was something they knew about. And then they would sit around telling stories about other wars and what the tough Serbs had done to the enemy with rifle and bayonet.

Harrelson's stories weren't so comforting. The Croats were being obstreperous. The old Croat leader, Matchek, who prided himself on never having worn a necktie and looking more like a peasant himself than the lowliest of his peasant followers, was making demands. Croatia must have more ministers in the cabinet, and jurisdiction over more territory, or else she wouldn't play ball. The Croats hadn't done any celebrating of the *coup d'état*. The Croats weren't a bit enthusiastic about the impending war.

And even in Belgrade the emotional drunk of a few days ago was beginning to wear off. The holiday spirit had disappeared quickly. People began to look worried now. Newspapers that hadn't been allowed to speak out for months, and then under the new freedom had lashed away at the overthrown traitors and the Nazis with strong language for a few days, now restrained themselves without any government order. Hitler must not be provoked. Some of the calmer minds began to argue that it would be better for Yugoslavia, and even for Britain and Greece, if Yugoslavia maintained a benevolent neutrality and thus prevented the Germans from using the country as a corridor through which to attack Greece and wind up the Albania sideshow.

Once more some of us were in trouble with the censors. The military ban against my making international telephone calls still existed, but Parker in Berne called me every hour of the day and night, giving me plenty of opportunity to keep a running story flowing to America. But now the civil censors started threatening me with expulsion, because I was writing as if war was inevitable. They knew it was. I knew it was. America probably knew it was. But we must play-act. We must not let Hitler know that Yugoslavia thought that war was inevitable. Otherwise we might be manufacturing the very excuse he needed to justify an attack. We pointed out that Hitler still had his agents in Yugoslavia and that he didn't need to read our dispatches to find out about the girding for war. But Simovich, in truly Balkan fashion, insisted we should help him play possum. It was disheartening to be in trouble with pro-British censors so soon after being ordered expelled by pro-German censors.

Late in the week the German Minister, Von Herren, got orders to pack up and get back to Berlin in a hurry. That looked like the tip-off that a break was due soon. I went down to the railroad station to see the Nazi diplomat off. The station was roped off. You had to have a special permit to get inside. Bayoneted soldiers kept back the mobs of men, women, and children, many in bright peasant dress, who had come with all their belongings, hoping to get transportation back to the towns of their birth, to the parts of this hodgepodge of a country where they felt they belonged, to get back to the soil from which they had sprung. Some were raw-boned Montenegrin hillbillies. Some were peasant farmers from the green hills of Bosnia. Others were fishermen from the Dalmatian coast, or Slovenes or Croats who had no sympathy for the Serbs' belligerency. Then there were the foreigners, Hungarians, Rumanians, Italians, and Bulgarians who feared they would go to concentration camps or perhaps even be shot if they stayed in Yugoslavia too long. The Germans had already been called home by their paternalistic government. Most of them had left on a big Danube River steamer the night before.

The streets around the depot were a nightmare of confusion. The *Queen Mary* herself couldn't have loaded into her hold all the baggage these frantic people wanted to take with them. It was piled in the big square in front of the depot and along the avenues branching out from the square. Trunks, mattresses, sacks made of bright handwoven peasant cloth, chickens, dogs, bags of cornmeal, even a sheep or two and a litter of baby pigs. Soldiers with bayonets on the ends of their rifles tried to explain that from now on there would be no rail transportation for civilians to any point in Yugoslavia; that the military had taken over all the lines for its own use; that all these people might as well go home, because the only train to move out of Belgrade tonight would be one international express. But none of them budged. That was the peasant in them. They didn't believe what they were told. They wanted to see for themselves. They were going to stay right there, forever if need be, waiting for trains to take them into the country, to what they thought would be safety.

We got through the cordon and into the depot. Hundreds of red-eyed women with their sullen husbands and sleepy children crowded the train shed, looking down the rails for trains which would never come. Somehow they had slipped through the cordon. A constant battle was going on as soldiers tried to push them out into the street.

The German Minister had a simple first-class compartment. He leaned from the window, chatting lightheartedly with members of his staff who were being left behind. I stood watching from behind a convenient post. Suddenly all conversation stopped. A group of young men was approaching Von Herren's car singing "Tipperary" and roaring with laughter. I recognized most of them as youths attached to the British Legation, many of them engaged in minor espionage and secret-service work. One of them, an assistant military or naval attaché, was going up to still neutral Hungary on some strange mission I was never able to get fully explained. He had—I wondered if it was by accident—the compartment next to Von Herren's. His pals boosted him through the window, threw his baggage in after him, and then followed for a farewell round of drinks. They pretended not to notice Von Herren. For nearly half an hour, until the train finally pulled out, they sang college songs and British war songs with such gusto that whatever last-minute instructions Von Herren may have had for his assistants were lost in the din. The Germans on the platform growled and grumbled and made some rather anti-British remarks under their breath. Von Herren stayed in the window with his jaws set and a forced smile on his lean, rather aristocratic face. The British boys were having the time of their lives. This was their country now, and to hell with Von Herren and all the other Nazis. This was their Roman holiday. They didn't have to worry about Gestapo agents in Belgrade any more. All of them had either fled, or been thrown in jail, or, as some whisperers said, been shot by hotheaded Serb patriots.

Two nights later I went back to the depot at midnight again. This time the rest of the German Legation staff was leaving. In the past few weeks I had gone to railroad stations in Bucharest and Sofia to see British diplomatic missions fleeing for their lives. This was a novel experience, seeing a German mission doing the same thing. In Bucharest, although the country teemed with three hundred thousand Nazi troops, the British had lived up to their tradition of diplomatic elegance by fleeing in a twelve-car train of beautifully appointed Wagons-Lits cars the like of which none of us had seen anywhere in Europe since the war began. In Sofia the train that carried the British mission, and also the infernal machines that later blew up and killed people in an Istanbul hotel, was also an all-sleeper train. But in Belgrade the best the Germans could afford, or obtain, was one second-class day coach in which forty-two diplomats had to sleep sitting up until they got to Berlin.

One of the departing diplomats was the German assistant air attaché, a pleasant young fellow who had been stationed at various times in London and Washington and who at heart was quite pro-American, although he didn't admit it to anyone. His room in the Srpski Kralj had been near mine, and he had been my chief source of information about what went on in Axis diplomatic circles. My British colleagues raised their eyebrows over my association with him, but most of them counted on me to supply them with any news I picked up in this way because of their own difficulty in finding out what was going on across the fence in the German and Italian camps.

"By morning," the assistant air attaché told me, as we stood beside the train, "there won't be a single German left in Yugoslavia except our military attaché and his assistant and their two servants. We've worked all day helping them make a fortress out of the legation. It's well armed and well stocked. They'll be ready for anything!"

"And what is 'anything' likely to mean?" I asked naïvely.

He just smiled, but as he jumped up the steps of the car a few minutes later and shook hands with me he said jovially:

"Cheer up, St. John, we'll be back soon. Probably very soon. And when we do come we'll bring a few souvenirs for you boys at the Srpski Kralj."

Then the train steamed away.

I stood on the platform for a full minute trying to figure out what he meant. "We'll be back soon." Did he expect Simovich would be forced to knuckle under to Germany and that normal diplomatic relations would soon be resumed? And what did he mean by that crack about "souvenirs"?

But this was no time to moon about things like that. There was news to be gathered, stories to be written, censors and telephone operators to be fought with. So I battled my way through the mobs inside the depot, and the mobs outside the depot, and the semihysterical people in the streets leading into railroad square. There were more of them there now than ever.

Belgrade those last two days of peace was a weird place. A heavy, depressing atmosphere hung over the city. Milan, our Srpski Kralj barman, was called into the army. Happy, well-informed little Milan, our font of wisdom. Milan, who was fat and thirty years too old to be a soldier. On Friday, when he appeared in his badly fitting uniform, we all bought drinks for this likable little fellow who for months had been mixing drinks for us. The liquor made him loquacious, and before he left he got quite confidential.

"I'm a good Serb," he said sadly, "and I'm no coward, God deliver me. I've fought in two wars already. I've got a few bayonet wounds on me I'll show you if you don't believe me. But I don't like this business. Not this war, the one that's going to start in a few days. We're going to catch hell, boys. War's different, you know, than when the best man with a bayonet could win. What can we do against these—these bastard Germans, with their planes and their tanks? We're brave, we Serbs. We're wildcats from hell when they set us loose. We don't know how to be afraid. But we're beaten before we start, this time. That's what I think."

So we bought Milan another drink and we told him he was crazy and of course the Serbs would make a good showing against the Germans. But we didn't look at one another when we said it, because we were beginning to have doubts of our own. Serious doubts.

When Milan went, the Srpski Kralj took on the atmosphere of a theater after the players have made their last bow, the curtain has gone down, the crowds have gone home, and there's no one left but a floor scrubber or two. A lot of the waiters had been called up, and even most of the bellhops, although some of them were so young they hadn't started to shave. We pressed buttons and nothing happened. A substitute telephone operator gave my calls to someone else and someone else's calls to me. The army started grabbing all the food in town, and the groaning tables of the Srpski Kralj dining room, where we used to eat with the gusto and relish of old Romans, didn't groan any more.

On Saturday I told Berne it looked like a matter of only a few days now, and Berne told me to be sure to get a thousand dollars' worth of dinars quickly, because once I left Belgrade it probably would be impossible to change American money into Yugoslav money, and I would of course need plenty of dinars to send off radio messages, or cablegrams, or to make telephone calls. I telephoned to the man who usually handled my money matters. He said he would be around Sunday noon with the bundle of dinars. Kay, of the United Press, said his office had given him the same instructions. His money man had already delivered a thousand dollars' worth of the Yugoslav dinars. Kay's pockets bulged with the stuff. He said he was all ready for the show. But I knew he hadn't sent anyone to Skoplje, so I thought I was one up on him.

Except for the dinars I was all set for action. Eda had gone to Istanbul. She hadn't wanted to go. She argued, quite logically, that she had stayed at my side through two years of riots, revolutions, earthquakes, and all manner of miscellaneous bloodshed such as only the Balkans can produce. Why shouldn't she stick on now? But I thought I knew what this Balkan war was going to be like. Balkan wars never had been ladylike parties. This one might be much worse.

If the Serbs really did hold out, we of the press would follow the government into the mountains. Living conditions would be tough. Food would be scarce. We might be stuck in those south Serbian hills for months. Maybe during one of their notoriously bitter winters. That was, if the Serbs held out. If they didn't, God only knows what hardships and privations and close shaves we might experience trying to keep ahead of the Germans. So I had insisted that Eda push off while there was still a chance. She got the last train that left Yugoslavia and crossed Bulgaria into Turkey. On Saturday I had a phone call from her. She was safe in Istanbul. That was one big worry canceled out. Yes, I thought I was all ready for the fun.

It was on Saturday that the Ministry of Propaganda decided I had embarrassed them once too often. Berlin had complained about Yugoslavia's military preparations. Belgrade had denied any military preparations. Berlin rebutted by quoting one of my dispatches. The minor functionary who gave me the bad news said the Minister of Propaganda would see me at three o'clock Sunday afternoon and tell me when my expulsion would go into effect. If I thought the action was unfair I could state my case then. But he doubted very much if it would do any good. So did I. I had had this trouble too many times before.

Once in Bulgaria and three times in Rumania the Germans had "suggested" that I be kicked out. Each time until now it had been because of some dispatch that hinted at the possibility of eventual war between Germany and Russia. That was what always made me so sure such a war was in the cards. Each time, some freak of luck had saved me from actually being escorted to a frontier. Once in Rumania I had had my bags all packed. The dead line for my departure was only a few hours off. And then, at almost the last moment, the government fell; and when the new cabinet was formed, a new Minister of Propaganda was picked, and he took office without being told anything about my case.

Another expulsion order had come directly from Carol's palace. The Rumanian king had tried to appease Berlin by personally ordering that I "henceforth be denied the hospitality of the country." But before they could expel me that time, Carol had abdicated; and instead of booting me out of the country, the new Iron Guard regime looked on me with great favor, because anyone Carol hadn't liked was their friend. In Bulgaria it was the excitement and confusion when the German army arrived that kept me from being ordered out of the country immediately. By the time they got down to business again I had been transferred to Belgrade.

The fall of the Cvetkovich government had saved me from expulsion here in Yugoslavia only a few days ago. But now Berlin was making the old demand again, and I knew that only war could save me this time. But it would have to come fast. Sunday afternoon at three o'clock was only twenty-four hours off. Some of my colleagues heard about it, and in the Srpski Kralj that Saturday afternoon they raised their glasses in a toast to "one more break for St. John."

We kept the lines to Berne humming all Saturday evening. Every few minutes there was another little development indicating that things were moving fast. Simovich issued an appeal to his people to stand firm, whatever happened, and to guard the thresholds of their homes with their lives if necessary. The streets were full of marching, singing troops. The stirring words and tune of "Oi, Serbia" rang out all evening. Every few hours sirens shrieked out the signal for another practice black-out or air-raid drill.

All the other countries in Europe had held such rehearsals so many times that all their people were equipped with headlight devices and blue-painted electric-light bulbs and black-out paper, but Yugoslavia had ignored this matter so long that now the only feasible black-out scheme was to pull a master switch in the power house and throw the whole city into indubitable darkness. It was all very annoying, especially if you were halfway through dictating a story to Berne when all the telephone lines, as well as the lights, were cut. Another thing that worried some of us was how the people would be able to tell a real air-raid warning from all these "wolf, wolf" scares.

Between the black-outs Saturday evening I went down to the Srpski Kralj dining room for dinner. Schmidt-Pop, Hungarian press attaché, was sitting at a table near the gypsy orchestra entertaining a tall, attractive girl with flashing brown eyes, a defiant tilt to her chin, and a crazy little thing she called a hat cocked over on one side of her mass of lovely black hair. He beckoned to me, introduced me to Sonia, and invited me to have dinner with them. Sonia was a well-traveled university graduate. She held an important government position in a country that boasts of five men's clothing stores to every woman's shop, thinks that a woman's place is in the home, and still follows the old rule of the animal kingdom that the male should do all the dazzling while the female sits back unobtrusively being dazzled. We chatted idly of the war, which all three of us agreed was just around the corner. Then a phone call came for Schmidt-Pop, and he had to leave the two of us to ourselves. I didn't mind.

Sonia had a flashing wit, an intriguing touch of fatalism, and that typically Slav attitude of enjoying the past, tolerating the present, and dreading the future. She was quietly telling me about her many British friends in Belgrade and how glad she was that they were on top again, and not the Germans, when the sirens went off and the lights went out again. A lot of the people in the dining room began laughing and fumbling for matches. The orchestra went into a wild gypsy dance tune. I was about to make some kind of a wisecrack when Sonia reached over and clutched my arm with the grip of a drowning man.

"Don't move!" It was a command the way she said it. "Don't move, because I'm terrified. Please hold my hand. Tighter! I hate all this. It . . . it frightens me so! The dark. Those horrible sirens. The . . ."

I wrapped my hand tightly around hers. She held it like a vise. But she suddenly stopped talking. I was glad. I never heard a voice packed with such utter despair.

Then the waiters began lighting candles, and I looked at Sonia. In the yellow of the flickering flame on our table I could see in her face what I had heard in her voice. I tried now to talk her out of it. I spoke as softly and soothingly as I could. Like you would to a little child.

"There's really nothing to fear, my dear girl. This is just a rehearsal."

"Yes, but the real show will come soon. Maybe tonight. Maybe tomorrow. Then what will we do?"

It was ten days later before I really realized what a great error I made in answering thoughtlessly:

"Well, I know what I'm going to do. I'm getting myself a car and following Mister Simovich and his putsch boys into the hills of south Serbia. If we're with the government we ought to be fairly safe and we ought to have some communications."

She clutched my hand tighter than ever. "Take me with you. Please take me with you! I can't stay here. You mustn't leave me behind. I'll die of fright, if I don't get killed by the bombs. I'll be good. I'll do anything for you you ask me to. And I won't make any demands. Just let me go along, too."

I tried to pass it off lightly. "You'll have to bribe me."

Just then the lights came on again. She let go of my hand as quickly as she had grabbed it. I could hear the little sigh as she released the breath she had been holding in her lungs. Her eyes began to sparkle again. She reached for her wine glass.

"You'll have to bribe me," I repeated maliciously.

"Bribe you?" she asked. She really seemed perplexed. "Why?"

"If you want me to take you along when hell breaks loose."

She looked serious for just a second, then she said lightly:

"Well, I'll promise to bring along three quarts of good Scotch and four bottles of French champagne, how's that?"

We shook hands on the bargain, then we talked of lighter things than war.

I hadn't been out of the Srpski Kralj since the day of the *coup d'état*, but that night I walked home with Sonia. She lived about a mile from the hotel. It was a pleasant walk. It was about one o'clock in the morning. Most of Belgrade had gone to bed. A bright moon flashed its reflection down on the Danube and the Sava where they met. It was spring in Kalemegdon Park. We sat for a few minutes on one of the benches. There was a clean, fresh smell to the air. You could see the forsythia blossoms in the moonlight.

"Nice, isn't it?" she asked softly.

"For how long?" I asked. "Next week this clean fresh air may smell of gunpowder, and burning buildings and burning people."

I knew as soon as I had said it that I shouldn't have. The words just slipped out. I was itching to cover a good war, but it made me bitter to think what a mess the Nazis would probably make of this little city on the Danube.

"Why do you always have to talk of war?"

"Because, my dear girl, war is my business. And it won't be long before it will be Yugoslavia's business too."

Sonia was quite calm all the way home, but as I said good night in the dark hallway of her apartment house she clutched my arm again as she had done at the Srpski Kralj.

"You promised on your honor, you know, to take me with you when you leave Belgrade."

I said, sure, and then she wrote her telephone number in my little black book, and on the way home to the hotel I tried to memorize the way to get to her apartment house. Telephone lines might not be working for long.

Back at the Srpski Kralj the operator said Berlin had been trying to get me for half an hour. She put the call on my room phone a few minutes later.

"What are you doing tonight?" someone in the Berlin office of the AP asked.

"I was just thinking of bed. So what? Have you got a little party on up there?"

"Seriously, St. John, if I were you I wouldn't go to bed tonight. So long."

"Hey, wait a minute. Why shouldn't I go to bed?"

"I don't have any idea," came back the voice from Berlin, "but we think up here it would be an excellent night for you to sit up listening to the music from the Berlin broadcasting station."

Something big was surely in the wind. The AP bureau in Berlin knew what was going to happen, but they didn't dare be specific over the telephone. I ran down to Brock's room. He was pounding out his Sunday-morning story. It was mostly based on some information that one of his usually reliable diplomatic informers had given him about how this Yugoslav mess would be patched up; how there was no immediate prospect of war. Brock wasn't very sold on the story himself, but he trusted the informer's judgment. We talked about my call from Berlin and decided Hitler was probably going to declare war on someone during the night, either Greece or Yugoslavia. So we ordered a dozen bottles of beer and started the death watch.

Just before two o'clock I made the last telephone calls I was ever going to make in Yugoslavia. First I called Harrelson up in Zagreb. He said everything was quiet. We discussed for the last time the plan for him to head for Budapest if and when the German troops swept through Croatia. Then I called Paul Vajda down in Skoplje. There was nothing quiet about Skoplje, Paul said. The streets and cafés and railroad depots were all packed with soldiers. The Serbs down there wanted to declare war on Germany without giving Hitler a chance to take the initiative. I told Paul about the message from Berlin.

"Well then, I may be seeing you down here in a couple of days! We're all set for you. Radio station has agreed to send our dispatches. I've got a swell office set up. But be sure to bring all the clothes and books and other stuff I left in the closet of your hotel room."

Then I called Berne with a new "top" for Sunday papers. If I had only known it was the last time I would ever talk to the Berne office, and the last time for a full month I would be in contact with the Associated Press, I would have sent off a few personal farewell messages. But all I said was to be sure to keep

a man on tap in the office all night because I probably would
have something more for them. Then I dictated a story that war
between Germany and Yugoslavia was without doubt now only
a matter of hours. (If I happened to be wrong I had little to
lose, because I was due for expulsion within thirteen hours anyway.) The latest straw in the wind, I told them, was an enig-
matic message sent over the Belgrade short-wave radio station.
Just before the transmission closed down for the night we heard
the announcer say:

"Calling the Yugoslav Legation in Sofia. Yugoslav Legation
in Sofia please stand by for an important message."

When the message was finally read it went something like this:

*"Cedam, pet, cedam, tcetere, iedan, cedam, dwa, cedam,
pet . . ."*

All Serbian numbers. Nothing but numbers. Of course it was
a message in diplomatic code. But the significant thing was that
the Belgrade government was being forced to use the radio to
get orders to its Sofia Legation. It meant that telephonic and
telegraphic communications had been cut between Belgrade and
Sofia. Cut by the Bulgarians. Cut for everyone. Not just for
journalists and private individuals, but even for the Yugoslav
government. Why had Bulgaria taken this drastic step? And why
was Belgrade so anxious to get this early morning message to its
legation in Sofia? Obviously the zero hour was almost here.

So Brock and I kept the radio tuned to Berlin, and every half-
hour we telephoned a few of our best contacts. Only one of them
laughed at us. A diplomat who must remain unnamed told us
to go to bed and stop being sensationalists. He was trying to sleep
and he wished we would, too. He was tired of these "newspaper
scares." But Arthur Lane, the American Minister, was of a different mind. He and his wife were taking turns at sleeping. One
of them would always be awake tonight. We must be sure to let
him know the minute we got anything definite.

We sent a man off to the government buildings in a taxi. He
came back about three o'clock with his report. No office lights
were burning. No automobiles were around the ministries. It

looked as if the unnamed diplomat was right. Why didn't we quit for the night and go to bed? But the AP office in Berlin had said to stay awake, and the AP in Berlin ought to know.

And so Brock and I opened another bottle of beer and kept the radio going.

CHAPTER THREE

Bloody Sunday

IT WAS ABOUT FOUR-THIRTY as I remember it when Brock and I
heard Ribbentrop begin to bellow over the radio. You couldn't
mistake that voice. Neither of us could make out very well exactly what he was saying, and so I phoned Max Merzljak. Max
was our permanent Yugoslav correspondent. If I could wake him
up he could listen over his radio and translate for us. But Max
wasn't asleep. He answered as soon as his phone started ringing.
I could hear his radio blaring away. Max could hardly talk, he
was so excited. It was hard to hear what he was trying to stam-
mer. He spoke English rather badly, anyway, and Ribbentrop's
voice over his radio, and ours, too, made an awful noise. What
I understood him to be repeating, over and over again, louder
and louder each time, sounded like:

"War! War! War is here, St. John. War, I tell you. Hitler
says it. Hitler tells his army to march. Ribbentrop reads the
orders. They march against Yugoslavia. Against Greece. I see
you at the Srpski Kralj when I dress. Maybe one hour. Maybe
sooner. My God, it is awful!"

43

That was the last time I ever heard from Max. We liked Max. He held half a dozen university degrees and he had written books in three or four languages. But the real reason we liked him was because he was the best poker player in the Balkans, and what was much more important, he was the best tipster any American newspaperman ever had in Belgrade. Or English newspaperman, either. I haven't heard yet what happened to Max. Maybe he was just hit by a bomb. All I know is that his name is on the list of the "missing."

Ribbentrop was still talking when the Belgrade air-raid sirens went off. We knew they meant business this time, but the rest of Belgrade didn't know it. There were three hundred thousand people in Belgrade that Sunday morning. Probably not more than three hundred of them, and maybe not more than three dozen, heard the declaration of war from Berlin. And so it's no wonder everybody woke up when they heard the sirens and then rolled over and went back to sleep again. Of course they thought it was just another one of those damned rehearsals.

We tried to telephone to Berne. We weren't very surprised when the operator said all international lines were cut. Our only chance to get a story out now was the radio. Brock and I pulled out our typewriters, and we each wrote a short dispatch. Ribbentrop hadn't finished his roaring when I started off for the radio station in a taxicab.

The radio operator didn't know about the declaration of war. His business was to send messages by radio, not to listen to the radio. I didn't tell him his country was being invaded. I wanted to get off the two dispatches I had in my pocket. There weren't any army officers around at that time of the morning, and so I slipped the operator a handful of dinars. Just forget there isn't any censor's mark on these messages, I said. Or put a stamp on them yourself, if you can. Anyway, send them off quickly. He took the dinars and promised to start tapping them out within the hour. I was sure he would, but then I didn't realize what hell would be popping around that radio station before the hour was up.

On the way back to the Srpski Kralj I saw an air-force officer waving his arms like mad at every car going by. He was trying to find a taxi, but my taxi was the only one around. He seemed very excited. Figuring that he might have some inside news, I picked him up. He asked me for God's sake, for Serbia's sake, please to take him to General Headquarters on Zrimskoga. He acted very dramatic. Very patriotic. Serbia was about to fight for her honor. Yes, I told him, I knew about the broadcast from Berlin. But did I know, he asked, about the formation of thirty-two German bombers that had just crossed the frontier? They must have taken the air before Ribbentrop finished talking. The air force had just got a report from one of the frontier posts. The officer was very excited. I couldn't understand everything he said, because he mixed French words and Serb words and English words all together. But I did understand the important thing. The big bombers were coming toward Belgrade. They ought to be here any minute.

When I got back to the Srpski Kralj, Brock had dragged a card table onto the balcony of the room we were using for an office. The balcony hung way over the street. You could see in almost every direction. A good place to watch an air raid, we had said, half jokingly, earlier in the night. Now that was just what we were going to use it for. Only Brock didn't know it yet. A waiter was setting delicate china cups on a clean white table-cloth. He was too old to carry a rifle. When I saw that white tablecloth I thought of the thirty-two bombers and what good bandages it would make. Brock was humming "Oi, Serbia." He was happy about the whole thing. He had been in Yugoslavia only six months, but he was more Serbian than the Serbs. He was sure Hitler had put his foot into a hornets' nest this time. When he saw me, Brock broke into one of the *Comitaji* battle songs. Brock should have been a member of the Comitaji himself. I was out of breath from running up the stairs. I told myself that maybe I was getting too old for this sort of business after all.

"Planes, Ray!" I yelled at him when I got my breath. I

pointed out the window toward the sun that was just daubing
some clouds with big globs of red and pink and scarlet.

"Nazi planes!" I yelled at him. "Thirty-two! Belgrade!"

Brock got the point. He grabbed his field glasses. The ones
with artillery markings so that you could figure out distances.
We went out onto the balcony. Somehow the card table got
knocked over. The two cups fell down on the sidewalk. They
landed just in front of a fellow carrying a big bundle of newspapers. He jumped at least a foot. Cheer up, brother, I yelled at
him, worse things than cups will be dropping around you soon.
Of course he didn't know what I was talking about. Not many
Serbs understand English. Then I laughed. Brock was too busy
looking into the clouds to pay any attention. What made me
laugh was that fellow with his newspapers. He thought he was
going to sell them.

We heard the planes before we saw them. At first it was just
a faint drone. Like a swarm of bees a long way off. Then louder.
Louder! LOUDER! Now they made a deep roar. Louder! Closer!
There they are, Brock yelled. Thirty or forty of them! What a
perfect formation! But why aren't there any Yugoslav fighters
up there heading them off? Look, they're coming right at us!
Right at the Srpski Kralj!

All at once a million machine guns began talking. They
seemed like a million to us, anyway. That deep-throated booming must be from Yugoslav pom-poms. We knew the next noise
came from ack-ack guns. A dozen of them must have gone off
all at the same time. Now the sky was full of black and white
puffs. They looked like little clouds. Then they disintegrated.
That was shrapnel from the ack-ack guns. Some of the stuff
went pretty close to the bombers, but the bombers didn't stop.
They didn't even get out of formation. They seemed to be laughing at these childish efforts of little men down on the earth to
bother them. We were breathing in short little jerks. The planes
seemed almost overhead. But suddenly they swerved away from
us. They were going over to the southwest. Brock was still following them with his glasses. They must have been flying at ten

thousand feet. All at once they broke formation. The leader went into a fast dive. We could tell about where he dropped his first bombs. Then the dull thuddy sound. And in a couple of seconds we heard the thick noise walls make when they fall into the street in pieces.

They've got the government buildings in Zrimskoga, Brock yelled above the noise. Probably the Prime Minister's office. Or the War Office.

Now we could see one plane, then another, then another, playing follow the leader. They were diving down into the smoke and fire set up by that first stick of bombs.

I spotted the second lot of planes while Brock was still watching what the first bunch was doing. The second three dozen came out of the clouds just like the first. Only this formation was flying lower. They were coming closer and closer. They were heading right for the Srpski Kralj, just like the others. But these didn't swerve off. I guess Brock and I went through the door and out into the hall and down the stairs side by side. Maybe we weren't exactly afraid, but I guess we both ran pretty fast. The lobby was packed with men and women. There wasn't any dugout in the cellar. Yugoslavia had planned to stay neutral. And besides, Belgrade was going to be declared an undefended city if war ever came. Only when it did come the bombers were over the city before anyone could make any declarations.

And so we stood in the lobby looking dumbly into each other's faces and listening to the God-damned roar up in the sky right over us. Then we heard the leader start his dive. I don't think anyone breathed during those few seconds. We knew the nose of that plane was pointed right at our hotel roof. We could hear the song a plane sings to you when it dives down from the clouds. I kept thinking the plane wasn't aiming just at the hotel but right at me, personally. It really was a relief when the bombs finally fell. Not that the bombs didn't affect us too. They made our insides do somersaults. But at least the suspense was over. The whole building shuddered when that first stick of bombs hit the roof. We could hear wagonloads of tiles falling into the street. No one screamed. No one spoke. We just stood riveted to the spots we had picked, like the book told us to, under arches or beams or in doorways.

When the second bomber came roaring down it wasn't so bad. Now we knew we could take it. After the third or fourth it began to get monotonous, except that I kept thinking the walls might fall in on us. I didn't count how many planes came at the Srpski Kralj. There must have been at least ten of them.

The last bomb landed in the street and blew out the big plate-glass windows in the lounge. Nobody was in there, and so it was all right. Only when the doors blew off, because of the air compression, a man standing ten feet away got hit by one of them when it flew across the lobby. Then the planes went off to some other part of the city, but we all continued standing there right where we had been all the time.

I remember I kept thinking about that German air attaché. "We'll be back soon." So these were the souvenirs! Nice little remembrance, thanks! The bastard! Or had he been trying to give me a tip? Should I have been smart enough to know what he meant and moved out of the Srpski Kralj?

They've gone away now. Not far, of course. You can still hear them droning up there in the sky. Maybe they'll be back in a minute or two. I had always thought I would be scared as hell in an air raid. Well, I guess I was scared all right now, but I was madder than I was scared. What disturbed me the most was why there wasn't any opposition up there in the sky. Why were these Nazi bombers having it all their own way? Where were the Yugoslav fighters? And how about those hundreds of British planes I had been writing about? They should have been here by now from their bases in Greece.

Then I looked around for the first time. I could see the blond head of Cecil Brown, of Columbia, sticking up above the crowd. Chinigo, of INS, was standing beside him. Leigh White, the other Columbia man, was there, too. Kay wasn't anywhere in sight. Then I saw Russell Hill hugging his little portable typewriter in a tin case under his arm, and I finally came back to

earth again. Of course! I had forgotten! We were newspapermen. We had a job to do, even if the planes were still up there.
Even if the phone lines were still cut.

So Russell and I went out into the street to look things over.
We had to dodge the tile shingles still falling off the roof. The
air was thick with clouds of plaster dust and some kind of white
smoke with a stench like sulphur. If we didn't stick close together we couldn't see each other. The street was so full of broken
glass and other debris that we didn't notice at first where the
sulphur smoke was coming from. But then we nearly stepped on
one of the crazy things. We bent down to look at it. Don't touch
it, Russell yelled. I didn't. It was a thin piece of metal about a
foot square, with wires attached to it. It must have been coated
with some kind of chemical that sent up the acrid white smoke.
Through the smoke you could occasionally see little spurts of
yellow-red fire. Now that we looked we could see that the streets
and sidewalks in every direction were covered with the incendiary plates. One had dropped on the roof of a trolley car,
one of those streamlined jobs built in Italy for the British and
then sold at bargain prices to the Yugoslavs when the British
refused to accept delivery because of the war. It had set the whole
roof on fire. Two taxicabs were burning, too. Nobody was doing
anything about the fires.

A man with an armband that must have said something like
"Air Raid Warden" in Serbian came running down the street.
I imagine he was trying to tell us to be careful not to step on the
chemical plates. We didn't understand him, but we were stepping gingerly anyway. I wanted to get off a little way and look
up at the Srpski Kralj to see what damage had been done. When
we did look up we saw. We saw that the roof was full of holes. Big,
jagged, round holes. Ugly holes, like you'd make if you poked
your fist through the head of a drum. The whole top story was
a mass of wreckage. While we stood there looking, fire began
to come out of a lot of the holes in the roof. Black smoke poured
out too. The boys who brought the souvenirs had dropped light
bombs on the roof to make holes through the steel and slate.

Then their pals had come out of the clouds and dropped the incendiary plates right through the holes. Of course all of them hadn't gone where they were supposed to go. Most of them had landed in the street, on the stone pavement where they did no harm. But enough had gone through the holes in the roof to make a furnace out of the inside of the hotel.

Hill and I went back into the lobby. You could tell by looking at them that these people didn't know the place was on fire. We decided not to tell them. And not even to tell the desk clerk. He was an excitable old fellow. Hill and I thought we could handle the situation alone, and so we ran upstairs to the fifth floor and started banging on doors to be sure no people were trapped in their rooms. The top floor, the sixth, was empty. This was the only time I was glad that even the best hotels in the Balkans have bugs. They had closed off the sixth floor a few days ago to try to get rid of the bugs. If there were any left up there after they got through disinfecting the rooms, Hill said, they're roasting now. We could feel the heat down on the fifth floor.

It was a good thing Hill and I got that idea about routing people out of their rooms. A lot of people had stayed in their beds. They seemed to think they were safer with their heads hidden under blankets than anywhere else. If they didn't open up when we knocked, Hill and I put our shoulders to the doors and broke in. You've got five minutes, we told them, to get dressed and pack up and get out of the hotel. Be fast! By the time we had covered the whole fifth floor the fire was running in little rivers down the staircase from the sixth floor.

A lot of people got angry at us for breaking into their rooms. Especially one woman, who said she was a countess. Well, we told her, you can burn as fast as anyone else. She wanted to know what we meant about burn. We told her the hotel was on fire. She gave a scream you could have heard a block if the planes hadn't still been making noises. She was trying to hide her bare legs with a bath towel. But Hill and I weren't interested in legs. Not even a countess's legs.

By the time we got down to the second floor we were damned

tired. We had routed people out of a dozen rooms. I think we saved a few of them from being trapped. Actually there wasn't much danger for us, because the planes were off in some other part of the city. We could hear the explosions of bombs every once in a while above the noise of the gunfire. If the planes had come back just then to the Srpski Kralj we probably would have run downstairs and let the countess and all the rest of them burn to death.

The door of Room 225 on the second floor was one of the locked ones. I asked Hill to help me break it down. You damn fool, Hill said, that's your own room. I pulled the key from my pocket and opened the door. That was the first time I remembered I hadn't packed any of my baggage. I had enough stuff of my own to fill two or three big suitcases, and then there was all of Paul Vajda's books and clothes.

Just then the old Serb servant who took care of my room came in. He said if I didn't get downstairs pretty soon it would be too late, because the fire was spreading fast, and there weren't any fire escapes on this side of the building. He was about seventy years old, but he was just learning English. I could see him looking at all my books with a hungry, begging expression. Take them, I told him. All of them. Then I gave him Vajda's books too. He went off happy. I wondered whether he and his books would survive the air raid. And if they did, whether he would have sense enough to hide the books before the Germans came in and occupied the city. If he didn't he probably would be shot as a spy, because one of the books was on how to identify German planes and another was *Inside Germany,* which he would have a hard time explaining, and some of the others were even worse. But he had grabbed them and gone off in such a hurry I hadn't had time to warn him.

Out of the window I could see the government buildings burning, but I didn't stop to do much looking. Smoke was beginning to fill the room. There wasn't much time to spare. I pulled down a little black overnight bag and started throwing things into it. It wouldn't hold much, but it might be all I would be able to get away with. It's funny what you decide is important when you look over all your worldly possessions and try to pick out eight or ten things to save. Just enough to go into one small bag. The first thing I threw in was my expense account for the last three months, a big wad of telephone receipts and other vouchers I would need to explain what had happened to the thousands of dollars I had been spending. Then an alarm clock. I can't explain that one, because I had a good watch strapped around my wrist. Then the *World Almanac,* which took up enough room for a couple of suits of underwear. Then a cream-colored pongee shirt that was nearly worn out and a brown necktie, because a girl in Bucharest had always admired them. Then an extra pair of shoes, because I thought I might have to do a lot of walking down in the hills of southern Serbia. I also chucked in a pencil sharpener, a cigarette holder a good friend had given me, a Martzishor charm that had a sentimental significance, twenty passport pictures—for what reason God only knows—and a lot of other foolish stuff. The only sensible things I took besides the shoes were one extra handkerchief, a bottle of whisky, and a French beret.

I was just throwing suits and shirts and things like that into one of my big suitcases when Hill showed up in the door with a huge knapsack on his back and his tin-can typewriter under his arm. Hill had been at the front in Greece, and he knew a thing or two about how a war correspondent should be equipped. When I saw his typewriter I stopped packing and tried to fit the case on my own typewriter. My hands were shaking and it took an eternity to get the job done. Hill kept telling me to hurry or it would be too late. I didn't try to do any more packing. I just closed the suitcase and took the three pieces of baggage and followed Hill down the smoky staircase into the lobby. I left behind about four-fifths of all my belongings.

The people in the lobby weren't calm any more. Just as we got down there the planes came over the hotel again. The assistant manager took the two of us aside and said please would we go into the dining room and order breakfast, because maybe if we did other people would too, and that would take their minds off what was happening. They might just as well be eating breakfast as standing doing nothing. The dining room, after all, was just as safe as the lobby. So Hill and I went in and ordered breakfast. I hope I never forget those Serb waiters. There were only two of them left, but they rustled cups of coffee just as if nothing were happening; just as if the capital they were so proud of wasn't being blown to bits; just as if they might not be killed any minute, and us too.

But all at once hell broke loose again. Bombs seemed to be falling around the hotel again. Everyone ran for cover. I made for the big grand piano. There was another fellow underneath it when I got there. I saw he had taken his cup of coffee with him, and by that I knew he must be another crazy newspaperman. He turned out to be Brock. We looked accusingly at each other. Brock said he really thought all this taking cover was foolish. If the bomb had your number on it, it would get you wherever you happened to be. I said, okay, then why are we staying under the piano? And so we got up and went out into the street again. The bombs actually were falling over near the river. When we looked up at the Srpski Kralj we could see it didn't have much longer to live. The fire was sweeping the building pretty fast. We went back and got our baggage. Hill and Chinigo and Brown and White brought theirs out too. We carried it all over into Kalemegdon Park and put it in a big pile. Just then the planes started re-forming right over our heads. We were near a big air-raid shelter dug into the ground. It was already packed, but we crowded our way in. After a few minutes it got so hot and it was so hard to breathe down there that we came out again. It was just as well. A hundred people were killed in that shelter and about a hundred more in another one when the planes landed direct hits on them.

More planes seemed to be taking the place of the first lot, which had to go back home for a fresh supply of bombs. Since it looked as if the raid was going to continue without much of a recess, we held a press conference and decided to try to get to the American Legation.

A few days before this we started sending envoys to intercede for the American press with the General Staff and try to arrange some kind of military transportation for us in case war came. We worked on the problem every day after that, but were always told there was no need to rush things. Now war had come, and we had no way to follow the government. But we knew that Lane, the Minister, would fix us up somehow. The only problem was getting our baggage to the legation. The taxi stand across the street was jammed with cabs, but the drivers had all taken it on the run. We found one cab with a key in the ignition switch. Brock started the engine. We were just loading in our luggage when the driver popped up from somewhere with two army officers. They pulled out their revolvers. We couldn't understand a word of what they were shouting at us, but we unloaded our suitcases anyway. Then someone spotted a horse pulling a milk wagon down a side street. We waved a lot of dinars in the driver's face, and for about twenty dollars' worth he agreed to take us the mile to the legation.

While we were packing the stuff inside the milk wagon, the Netherlands Minister, who lived at the Srpski Kralj, kept insisting we take his luggage too. The poor fellow was almost hysterical. But he had a dozen big suitcases that couldn't possibly have been fitted in. And anyway he didn't even know where he wanted to go. In the confusion one piece of his luggage, a big hatbox, got into the cart by mistake, under all our suitcases and typewriters. When we tried to lock the back of the cart, he changed his tune and wanted the hatbox back. He kept yelling it was full of valuable diplomatic documents. Just then some shrapnel from one of the ack-ack guns dropped right near us. The horse started away on the run. Brown, Brock, Hill, and White jumped on top of the wagon. Chinigo and I tried to run on behind, but we were tired, and the horse was galloping because of the noise, and so we let them go. The wagon had to detour around the center of the city because the streets were full of wrecked buildings, but Chinigo and I picked our way through the debris. We hugged the sides of buildings, because glass and slate and cornices and balconies were still falling from the bombed houses and office buildings.

Almost everybody had been sleeping when the first bombers came, and the sensible ones had stayed in their beds all morning. But some people had been worried about sons and daughters or mothers and fathers in other parts of the city. They had tried to go through the streets. We could see now how foolish this was. The bodies lay where they had fallen. Most of them were dead. Some were just wounded, but they might better have been dead. A few ambulances screamed around the city, but what good are a few ambulances when streets are full of bodies? Some small delivery trucks were trying to circle through the debris. Improvised ambulances. One man would drive and another would keep his hand on the button of the horn.

The din was something to tell your children and grandchildren about. The drone of the planes. The scream of their wings when they dived. The thud of the bombs. The crazy noise all the different kinds of ack-ack guns and pom-poms and machine guns made. Then the automobile horns and the sirens on ambulances. And when you got close to a badly hit area the screams of people with pieces blown from their bodies by pieces of steel dropped from the sky. Off in the distance somewhere I heard a church bell. It was a strange noise, different from all the others. Ding-dong. Slow. Majestic. A sound from another world. A sound from what seemed like the dim past. Church bells. Of course, it was Sunday.

Chinigo and I were making slow progress. We began to be afraid Hill and White and Brock and Brown might get out of the city without us. We were going along a street of shops and office buildings without knowing quite where we were. Every once in a while a bomb dropped around the corner or down the street. Each time, we flattened ourselves against the wall of a building and watched helpless little people, who looked like ants scurrying around. They dodged first here, then there, looking for a safer place than where they were. They seemed so pathetically impotent against this enemy in the sky. Impotent even to think.

We were just crossing a side street when a big black limousine stopped right in our path. There was a chauffeur in a white coat sitting at the wheel, very stiffly. A young man sat fidgeting in the back seat. The other five seats were empty. A grocery-store delivery truck up ahead had forced the limousine to stop because it had stopped. Its back doors were open. They couldn't be closed because the little truck was full of bodies, and all the legs stuck out the back. Most of them were men's legs, but one belonged to a young woman. There was a silver slipper on the foot. We stood there waiting for the truck and the limousine to go on so that we could cross the street. It didn't seem to occur to either of us to go around the limousine.

I stared at the back of the truck without really thinking about anything. I wondered rather mechanically what had happened to the other leg of the girl with the silver slipper. Then I saw. She was on the top of the pile. I guess she hadn't had time to put on her dress before it happened. All I could see was a pair of white pants. That is, they were white before something had chewed off her left leg, just like a fox would chew off the leg of a bird. The flesh—well, it wasn't a pretty picture.

Two men who seemed to be running this improvised ambulance were trying to wedge one more body in on top of the others. Their hands were dripping with blood. Finally they gave up. There just wasn't room, because the truck had a top on it. But two soldiers stood there with guns and said they had to make room. My stomach started coming up into my throat as they bent and pushed those bodies around. I kept saying to myself, I guess you aren't as tough and hard-boiled as you thought you were.

Finally I had to look the other way. When I did, I noticed something. It was just a small piece of silk, about a foot square, fastened on a stick on the front left fender of the limousine, but it sent a funny feeling running up and down my spine. The stripes were red, like the blood on the ambulance drivers' hands. Some of the stripes were white, like that girl's pants had been before they got all stained. The square in the corner looked like the sky did over Belgrade just before Ribbentrop began hollering over the radio and the bombers started coming. Maybe that sounds like a high school oration, but I can't help it. I'm telling you just how it was, and that's just what I thought when I looked at it. Life had suddenly become nothing but blood and stained white pants and pieces of sky that once upon a time had stars in them but now were full of black dots that made a noise like bees.

When I saw the flag, I knew the limousine must be an American diplomatic car. I looked at the fidgety young man in the back seat again. He appeared to be a diplomat all right, probably from Harvard, but he wasn't anyone I had ever seen before. He was sitting on the other side of the car. I walked around to that side and opened the door and said we were two American newspapermen trying to get to the American Legation and was he going there by any chance? He looked frightened when I opened the door. He moved quickly over to the other side of the seat, until he was right behind the big Serb chauffeur. Then he leaned over and grabbed the door I had opened and shut it and bent forward and said something to the chauffeur I couldn't hear. Chinigo was as mad as I was; he opened the door on his side and said, "Say, we don't want to ride with you, but just tell us which way the legation is; we're sort of lost, we've been twisting through so many streets."

He slammed the door in Chinigo's face too. Just then the two men running the ambulance convinced the two soldiers they really couldn't get anyone else in the truck, and they drove off. A woman who wanted to be taken to the hospital came over to the American diplomatic car. There was a lot of blood on her head. I was still standing by the back door on the right side. She came over and opened it. She knew that the man inside probably didn't talk Serbian, because she asked him in French and then in English to take her to a hospital. He grabbed the door out of her hand and yelled at the chauffeur to go on.

The truck was out of the way now, and the limousine with the little silk flag shot down the street. The two soldiers and the woman with blood on her head and some other people started shouting. They stood there in the center of the street shouting and shaking their fists in the air at the limousine, which we could hardly see now, it was going so fast.

I wanted to shake my fist, too, but I didn't. If you had been there you would always remember, as I'll always remember, how they all yelled "Amerikanski!" when they shook their fists. It wasn't a pretty word, the way they said it. It gave me a funny feeling inside my head and inside my stomach. I was too tired to figure out how to ask these people standing in the center of the street not to blame America. To tell them that all Americans aren't like that. I wanted to say something, anything, to make them forget what had happened. I tried to say in French to the woman with the blood on her head that I was sorry. She could tell, no doubt, from the way I talked French that I was an American, too. She told the other people standing there, and Chinigo and I had to get away fast, because all of them started shaking their fists at us and saying "Amerikanski!" between their teeth, just as they had said it to the back of the limousine.

We were really lost now. Neither of us had been in Belgrade very long, and I had hardly been out of the Srpski Kralj in a month. Besides, the bombs had made such a mess of everything that buildings you should have recognized looked so different now that you didn't remember ever seeing them, or else they were only piles of rubble. But when we saw the shining fifteen-story Albania Building in the distance we were all right. I told Chinigo how I had watched the putsch celebration from Nicky's apartment up in the Albania and how when I left, Nicky said jokingly, come back and watch the bombing from here too. Chinigo said, too bad you didn't; it looks as if it hadn't been touched. He was right, but what we saw when we got in front of the Albania was something to remember.

The Albania was at the head of Terrazia, the Times Square of Belgrade. You remember Terrazia, don't you? That was where those tens of thousands of people had gone crazy with emotion ten days ago over what King Peter and General Simovich had done. That was where they wrecked the Italian Travel Agency. It was one of the most beautiful spots in the whole city. Now it was the ugliest spot in the whole world.

There was a trolley car right in the center of the square over on its side. A lot of big busses were scattered in pieces all over the landscape. On the sidewalk just around the corner from the square was a big aerial mine. I don't know how many tons it weighed. But it was big all right. Somehow it hadn't gone off. It had just made a hole in the cement where its nose hit; that was all. I went over to look closely at it. It wasn't much to look at. Just a big chunk of metal. I don't know why, but I wanted to touch it. I was beginning to feel sort of goofy. The planes were still raising hell. The noise was worse than ever. And smoke from fires all around the city made it hard to breathe. I didn't just touch it. I kicked it. I was sorry as soon as I did it, because I banged my toe so badly it was hard to walk after that. But I think I felt better inside because I kicked it. My stomach went down where it belonged.

Back in the square we saw one place where a bomb had made a hole in the street big enough to bury a couple of railroad cars. I mean big American railroad cars. We walked up as close as we could to it, but still we couldn't see down to the bottom. You never saw such a mess as Terrazia was. I don't think there was a piece of glass more than a few inches square within half a mile. The bombs had torn the fronts right off a lot of buildings. I know that's old stuff. Everyone's seen pictures of buildings like that in Spain and in France and Rotterdam and, of course, in London. But it was different seeing it right in front of your eyes. Especially when the bombers were still over your head and you didn't know if they were through with the job or not. Those naked buildings made us think of Eugene O'Neill's *Desire under the Elms*, where they had a house on the stage and took away parts of the front wall so you could see what went on inside.

We picked our way gingerly through the stuff on the sidewalks.

Pieces of people's bodies. Jewelry and groceries and clothing out of shop windows. Glass and stone. Chunks of bombs and jagged pieces of tin roofing. There were plenty of people around, but nobody paid any attention to the stuff on the sidewalks. Once Chinigo or I kicked a cardboard box in front of a jewelry store and saw diamond rings and watches and other glittering baubles go sailing into the street. It wasn't any phenomenal honesty on the part of the Serbs that made them ignore all this wealth that lay around. It was just that diamond rings don't help you when you're trying to dodge bombs. The important thing, the only thing that counted now, was trying to save your own life and the lives of your own people.

Weeks later a friend of mine who stayed in Belgrade until the German troops actually arrived said German cameramen took newsreel shots of people looting bombed buildings. The pictures were shown all over the Balkans, and they made Rumanians and Hungarians and Bulgars hate the Serbs more than ever for looting their own city. But the inside story was that the scenes were all staged. Gypsies had been ordered by German soldiers at the point of guns to rummage among the debris for jewelry and money, and they got shot if they didn't keep their backs to the camera.

There was one line of little shops on Terrazia, on the west side of the street, run for the most part by Jews. They were clothing stores and novelty shops and places that sold things like women's lingerie and men's shirts and lottery tickets. Most of the owners lived in back rooms or upstairs. When the planes came, these small-time merchants must have pulled on a few clothes and rushed out to see what was happening. Not many of them had gone out of their doorways, because that was where most of them got it. The bodies looked as if they had been placed there by some master stage manager. The feet were all out, toward the street. The heads were all in, almost touching the doors. The faces and hands were a crazy blue-white, all the same, as if some make-up expert had just finished getting these people ready to play ghost roles.

Chinigo got angry because I stopped to turn one of them over.

What I wanted to find out was what had killed these people. The one I examined didn't have a single wound you could see. They had probably all been killed just by the repercussion that knocked them down, like ninepins, and did a swift merciful bloodless job of it. I kept thinking it was too bad that everyone hadn't been killed that way. It was clean.

I told you that all the bodies lay in the doorways. That isn't exactly true. There was one body on the sidewalk. I couldn't help stopping to look at it. She lay on her side. She had on a sky-blue shimmery evening dress. Her hair was rich brown and perfectly combed. I looked down at her and wondered where she had been last night, to still have on an evening dress at five o'clock in the morning. The gown had slipped down off her right shoulder. It was the kind of a shoulder a sculptor would have chiseled. Then I noticed her right leg. Half of it was gone. Sawdust trickled out of the stump. My lovely brunette had been blown out of a shop window.

While I was catching up with Chinigo I thought if only it turned out that all these bodies were just shop-window dummies! But they weren't, because the next one we passed was moaning. I felt heartsick, going by without stopping when we passed these half-living, half-dead people. But we didn't have a car and we didn't have any bandages or medicine, and I don't know what we could have done. I should have had a bottle of slivo in my back pocket, but I didn't even have that.

We counted two or three hundred bodies right in Terrazia. And Terrazia isn't half as big as Times Square. Terrazia proved to me that this was all intentional. These planes that were bombing Belgrade had everything their own way. They weren't releasing bombs from up in the clouds. Every one of them came down in a dive or a glide and planted his bombs just where the crew wanted to plant them. From what we saw in Belgrade that day we decided they could have dropped a bomb right down the flue of a chimney, their aiming was so accurate. There wasn't any mystery about why Terrazia was one of the "military objectives" they hit, as Berlin called them in the communiqués after it was all over. Hitler was getting his revenge for the humiliation of ten days ago. He was showing the Serbs that no one could tear up his picture in public and get away with it. This was a mass execution of the guilty, of those who had demonstrated in Terrazia. It was a mass execution carried out on orders from Berlin, with the executioners riding the clouds.

We saw one piece of irony. The Italian Travel Agency had fixed its place all up during the last week. New plate-glass windows had been put in, and all the wreckage had been cleared away, and they had even put up new signs. But Hitler's pilots this morning had done a better job of wrecking the place with bombs than the Serbs had been able to do with stones. The plate-glass windows were broken all over again. The new signs lay on the sidewalk in splinters. I guess they won't be able to sell any tickets to Italy there today, I said to Chinigo. Chinigo said he wondered what the German Travel Agency looked like. So we stumbled around the corner to look at it. It was just as much a mess as the Italian place. We wondered why Berlin hadn't warned them not to replace the broken windows. Or maybe the pilots were supposed to have destroyed the buildings all around, without hurting the Nazi place.

The big laugh was the German Legation. That was a wreck too. They had barricaded it against attacks from the Serbs on the ground, but there wasn't anything they could do to barricade it against attacks by their own pilots from the air. I wondered what had happened to the two attachés who swore they would stay locked up in the place until the German army captured the city. Maybe they were buried alive in the wreckage. I don't know. That's one of those little historical matters we'll have to straighten out when we go back to Belgrade some day after the war is all over.

Except for those three Axis buildings, the German pilots seemed to have landed their bombs exactly where they wanted to.

The bombed Terrazia area ended in a clean line. On one side, the wreckage of bodies and the wreckage of buildings. Then you stepped across this invisible line, and there wasn't a scar of any kind. Not many, anyway. It was just as if someone up in the sky had taken a compass and put one point right in the fountain in the center of Terrazia and had drawn a chalk circle with the other point, and then had said to the bombers, go to it, boys, but don't go outside the mark. I don't mean Terrazia was the only target. There was the Srpski Kralj, of course, and when we saw what had happened to the Greek and British Legations we knew they had been on the list, too.

Then when we got to our own legation we found it had also been badly banged up by bombs. Louis Fortier, U.S. military attaché, was there burning all the legation's confidential papers. Kay was with him. Kay said he had spent the night away from the hotel and that was why we hadn't seen him in the lobby. He had had just as much luck as we had had in not getting hit, and he had had just as little luck as we had had in trying to get a story to Switzerland. He said the legation had been evacuated, and the Minister's house was going to be headquarters for the Americans. He was going over to Lane's house with Fortier in a few minutes. That was where the milk wagon with all our baggage had gone. So Chinigo and I started on foot for Lane's house.

On the way we saw where a lot of the smoke was coming from that made it almost like night all over the city. Down the hill, on Zrimskoga, were most of the government buildings. The Prime Minister's office and, across the street, the War Office, and a little farther down the Press and Propaganda. They were all burning. Nearly all the fire engines in Belgrade were there. But now there wasn't any water, and they just stood there letting the big buildings burn. So much debris had fallen since they answered the first alarm that no one would ever be able to get the engines out of the mess of stone and brick to fight any of the fires in other parts of the city, even if someone found a way to repair the broken mains and get water.

Chinigo and I tried to get down there. First the thick black smoke stopped us. We soaked our handkerchiefs in some water running in the gutter from a broken pipe somewhere and put them over our faces and went on. Then the heat got so bad we said, what the hell's the use, and turned around. I looked over my shoulder and saw for certain that the Press and Propaganda was going to be nothing but a charred shell by night. That was the only thing I saw all day that made me happy. My expulsion order and the calendar on the Minister's desk marked, "St. John, 15:00 Sunday," were certainly in there burning now. It was the first time I had remembered this was Sunday, Expulsion Day for me. The war had saved me.

By the time we got to the Lane house things had quieted down, although there were still a few planes flying around. All the newspaper boys were there with our baggage. Mrs. Lane was as soft-spoken and regal and calm as ever. The Minister was trying to work out evacuation plans for the rest of us. He couldn't leave the city himself. After Mrs. Daisy Harriman had tried to follow the Norwegian government, Papa Hull (as all the diplomatic boys called the Secretary of State) had sent an order out from Washington that if (he should have said "when") there was another evacuation, the Minister was to remain in the capital and appoint an assistant to follow the government. (In view of what happened later, the Hull order should have said, "try to follow the government.")

Days ago Lane told us he had picked Macatee, the first secretary, for the job. During the week, while we were getting the run-around on our transportation problem, we had gone to Lane and asked him what he could do for us when war came. He agreed one man could go along with Macatee to represent all of us. We must decide among ourselves who it was to be. We drew straws in Lane's office that same day. I got the short one. Then we drew up an agreement in which I promised to file stories for all the rest when Macatee and I caught up with the government and found communications. But now the whole plan was revised. Fortier suddenly appeared with Kay and said he was taking Kay off with him. He was going to try to follow the General Staff, which already had gone off somewhere. Just where was a great secret; he said he had room for one more man.

Leigh White jumped at the chance, and Fortier said okay. Hill and Brock and Brown and Chinigo started to raise a rumpus. Lane straightened it all out in good diplomatic fashion by saying there was no reason why all four of them shouldn't go along with Macatee and me. That meant we all had to trim our baggage down to the bare minimum, and we agreed to take nothing but one small bag apiece and a typewriter. It's funny how a newspaperman will sacrifice almost anything else before he gives up his typewriter. You'd think we hadn't ever learned to write with a pen or pencil.

Lane's house was in bad shape. Part of the roof lay on the sidewalk. Some of the windows were smashed. The inside was a mess. A lot of bombs had dropped close by. The courtyard was beginning to fill up with Americans. Every few minutes someone would come along with some kind of a pseudo claim to American protection. They kept delaying Lane and his staff in their job of trying to take care of legitimate Americans.

In places like the Balkans about seventy per cent of the people with American passports haven't ever lived in the United States, and a lot of them don't even speak English. They got their passports by being children of American sailors, or by marrying an American who may have scooted back home soon after the wedding and never returned, or thanks to some strange technicality of American law. All diplomats say these people cause them more grief than even the fussiest old-maid tourist. That was surely true in Belgrade on Sunday, April 6, 1941.

One of them we did feel sorry for was a boy about sixteen. He spoke English rather well, because he had once been in the United States. When the bombing started he made right for Lane's home. On the way a piece of bomb got him in the leg. He was bleeding badly when he limped into the courtyard. His blood made a deep crimson trail wherever he went. We put a tourniquet around his leg, and then someone drove him to a hospital. He cried like a baby, not over the pain, which must have been bad, but because he didn't want to leave what he called "all you other Americans." He figured that if he ever got into a hospital they would think he was just another Serb and treat him accordingly.

When he said "they" he didn't explain whom he meant, but we all knew.

Another person who stumbled into the courtyard was Ruth Mitchell, the sister of Billy Mitchell, the World War ace. She was all dressed up in her Comitaji uniform, with big leather boots and a fur hat covered with the skulls and cross bones the Comitaji use for an emblem. Just two days ago I had sent off a story about how the chief of the Comitaji had accepted her as a member of the outlaw organization and had appointed her his personal dispatch rider. The chief was an old man. A lot of people thought he was cracked. But he claimed to have tens of thousands of followers who were going to do in this war just what they had done in all other Balkan wars. That meant hiding by day and doing plenty of dirty work by night. This dirty work consisted principally of sneaking through enemy lines, putting poison in the drinking water, ruining the artillery, getting all the military secrets they could, and then sneaking back to their own lines. Sometimes they lived in enemy-occupied country for days or weeks, getting their job done. There were special Yugoslav laws that allowed them to demand food and lodging from anyone in the country and exempted them from punishment for murdering anyone they chose in time of war. When Miss Mitchell took the Comitaji oath they gave her the usual dose of poison that all members got. She was supposed to sew it in the lapel of her coat so that if she was ever captured she could suck the lapel and kill herself, even if her hands were tied behind her back. That was because no Comitaji was ever supposed to be taken alive, or to live after being captured.

Where's your horse? I asked her. She didn't laugh. That horse gag was no joking matter to her, because she still expected the old man to supply her with a horse so that she could go galloping around delivering messages for him. She just frowned a little and said, I'll get it just as soon as I catch up with the chief. Then she did grin. But I have the poison sewed in my coat collar; feel! I felt the lapel. She had something sewed in it all right.

Although Miss Mitchell had married an Englishman and lost

her American citizenship, she was divorced now. Technically she was still a British subject, but today she was looking to the American Legation to help her get out of town so that she could find the chief somewhere. I wondered as I looked at her in the rather silly fur hat and man's coat whether she and the rest of the Comitaji really thought they could use the old guerrilla tactics against the Nazi army of steel tanks and bombing planes. It seemed to me that Miss Mitchell was just looking for some à la Hollywood adventure. Well, I thought, she'll probably get all she wants and more before long.

While we were talking together the Minister said did anyone want a drink, and so we went into the kitchen and Brock found a vase about two feet tall and we filled it with ice and then poured in about a quart of good Scotch and called it a loving cup, and as fast as it got empty we filled it up again. We needed that Scotch all right. All of us were pretty jittery. Then we decided the Lanes had to have a good air-raid shelter if they were going to stay in Belgrade, and we spent an hour hauling cots and mattresses and about a ton of food and water down into the deep cellar. It had walls five feet thick and tremendous beams across the ceiling. It looked so safe to me that I thought of my big suitcase. Since I could only take the little bag and my typewriter in Macatee's car, I put the big suitcase in the cellar with the cots and the food. Some of the other boys thought it was a good idea, and they stored their stuff down there with mine.

A few planes were still dropping bombs around the city. But we were used to it now, and it didn't bother us very much. Lane told Macatee to leave his own Chevrolet behind and to take the five of us in the Buick. This was a big car, Lane said, that some rich American tourist had presented to the legation when he went back home to the United States last summer. Macatee thought that was a good idea, and Lane said the only trouble was that he had had a fight with his own chauffeur during the worst of the raid, and the chauffeur had gone off with the keys to the garage. The trouble started, it seemed, because the bombs scared hell out of the chauffeur, and he insisted that his pay ought to be doubled, beginning immediately, or he'd resign. Lane called him a yellow coward and told him a man wasn't worth much if he tried to run out just when he was most needed. Lane didn't double his pay because he was sure the chauffeur would still be yellow, no matter how much money anyone gave him. Just before we came along, the chauffeur had locked the Buick in the garage and had gone off with the garage key. We all went out and worked with a sledge hammer and finally broke down the steel garage doors, and someone drove the Buick out into the courtyard.

When we saw it, Chinigo and I looked at each other quickly, and I knew he was thinking the same thing I was thinking. But just to make sure we were right I asked Lane if the big black limousine had been through the center of Belgrade about an hour or two ago. He said, yes, the chauffeur had just driven the Buick back from the frontier. We asked who the fellow in the back seat was when the car went through the city? Lane said it was a secretary from an American legation in one of the other Balkan capitals. He had been trying to get to Belgrade and got stuck on the frontier during the night, and so Lane had sent the Buick for him. Then we told Lane what had happened, about the woman with the bloody head, about the people who shook their fists and said, "Amerikanski," so bitterly. Lane was disturbed by the story, but he said probably the young fellow was pretty excited because of all the bombs and he hadn't had any sleep all night and why didn't we just forget it. So we did. Weeks later we heard that before the Balkan war was really over, that same scared young diplomat had risked his life taking an important American diplomatic message through the battle lines. That feat made up for a lot of things.

To go back to April sixth and Belgrade, somebody asked, as we stood in the Minister's courtyard, what time it was. When somebody else said nine o'clock, no one would believe him until we all looked at our own watches. It seemed as if it must be almost night, so much had happened in the last four hours. Lane said he had heard that the government, right after the bombers came over Belgrade, had left for Vranyska Banya, about a hundred and fifty miles to the south in the foothills of the south Serb mountains.

He suggested that Macatee and the five of us start off as soon as possible, but for about an hour he wanted to use the Buick himself. We all agreed to meet in the courtyard in exactly an hour. Hill said he was going off to the radio station to try to send a story. The rest of us thought there was only one chance in a thousand that the radio station would be working, even if it hadn't been hit. But Hill said he was going anyway, and then he whispered that he would send a short dispatch to the AP for me if they were accepting messages. I told him thanks, because I couldn't go with him; I had a job to do. I didn't tell him what it was, but I had suddenly remembered Sonia and how I had promised not to leave Belgrade without her.

Until that very minute I had forgotten all about her. She had been so terrified about a few sirens going off last night. If she hadn't been killed by some of the bombs she must be a nervous wreck by now. I began to be sorry for her and I started out for her apartment on foot. Unfortunately for me, Lane's house was a long way from her place, and I didn't even know the name of her street. If I went back to the Srpski Kralj Hotel and started out from there I could find the way all right, because I had memorized it last night, but I could never get back in an hour if I had to cover that much ground, and then both of us would be stuck in Belgrade, which wouldn't help anyone. I didn't know Sonia well enough then or care enough for her to sacrifice my life or even my job for her, but I did want to make a real attempt to live up to my promise.

I had my Rolliflex camera with me, slung over my shoulder on a strap, and I stopped in Lane's street to use it. Right next door there was a private two-car garage. Someone during the first bombing had tried to drive an Austin out of the garage into the street. It was half out when a bomb hit the house next door and landed about two tons of brick on top of the little car. I took a picture of it; then I tried to look inside to see what had happened to whoever was behind the wheel, but the body of the car was smashed so badly you couldn't see inside. A little farther on there was one of those naked houses with the front all ripped away and some bodies hanging on splintered pieces of timber, just as if they had been crucified there by a bloodthirsty god.

I was squinting through the finder of the camera when I heard an angry yell. I looked up just in time to see half a dozen men rushing at me, shaking their fists. They were hollering bloody murder. I couldn't figure out what they meant. They got in a circle around me. When they tried to smash my camera I thought I knew what the trouble was. Then when I heard them yelling the Serbian word for German I was sure. It was the same old story. They thought I was a Nazi agent. There was no use arguing with them, even if I had known enough Serbian to do it, which I didn't. I didn't want my camera smashed, and so I started to run. It took me about half a mile to outdistance them, and then I was lost and awfully tired. I remembered for the first time that I hadn't had anything in my stomach but beer and whisky since my dinner with Sonia last night, and then I hadn't done much eating.

Last night? The white tablecloths and peace of the Srpski Kralj dining room seemed eons in the past. Thinking of Sonia made me remember where I was supposed to be going, but I knew now I could never find the place, and so I went back to Lane's house and tried to telephone her. The line wasn't working. Then I wrote a note to her and addressed it to Schmidt-Pop, at the Hungarian Legation, and gave it to someone who was staying behind in Belgrade, to be delivered sometime. I told her I'd miss the champagne she had agreed to bring along. I tried to pass it off lightly, just in case she was stuck in Belgrade when she got the note and had to live through any more of this hell.

The hour ended just about the time I finished the note. Hill still hadn't come back from the radio station. The rest of us began to pack our stuff in the Buick. We had less than half a tank of gasoline, but we figured in our ignorance that we would be able to get all we wanted when we got to Vranyska Banya, in case

we had to do any more moving. We checked the oil and filled up
with water and then sat down to wait for Hill. We waited more
than half an hour. Then Macatee got impatient and said maybe
something had happened to Hill, which would be too bad, but
after all we couldn't wait forever. The government already had a
long start on us, and there was a chance they might go right on
through Vranyska Banya and we might never catch up with
them. But Macatee wanted to stop at his own house, out in the
suburbs, and Lane said that if Hill showed up within half an hour
he would get him out to Macatee's house somehow. So we started
on our flight from Belgrade.

We didn't see much on our way to Macatee's house, because
we had to detour around big areas of the city where the damage
was so bad you couldn't drive a car through the streets. But we
did get a last look at what was left of the government buildings.
They were still burning as if they had been soaked with gasoline.

Macatee's place was a villa in Dedinje, on a hill looking out
over the Danube. Right near the edge of the river was the big
military airport. While Macatee was inside the house giving
final orders to his servants, we heard that same drone Brock and I
had heard just as the sun was coming up. Then off in the distance
we saw the planes. I was too tired to count them. And anyway,
they were coming in a single column, about a mile apart. The
first plane circled once over the airport and then dived. It seemed
to keep going straight down at three or four hundred miles an
hour until its nose got within a few inches of the ground. Then it
straightened out and glided away. One plane after another did
that. It was all as mechanically perfect, as systematic, and as well
timed as if they had been robots worked by some fellow a million
miles away with a switch. Each plane had its own target. Mostly
they were dropping bombs on a lot of Yugoslav fighter planes and
a few bombers parked on the field. But some of the Nazi planes
dropped incendiaries on the hangars and the other airport buildings. Then, after all the bombs had been unloaded, they came
back, flying just off the ground, and machine-gunned hell out of
all the men trying to put out the fires or get planes off the ground.

When they finally left, the whole field was dotted with globs of fire where the Yugoslav machines were burning. Thick black smoke was going up from the buildings.

The show was about over when Macatee came hurrying out of the house and said, Hill or no Hill, we had to get going. He had just received word that a lot of bombing had been done around Dedinje that morning. They had been trying to hit the military barracks and the White Palace. He said the military people had just told him a new wave of Nazi planes was heading this way, and there was no sense sticking our necks out and inviting trouble. So we started.

CHAPTER FOUR

Oxcart Army

———◆◈◆———

I GOT A FUNNY FEELING, driving in that big Buick out of Belgrade. I couldn't help remembering that it was the same car that refused to stop to pick up the woman who wanted to go to a hospital. Only this time the young diplomat who looked as if he came from Harvard wasn't in the car. And there weren't a lot of vacant seats, because Brock and Brown and Chinigo and Macatee and I and all our luggage took up every inch of space. But it didn't seem right, anyway, to be racing down a highway jammed with so many people. Most of them were on foot. A lot of them had been automobile owners, but now their cars were wrecked, because all the big garages in town seemed to have been hit. Later we talked to people who had tried to buy or steal automobiles that bloody Sunday in Belgrade. And some of the British newspapermen who owned cars of their own told us how they had run over to their garages the first thing, only to find them on fire or flattened out.

The vehicles on that road leading out of Belgrade were a strange sight. There was everything in the parade that man had

ever invented to run on wheels, from the crudest kind of oxcart
you ever saw, up to some diplomatic limousines fancy enough for
an Indian Maharajah. Some carts were pulled by donkeys, some
by horses, some by oxen, but most of them by human beings.
They were all loaded high with—well, stuff. Stuff is what you
take with you when you flee from a bombed city. If you're a
peasant, like a lot of these people were, stuff is a mattress, and a
few blankets, and a couple of chickens, and some sacks of cornmeal, and a few pots and pans, and the skirt with the big frills
and the elaborate embroidery that your great-grandmother spent
half her life working on and that your little daughter will wear
some day when she's big enough. Those are the kind of things
peasants salvage when they have to run for their lives. Of course if
you're a government official you take a case of fancy liquor, and a
few extra cans of gasoline, and some tins of Black Sea caviar, and
a big box with all your wife's jewelry, and the decoration the
Regent gave you last year, after you sided in with him on that
suppression of the press law, and maybe a few suitcases of things
like socks and ties and shirts and suits, and then an armload of
dresses your wife said she had to have.

The people we felt really sorry for were those who had everything they owned tied in bundles on the ends of sticks they carried
over their shoulders. Instead of following the winding highway,
these footloose people trudged across the fields, because that way
was shorter, even though they did have to struggle down
through little valleys and then up steep hills. That ribbon of
people is still one of the most vivid pictures of the whole war.

About ten miles from Belgrade there was a spot where the
highway circled around a hill. When we got up there we could
get a good view of the whole scene. Behind us we could see
Belgrade. Burning Belgrade. Belgrade already well on the way to
becoming a city of silent people. Except that a lot of those men
and women lying around the streets were probably still moaning
for help and a drink and something to stop the pain. We could
see the smoke from dozens of fires. And up through the smoke the
red flames. It looked as if there was another air raid going on. We

were too far away now to hear sounds distinctly, but what we did hear was a dull noise that probably was a brew of all the noises of war mixed together. The noises of planes and guns and sirens and falling buildings. But what made us think the raid was going on in earnest again were the little black dots in the sky and the puffs of white smoke, which we knew came from the shrapnel sent up by the ack-ack guns as they tried so hard and generally so futilely to pin one on the bombers.

Then from the hill we could see that human ribbon stretching across the countryside. We couldn't see individual people and we couldn't see any single movement, but the ribbon seemed to move just like a piece of string as you drag it across the floor when you're playing with a cat. Or like a snake slithering slowly through the grass. One end of that ribbon was back ten miles, in Belgrade. The other end was lost in the distance the other way. We figured that some of those people way up ahead must have started out the minute the first bombs fell, to be that far by afternoon. Silent, resigned people who knew it wouldn't be any use staying in their own city. Once out in the country they'd be safe from bombs, probably, but where would they sleep tonight? I kept thinking, where will they sleep tonight? And I kept wondering what they would do for food when they had cooked up all the cornmeal they had and there was nothing else left.

Going up the hill we passed a big black hearse that was just about making the grade. In the place where the coffin was supposed to be, the undertaker had packed his whole family. The six or seven small children seemed to be having the time of their lives, but the father looked as if he might be superstitious about using a hearse to rescue his family.

That evacuation of thousands and maybe tens of thousands of people from Belgrade was about as orderly as you could imagine. No hysteria. No pandemonium. Which made me wonder whether we Americans would be as calm if we were rushing for our lives out of one of our cities. My guess was that we wouldn't be. The difference, I suppose, is that these poor Europeans, and especially people like the Serbs, are so used to war and destruction that they've got resignation bred into their bones. They just take it. There isn't much else they can do.

Macatee didn't like to drive, and so the rest of us took turns at the wheel. We couldn't make much time, because there were a lot of other people with cars who seemed just as eager as we were to get out of Belgrade. We all thought, I guess, about Rotterdam, and how Belgrade was already well on the road to being another Rotterdam. There seemed to be something especially vicious about that bombing of Belgrade. Somehow we felt that Mister H, as so many people called him, had a personal interest in Belgrade. Well, you could understand it, as much as you despised what he was doing to the poor damned city. Belgrade had thumbed its collective nose at Mister H last week in no uncertain way. If Belgrade wasn't made to pay, and pay dearly, a lot of other countries scattered around Europe might take up the nose-thumbing habit, and then what?

While one of us drove, the rest of us were busy scratching notes on pieces of paper, or in the backs of passports. Notes from which we would write the stories we expected to send off that night, just as soon as we located the new seat of the government and found communications.

Vranyska Banya was a quiet little place. In normal times it was a summer resort. But this was only April, and none of the hotels were open and the place had a bleak look about it. The little town was jammed with cars. Macatee said he'd start looking right away for the government, and we should find a place to live, because this might be our home for quite a while. At that stage of the game Macatee agreed with Brock that the Serbs would probably hold out pretty well.

We found a villa on the edge of the city with three rooms. But Macatee didn't find the government. All he found was a minor functionary of the Foreign Office who kept putting his finger to his lips and saying "Sh! Sh!" every time Macatee asked where the government was. Only he didn't just say "Sh! Sh!" In French it takes a couple of hundred words to say just "Sh! Sh!" But that's what it amounted to.

When Macatee said something about maybe we'd better go on if the government wasn't there in Vranyska Banya, the little Foreign Office guy got quite jittery and said, oh no, you mustn't do that. This is the place to stay.

He could assure Macatee that none of us would make any mistake if we stayed right here in Vranyska Banya.

We sat up most of the night writing stories, but of course after we signed our names at the end there was nothing we could do with them except to pass them around in a circle and do a mutual admiration job on them. They really were good stories. Thinking about them now, I'm sure they were the most graphic, the best-written newspaper stories that ever came from any of our typewriters. But those dispatches about the bombing of Belgrade were doomed never to be sent over cable wires and never to be set up in type. Of course we didn't know that on Monday morning, April seventh, when the four of us, fresh from all that had happened in Belgrade, sat at our typewriters in little Vranyska Banya.

That Monday morning we had breakfast in a sidewalk *cafana*. The peasants were in from the country with their eggs and butter and chickens. They crowded into the market place, but they didn't do much business. Most of them gathered in busy little knots and kept looking up over their shoulders at the sky and whispering the dreadful news. Yugoslavia was at war! God help Yugoslavia! The younger people had a bright look in their eyes. The older people looked frightened. But I kept thinking that if they only knew all we knew they would look a lot more frightened. If they only knew what had already happened in Belgrade. If they only knew that we hadn't seen a single Yugoslav fighter in the air over the capital, and no British planes either. Then I wondered how many of those younger people with a bright look in their eyes had ever heard of tanks.

The only way we could get any real food in that sidewalk restaurant was to go out into the market place and buy eggs and meat and take them back to the *cafana* and get someone to cook them for us. But even that was difficult, because the peasants, as soon as they got the news that war had come to Yugoslavia, wanted to take all their produce right back home with them.

After eating all the eggs we could buy, Brock and I went wandering around the village and found a little shoemaker who had hundreds of pairs of Serbian peasant sandals hanging on the wall of his place. If you have never seen Serbian peasant sandals it will tax your imagination to try to picture them. They are made out of a single piece of leather, which forms the sole and the sides too, and then ends up in a horn at the toe—a queer-looking horn; and if the horn doesn't point in just the right direction, rain and snow pour into it, just as if it were a funnel, and you don't keep your feet very dry.

Brock and I decided it might be a good thing if we went completely native. In the first place, native costumes anywhere are designed to meet the conditions of the locality—to make the people who wear them as comfortable as possible in the circumstances under which they are forced to live. And another thing, we thought that if we got into some native costumes we wouldn't stand out from the rest of the people as much as we did in our New York clothes. And maybe that would save us from getting into so much trouble. Chinigo and Brown agreed halfheartedly with us. Macatee felt that being a diplomat he'd better continue to look Western.

The rest of us bought the crazy-looking shoes and some bright-colored peasant socks and then sallied out into the market place. If we thought we were going to be less conspicuous we surely were wrong. The whole town ignored everything else to stare at us. We tried to duck down the street, but people followed us, and everyone kept snickering. Even a lot of Serb soldiers, who probably were going to be killed a few days later when the Germans swept through that section, quit loading guns and equipment into carts and just gaped.

We tried to avoid the crowd by going into the first little shop we came to. It turned out that the shopkeeper had been in America for a few weeks almost twenty years ago. But like all those Europeans who have ever been over here, he remembered most of the English words he had learned. His vocabulary wouldn't have done for a conversation on politics or physics, but he was able to explain why the people were laughing at us. It seems it was all because of the knee-length stockings we bought and were so proud of that we rolled them up over the cuffs of our trousers, like golf socks. We had chosen a peculiar design, which, our shopkeeper explained in his faltering English, was worn, according to custom, only by Serbian virgins who were advertising for husbands.

That same morning Russell Hill showed up. He looked like the wrath of God. He was driving Macatee's Chevrolet. Lane had turned it over to him. His story was that after he left us Sunday noon he had found the Belgrade radio station operating, in a fashion, but before he could file his dispatch and get away, those same planes we saw demolish the military airport started bombing the center of the city again. Everyone was forced at the point of guns to go into basement shelters. And so Hill had spent an hour or two down under the radio station while we were pacing around the Minister's courtyard waiting for him. When he was finally released and got back, we were gone. But Hill was cheerful, because he thought he had scooped the world with his dispatch from Belgrade. It was months later, of course, before we confirmed what we suspected then: that no dispatch left Belgrade after dawn that first day of the war. Neither the one I had sent early in the morning nor those Hill had sent at noon.

Hill had brought along some people the British Minister had asked the American Minister to help him evacuate. I think they were Greeks who had been doing some secret work for the British. And then there was a Jewish Yugoslav newspaperman called Aroeti, who was quite panicky, and an English correspondent, Edwards, who had lived for years in Yugoslavia and had written several books on the country, and his wife, a Serbian girl we called Duka. Hill had been lost on the blacked-out road all night because the Greek refugees insisted on telling him how to go, and their sense of direction had been rather peculiar.

After we listened to Hill's story we held a consultation of

war and decided we had to get serious about this problem of communications. My God, yes! The war had been going on for twenty-four hours, and as far as we knew none of us had gotten a single word off to America yet! Then someone whispered a dark secret. He knew, definitely, that the British air attaché, somewhat contrary to international law and custom, had a portable short-wave sending set. And the British air attaché was right here in Vranyska Banya. Someone had seen him. And so we split up and all went out in different directions searching for the elusive Tom Maplebeck, British air attaché.

Someone finally found him. He did considerable hemming and hawing, and then he broke down and admitted, yes, he did have a radio set. But believe it or not, General Simovich, the Prime Minister, the dictator of the country and the head of the army, had absolutely no means of communicating with his British and Greek allies, or with his own six armies scattered in various parts of Yugoslavia, no way at all, unless Maplebeck let him use the little portable radio set for his messages. So, Maplebeck told, his radio operator was busy twenty-four hours a day tapping out pleas to the British in Greece to hurry up with some help—with some of those three hundred thousand troops and hundreds of planes. And the little sending set was also trying to get into communication with the six Yugoslav armies, because civil phone lines were all cut and military communications hadn't yet been set up.

Each one of us had thousands of words we wanted to send. Graphic word pictures of what the Nazis had done to Belgrade. But Maplebeck just looked at our sheafs of copy paper and laughed. Impossible. Ridiculous. A war is on. Wait until the war is over and then write about it. The job now is to win the war. To get orders to the six Yugoslav armies. To try to establish contact with the British and the Greeks. Military men seldom see a news-paperman's point of view. We moaned and groaned and begged and pleaded. We finally reached a compromise. Maplebeck agreed that if we would write about one hundred words and address the dispatch to all our American papers and news agen-

cies and sign all our names, he'd try—yes, he'd promise to try—
to get it out. Well, you can't describe much about the bombing of
a city and the beginning of a war in a hundred words. We sat
around trying to figure out what to say. Someone remembered
that his first city editor used to impress cub reporters with the
value of brevity by pointing out that the story of the creation of
the world was told in the Bible in thirty-two, or was it sixty-seven,
words? And so we tried to tell about the first thirty-six hours of
the Balkan war in a hundred words. It wasn't very hot stuff.
Everyone had a different idea as to what was important. But we
finally got it written and signed our names and gave the piece of
paper to Maplebeck, and he agreed to have his operator tap it out.

Well, we relaxed a little then. Our employers over in New York
and Chicago wouldn't pin any medals on us for a joint dispatch
of a hundred words, but at least it would let them know we were
trying.

That afternoon some of us took a trip into Kraljevo, where
the Yugoslavs had their largest airplane factory. One of the biggest in all the Balkans. We had heard Kraljevo had been bombed,
and we wanted to see for ourselves. It had been all right, but the
big plane factory was still undamaged. We talked to a local
official. We asked him, what about the factory when the Germans get here? He didn't like that word "when." He kept saying "if." He said, if the Germans come here they won't find any
factory. We're going to take care of that. We don't have any
regular explosive, but we've got the building loaded with bombs
and hand grenades. They're all tied together with a big fuse. All
we have to do is to light one match. Just as soon as we get the
order. We wait for the order. Then we light the fuse. Then,
good-by factory. The joke will be on Hitler. He will never make
airplanes in Kraljevo.

I was impressed by that little speech. I remembered every
word of it. Weeks later I found out what did happen when the
Germans got to Kraljevo, but that's getting ahead of the story.

That night more refugees streamed in from Belgrade. They
told some pretty grisly stories of what had happened after we

had left. It was just more of the same thing. More bombs. More fires. More deaths. More destruction. Only now the city was really a place of lost souls. It was another Rotterdam all right. Hitler had had his revenge. He was wiping Belgrade on the Danube right off the map.

We spent most of the night interviewing each new arrival, jotting down figures and facts and stories in our notebooks, and writing fresh dispatches, just in case we ever did get a chance to send them. And all the time one or two of us kept after Macatee to try to locate the government and find out what the hell the communication situation was going to be. Where was the government going to set up shop? When would they have a radio station in operation so that we could get the story of the plight of Yugoslavia to America?

Tuesday morning we watched the British and Greek diplomats pack all of their cases of documents and their short-wave radio set and their personal luggage into their automobiles and make off. They did it in the stage-whisper manner. They were so obvious with their secrecy that before they ever started out of town all of Vranyska Banya knew they were going.

When we saw that caravan of *Corps Diplomatique* cars tear off in a cloud of dust we knew it was the tip-off that the Yugoslav government, if it ever had been in Vranyska Banya, surely wasn't there any longer.

So we badgered Macatee about pushing off too. And Macatee badgered the little Foreign Office fellow, who still acted very confidential and said he didn't want us to go on any wild-goose chase. The British and Greeks? Oh yes, they were, he implied, just going off on a little cross-country inspection of the scenery. They'd be back very soon. We mustn't pay any attention to them.

While this was going on we got a very good tip that the Yugoslav government had gone to the town of Užice the night before. And it made sense when someone told us that the little Foreign Office fellow had been given the job of seeing that the diplomats were kept behind as long as possible, because the government people were afraid that long lines of diplomatic cars might attract the Nazi bombing planes and give away where the new seat of government was. With the British and Greeks it was different. They were allies, the countries that were going to give Yugoslavia so much help. And then, the British had that all-important short-wave set. We could see the Yugoslav point of view. They were right of course. But we were newspapermen. We had a story to send. The only possible chance of ever being able to send it would be to get where the government was and try to impress on Simovich himself the importance to Yugoslavia, as well as to us, of letting America know what was happening.

So we ganged up on poor Macatee, and finally he threw up his hands and said all right, he'd go. But as we started off he was still worrying out loud about whether he was getting in bad with the little Foreign Office fellow, who, of course, wouldn't approve what we were doing.

It was a nasty night. Pouring rain. Roads jammed with cars. Shots rang out from the darkness every time we tried to use our headlights. Then the Chevvie, which Hill was driving, had a flat tire on a road so deep with mud we couldn't use the jack. And anyway the gadget that turned the screw of the jack was missing. So we had to get a lot of soldiers, who were sitting around a cafana talking about what the Yugoslav army was going to do to the Germans, to play human jack while we put chunks of wood under the axle. We were caked with mud from head to foot by the time we got the wheel changed. Then we took a wrong turn somewhere and got on a pure mud road. There weren't any natives to ask about directions, because it was late at night. But the road seemed to be going in the general direction of Užice, and so we kept right on.

After a few miles I suddenly grabbed Brock's arm. Brock was driving the Buick, and I was sitting beside him. He slapped on the brakes just in time. Right in front of us were two of the biggest heads I had ever seen. Oxen heads. A team of oxen pulling a peasant wagon. Behind that first team was another and then another. As far as we could see in the light of the headlights were oxen and peasant carts. Two soldiers walked beside the

head of each of those lumbering, plodding animals. Inside each
wagon there were a few cans of gasoline, or some hay, or some
sacks of bread. Supplies for the Yugoslav army. Supplies going
to the battle front. A military supply train of oxcarts. One strong
man could have carried all they had loaded in one of those oxcarts. I never had been able to figure out why the Yugoslavs,
who aren't especially kind to animals, never, even in peace time,
gave their oxen decent, manly loads to pull. Tonight the carts
seemed to have a bare minimum of weight in them.

The road was narrow and slippery with mud, and since the
headlights bothered the oxen we stopped the engine and turned
on the parking lights and sat waiting for this primordial military
train to pass. While we waited we counted. We waited there for
more than an hour. And we counted one hundred, two hundred,
three hundred oxcarts. When somebody got tired of counting,
Brown suggested it might be easier if we should just count the
oxen and divide by two. It was a stale joke, but it was the only
time anyone even smiled. I guess the rest of them were thinking
the same thing I was thinking. Most of us had been up in
Rumania while the German army was getting ready for this
show. We'd seen the German military supply trains. Tremendous
motor trucks. Any one truck would have held almost as much as
all these oxcarts put together. And the truck would have covered
in an hour the distance these oxen would cover in a whole day
and night.

Of course, in a way it had been the same story the year before
in France. But why hadn't anyone learned the lesson of France?
Why had the British urged or even allowed these Yugoslavs to
commit suicide this way? Surely the British, with all the espionage
agents and military intelligence people they had had in Yugoslavia, knew that this was an oxcart army? And there had been
some British in France, and there had been plenty of British
espionage agents in Rumania when the Germans were preparing
for this Balkan war, so that they knew that the German army
was no oxcart outfit.

Oxen, oxen, oxen. They trudged past us for hours. Finally

we decided to buck the stream and try to make some headway. We went slowly with dim lights, traveling in second gear, but even at that some of the oxen got frightened and shied off to the left and overturned their carts. Whenever that happened there was complete bedlam for half an hour. The peasant soldiers would ignore the accident and swarm around the car cursing us out in a language we barely understood. Then they would argue about which way the cart ought to be picked up. And they generally wound up by taking the cart all to pieces. Then, of course, it had to be reassembled back on the road. I remembered how the Germans, with their cold efficiency, abandon any truck that breaks down, for the slightest reason, knowing that the repair outfits that always trail along after each motorized column will take care of it later.

Oxen. Oxen. Oxen. By the time the last team finally went by, our count had reached one thousand five hundred carts. Three thousand head of oxen!

Užice was a filthy little town. I said was. I don't think there's much left of it now. We arrived there while it was still dark, and we were dog-tired. This was the fourth night without sleep and the beginning of the fourth day without a real meal. At the town's only hotel they just laughed when we asked about the possibility of a room or two. We went into a dirty café and had some Turkish coffee; then we each arranged five chairs to form a bed. We got to be past masters at chair-dozing before it was all over. The trick is to face the first chair to the left, the second to the right, etc. It prevents rolling onto the floor.

But after an hour or two, other refugees started pouring into the café, and sleep was murdered for that night.

There were two cafés in Užice. And there were thousands of refugees. We could tell in the morning that we had caught up with the government all right, because of the faces we began to recognize. Undersecretaries in various ministries, court attachés, the British and Greek ministers, the head of the Press Department, who was supposed to have expelled me on Sunday but who had forgotten all about that now. Then I spotted Nicky. Good old Nicky! It was in his apartment that we had watched the *coup d'état*. Sorry, I said, I didn't accept that invitation to watch the bombing from your place.

But Nicky wasn't in any joking mood. He had just come from Belgrade. He had seen a lot more than we had. Nicky said two or three direct hits had landed right on the Albania Building, that tall white skyscraper where he lived. The top two or three stories had been completely wrecked. A lot of people up there had been killed. Nicky's own apartment was up near the top of the building. Everything he owned was gone. But fortunately he hadn't been in the Albania at the time. The safest place in the world in an air raid, Nicky said, is some place halfway up in a skyscraper. If you ever get back to New York tell your friends to take a lease on an office in the Empire State or the Chrysler Building or one of those big things. Not on the first five stories, because they get wrecked by the repercussion of bombs that land in the street. And not on the top five or ten stories, because they get wrecked by direct hits. But anywhere else in a big building is as safe as an air-raid shelter. Really a lot safer. I knew he was right because I had seen what happened in Belgrade.

Then Nicky asked, "Do you know a girl who worked for me in the Senate, called Sonia?"

I said, sure, and then I held my breath, because I was afraid of what he was going to say. I knew that if he said what I expected he was going to say I wouldn't be able to sleep, even if I ever got a chance again.

"Well," Nicky said, "I saw her just before I left Belgrade, and she was looking for you all over what was left of the city. I tried to get her to come with us, but she said the two of you had made a deal of some kind. I'm afraid the raids busted her up pretty badly, but she still hadn't been injured in any way."

I didn't like myself very well the rest of that day. I kept calling myself a dirty rotter and a God-damned selfish coward. Poor Sonia, with her sickening fear of sirens and strange noises and darkness! Where in hell was she now? Nicky didn't know.

The other newspapermen were impatient with that talk about

a woman. This isn't any time, Brock said, to talk women. What about the government, Nicky?

So Nicky told us. The government was here. Well, not right in Užice but within a few miles of the town. But it wouldn't do us any good to hunt for them. In the first place, their hide-out was guarded by soldiers who wouldn't even let a Yugoslav near the place unless he was at least a minister or an undersecretary of state.

That's okay with us, I told Nicky, because we haven't the slightest desire to see them. I can live happily the rest of my life without ever seeing a cabinet minister again. All we want them for is to get communications.

Nicky's answer was that he knew they had done nothing about communications yet. They had been too busy moving. Too busy jumping around trying to keep out of reach of the Germans. Too busy trying to keep their hide-out a secret.

The government itself was still relying on the little British radio set. They had a big short-wave station on a truck in pieces, but it hadn't been set up yet. In fact, the truck was lost somewhere along the line. When it did arrive and when the station was ready for operation, Nicky said he would let us know.

Then we met a Yugoslav officer who had just come from the boy king's palace in Dedinje, on the edge of Belgrade. He told us all about being in the palace when bombs were landing on the gardens and close to the royal home. Some damage had been done, but when he left, the house was still standing. His job had been to get Peter out of Belgrade. First, the boy didn't want to go at all. Then he agreed on the condition that he be allowed to drive the car himself. They had come over the same winding road we had taken. Only by that time the German planes were working on the refugees. The army officer said they kept the main highway under constant machine-gun fire, swooping down and riddling almost every car that tried to leave Belgrade, as well as pouring lead into the thin black ribbon of foot-loose people. But Peter refused to take any easy way out. He drove straight down the lead-sprinkled road at sixty miles an hour. Some lucky

star apparently was looking over him, the officer said, because
the bullets came close yet never hit the car. It made a good story.
Another story for the book, Hill called it. From then on about
all we were doing was collecting stories for the book, because we
were getting pretty damned despondent about ever writing
stories for newspapers again.

We spent the day going from one café to the other, trying to
get food and watching thousands of refugees, some completely
unnerved, some wounded, all of them hungry, all of them worn
ragged from lack of sleep, and a few of them hysterical. The
cafés were jammed to the doors. Gregarious instincts shatter the
veneer of self-sufficiency at a time like this, when life and death
are in the delicate balance. People want company in their
misery. Even if their misery and their chances of death are
multiplied by their foolish gregariousness. And so they jammed
themselves into the two cafés and told one another what they had
seen in Belgrade and told one another that things looked black
for Yugoslavia and for all of us who happened to be in Yugoslavia.

Of course the Yugoslavs were the calmest of the lot. The
people who stood to lose the most crabbed the least. None of these
Yugoslavs we sat around talking to were ever going to get out of
the country. And before it was all over a lot of them were going
to be strung up in trees, like American Negroes accused of rape,
but they were fatalists. The hysteria all came from Poles and
Czechs and other foreigners. Yes, and from a lot of British and
American refugees too.

I remember one woman. She was sitting at a table with half
a dozen girls who used to work in the Press and Propaganda
Office. They were all Serbs and Croats, but she was a foreigner.
Suddenly she started screaming. There were a thousand or two
of us in there, and our nerves were drawn pretty tight. And we
had all gone through a lot already. We couldn't stand things like
hysterical screaming. Just as soon as she began, people started
heading for the door. But it was a little door, and there were
people trying to get in, too, and so most of us just had to stand

there and let that screaming file away at our raw nerves. Someone said she was screaming because a man had just come from
Belgrade with the news that her husband had been blown into
little pieces by a bomb. Anyway someone had some pills that
were supposed to quiet down hysterical people, and he also had
some smelling salts.

Between the two the woman stopped shrieking after a while,
but just before she stopped, two other women started. It was like
one of those rounds that children sing in school, where you divide
the class in three sections and one section starts a tune and then
after a while another joins in and then another, until you get a
bedlam of noise. That's the way it was in the café in Užice on
the morning of Wednesday, April ninth. Well, we finally got
out of the place. We had given up any hope of getting anything
to eat anyway.

Out in the street we watched owners of automobiles taking
handfuls of mud and plastering the stuff all over their cars until
not a square inch of the surface showed. Then there were eight
or ten boys who had bought up all the canned paint in town.
They were charging the equivalent of a dollar or two to cover the
chromium parts of your automobile with paint so that they
wouldn't reflect the sun and attract the attention of Nazi planes.

Then we met an army officer we knew, and he said they had
just executed one of their own Yugoslav majors. Shot him down
without even a perfunctory court-martial. They had found him
working a little radio set, sending messages to Berlin about just
where the government was hiding.

Then an hour or two later someone listening to the radio
heard an announcer up in Budapest boast in both Hungarian
and Serbian that the Germans had located the seat of the Yugoslav government in Užice and that that little town was going to
be bombed tonight or tomorrow.

We tried to keep the news a secret, because we knew what
would happen if it got spread around town. But a lot of other
people had heard it, and by night Užice was a city of confusion.
A madhouse of hysteria. Another place of lost souls.

Nicky whispered during the evening that the government was getting ready to move along. They were probably going to Sarajevo, that old Bosnian capital where the last war started when the Archduke, Franz Ferdinand, was assassinated there. Sarajevo was in a cup of the mountains. It was far away. Surely the government would be safe in Sarajevo, and maybe they would get a chance to set up their big radio station. And then maybe we could get some news out.

But now we had some problems. The principal one was gasoline. The tanks of both cars were empty. There was, of course, no gasoline for sale anywhere. Almost every drop had been commandeered by the military. The British and Greek diplomats, representing countries that were expected to help Yugoslavia out of her difficulties, were given all they wanted. But the rest of the diplomats begged in vain. Macatee saw everyone in authority whom he could possibly buttonhole. But he didn't have any luck. At that moment the government wasn't much interested in whether American diplomats and newspapermen went places or not. It was the first time in our whole European experience that the word American didn't have some sort of magic spell about it.

It was a desperate situation, because that bombing we had been promised by the Hungarian radio might come any moment now. And without gasoline we were trapped in this filthy little town of Užice. And so we held a council of war. We decided drastic situations needed drastic action. Then we split up and went out foraging. We pledged our word to one another that we'd be drastic. Brock came back first. He had located a government gasoline dump. The stuff was in big fifteen-liter cans. A high fence surrounded the storage grounds, but there were no guards. Come nightfall, Brock said, there wouldn't be anything to it.

Then someone found a dirty little cafana on the edge of the city, where they had one bedroom to rent. We drove out there, but somehow the car skidded off the road on the edge of a ravine over a roaring little river. We didn't dare use the engine to try to get back on the road, because it seemed to us that the weight of a feather would have sent the car catapulting down the ravine. It was a job for a towing truck, but people just laughed when we asked where we could hire one. All that sort of equipment had been taken by the army days ago. We finally rounded up about twenty husky Serbs, who lifted the car by sheer man power and placed it back on the road. They refused to accept money, but they were willing to have a few drinks.

We took them to the cafana and ordered slivovich, and the patron brought out some bitter cabbage salad designed to make you want more slivo. But it tasted damned good to a bunch of hungry newspapermen, and we sat there for hours drinking slivo and eating sour cabbage salad while our twenty guests toasted *Amerika* and the *Amerikanskis,* and the *Angleskis* and the Serbs, who were going to drive the Germans right back to Berlin. Oh, it was going to be a glorious war. Serbia would fight as she had never fought before. God help Hitler now! Then Brock started singing some of the Comitaji battle songs, and the Serbs grinned and joined in, and we slapped one another on the back, and we even forgot to ask why, with Yugoslavia fighting a life-and-death struggle at that very moment, these twenty husky sons of the soil weren't out on some frontier in khaki uniform instead of sitting around a cafana talking about it.

After they staggered home, pretty drunk, we went out to steal that gasoline. We got over the fence and had two of the fifteen-liter cans in our car before anything happened. But then a carload of officers drove up and got suspicious, and we decided that two cans were better than no cans at all, and we got away from that place fast. The thirty liters, we figured, would get the Buick part way to Sarajevo anyway. Now the problem was to get gas for the Chevrolet. But we were too tired by then even to think. It looked as if this might be the night to get some sleep, and so we went up to our one room above the cafana.

There were two beds for the five of us. Hill and I shared the narrowest single bed ever made. Hill slept a few hours. That was the trouble. He slept, and apparently had nightmares about

Belgrade, because he thrashed his legs around as if he were running from bombs. So I spent the few hours we were in that bed together dodging the Hill legs and thinking about comfortable hotels like the Srpski Kralj and the Athenee Palace in Bucharest and the Ritz in Budapest and the Grand Bulgaria in Sofia, where they have a gadget by which you can wake yourself up with musical bells at any hour you wish simply by putting two plugs in holes marked with the hours and the minutes.

I was the only one awake when the excited little patron rushed in shortly after dawn shouting in Serbian that we'd better get out in a hurry, because the German motorized columns were bearing down fast on Užice.

We were out of the place in a couple of minutes. Brock and Macatee took the Chevrolet into town to try to find the people Hill had been carting along. We felt no more responsibility for Hill's Greek passengers, but we did want to save Aroeti and Edwards and his wife. They had left their luggage with us and had found quarters somewhere in the town. Also there was gas to get for the Chevrolet unless we were going to abandon it.

While they were gone the rest of us watched the parade go by. The Hungarian report that Užice was going to be bombed, and then the rumor that the German army was approaching, must have spread all over town, because the highway leading toward Sarajevo, which went right past the door of the cafana, was one solid line of cars. Up near the head of the procession we saw the square, boxlike limousine of Campbell, the British Minister, with a big Union Jack flying from the left fender and a lot of cans of gasoline tied on behind. He was followed by several dozen other British cars.

The Campbell car made me think of Bucharest a few weeks before, after the German army had moved in. The German generals in charge of that expeditionary force paid a visit to the royal palace and took a fancy to Rumania's boy king, Michael, but they found he was rather glum and despondent about the abdication of his father, Carol, and the general state of things in the country. They decided to put on a show for him, knowing

his love of military things. That was the explanation back of the
sudden announcement that for no particular reason the Germans
would parade a whole division of their motorized equipment
down the Chaussee Kisselef. For an hour or two the mobile might
of the Nazis swept by the grandstand where little Michael sat
goggle-eyed. After the parade was all over, and just as Michael
and the other dignitaries were getting ready to leave the grandstand and go home, there was a sudden piercing toot of an automobile horn, and down the street sailed the square boxlike Rolls-
Royce of Sir Reginald Hoare, British Minister, with its Union
Jack flying in the breeze as a brief reminder to Michael and the
people of Bucharest that the British were still around those parts.
The British Legation that afternoon slyly refused to say whether
it had just been a coincidence or whether it really was a well-
planned propaganda trick.

Anyway, Campbell in his car that looked so much like Sir
Reginald's was up near the head of the parade out of Užice that
morning, and there were a lot of other diplomats not far behind
him. Then came refugees of various nationalities, and hundreds
of government cars and then the army. It wasn't anything like
that German parade we had seen on Bucharest's tree-lined
Chaussee Kisselef. This was an army in rout. The soldiers had
commandeered any vehicle they could get their hands on. Motorcycles, grocery-store trucks, everything in the way of private cars
from new limousines down to model T Fords, moving vans, gar-
bage carts—anything with a motor in it. This was different from
the flight out of Belgrade, because on this road there was no room
for anything that wouldn't run on its own power. Horse-drawn
carts and ox-drawn peasant wagons were shoved off the highway.
The people were mad. They fought like New York taxi drivers
for places on the road. And whenever the traffic came to a halt
men and women popped up from nowhere and tried to jump on
running boards or on the tailboards of trucks or even on the
handlebars of motorcycles.

Some of the soldiers had shed their uniforms and put on ill-
fitting civilian clothes that they had picked up somewhere. Some

of them still carried their guns, but most of them were completely unarmed. In some of the trucks they had broken-down motorcycles that had once belonged to army dispatch riders. In other trucks they had mounds of assorted military stuff, such as tents and cans of rations.

All the passengers and most of the drivers kept looking back toward Užice, probably to see if the Germans were catching up with them. But there was no sign of the Germans except a reconnaissance plane that flew low over the road. It didn't drop any bombs or use its machine gun, but it gave us the jitters, because Macatee and Brock weren't back yet, and we were afraid that by the time they did come the road might be under real attack from the air. The reconnaissance plane would surely send word to the nearest German base that there was a swell target here.

While we stood in the door of the cafana waiting, the patron ran up and said, "For God's sake, are you men crazy, leaving that Buick standing out on the road unguarded?"

We told him that all the doors were locked, but he shot back that it was our car and we could do anything we wanted to with it, but maybe we'd like to know that there were two soldiers right now trying to break into it and steal it.

Chinigo and I ran out to the car, and the soldiers acted considerably embarrassed. We felt sorry for the pair of them. They seemed so tired and depressed. They had such a hunted look in their eyes. We tried to explain to them, largely by gestures, that the car belonged to us and that we were going to use it pretty soon and that we were sorry but we couldn't even offer them a place in it because we were going to be full up. Then we had the patron of the cafana bring them out a glass of slivo apiece. They sat on the running board drinking the fire water and chewing on some stale pieces of black bread. When they finished they shook hands with us and started trudging down the road. They seemed symbols of Yugoslavia's impending defeat.

Finally Macatee and Brock showed up. They had a pretty Serb girl with them. They introduced her to us as Millie. She seemed to be in her early twenties. Macatee took the rest of us aside and explained the situation. Her family, he said, was quite prominent in Belgrade. Macatee had known them well. Millie had gotten as far as Užice with her mother. Now her mother wanted to stay there. She knew German and she figured she could get along with the enemy when and if they arrived. But Millie was of a different mind. She wanted to keep going. So Macatee, subject to the approval of the rest of us, thought we ought to take Millie along. Especially because she was the one who had gotten gas for the Chevrolet. When she found that that was our chief problem she had gone to an influential army officer she knew in Užice and had pleaded until he filled the tank half full. And besides, Macatee said, we had extra room now because he and Brock had searched the town without finding a trace of Edwards and his wife and Aroeti. No one knew just where they had spent the night, and no one had seen them all morning.

While we stood there talking, a woman came up, kissed the American flag fastened to the fender, and started whining in English that we simply had to save her and her four small children, who were trailing after her like chickens after a mother hen. Her eldest son was in America. She herself had been in America once. Here was a letter from the son. See, he says, please Mother take care of yourself. I won't be able to help you if anything happens.

The reason you must save me, she said, is because I myself served in the American and British armies at Salonika in the last war and the Germans know it, and so you can see what's going to happen to me when they catch me.

That story about how she had served in the American army at Salonika gives you an idea how desperate these people were that day when everyone was trying to get out of Užice. They were grasping at any straw, using any argument, no matter how illogical.

We had a lot of trouble getting the two cars into the procession, because a crowd had gathered and they all thought there was room for at least a dozen or two of them in the two cars. The woman with the son in America was especially troublesome. She got hysterical when she saw we were going to turn down her appeal. But she quieted down and finally went off into the woods with her children after Macatee took her son's address and promised to write to him and say she was all right, and after the rest of us took up a little collection among ourselves and gave her a handful of Yugoslav banknotes to keep her going.

It hurt to have to be so gruff with all these people who wanted only to live and let live, but there were millions of them in the country, and we couldn't save them all; and we were beginning to wonder whether we could even get away fast enough ourselves, because it was about time for those bombers to be coming over to work on the target the reconnaissance plane had discovered.

CHAPTER FIVE

Welcome to Sarajevo

———————◄◆►———————

From užice to sarajevo doesn't look far on a map, but the road twists and turns in dizzy hairpin fashion around and around and over some of the steepest mountains in that part of the world. Also, don't forget what was ahead of us. Anything that anyone thought might run, with luck. And remember, too, that even if it was April it was still winter up in those mountains. The road was deep with snow, so that there was room for only one line of traffic, with no passing. If something up ahead broke down, thousands of cars behind had to stop until it was repaired or pushed off the road over a ravine. Some of the cars went over the ravine without being pushed. There were a lot of accidents that night, and everybody was too busy trying to save his own life to bother much about what happened to other people. Unless, of course, the accident blocked the road. One big gasoline truck, fully loaded, went over a precipice and caught on fire. It was still burning, down in the valley, when we went by. It was upside down, with the driver's cab buried in the dirt, which made me think the driver and his passengers probably were still trapped underneath. But nobody seemed to be bothered.

One thing that made it a tough drive was that the road was covered with a thin layer of ice, and few of us had chains. When we came to a steep grade we'd stop and get out and help push two or three cars ahead of us up the hill. Sometimes those hills were two or three miles long, which meant we had quite a hike back to our own cars, and then we had to beg those behind us to do us the same favor.

Not far out of Užice we were stopped for a long time, and some of us walked a mile or two ahead to see what the trouble was. On a very steep hill we found half a dozen big trucks parked in the center of the road. While soldiers with rifles stood guard, gangs of men hauled huge packing cases from the trucks down into a valley. When they ripped the wooden boxes to pieces we saw that there were big tin boxes inside, all neatly soldered together. The tin boxes were filled with bundles of legal-looking papers, many of them covered with large red seals. By the time they had all five or six truckloads of packing cases and tin containers ripped open, and all the papers piled up in the center of the valley, they had a real mountain of documents. Almost as big as a two-story house. While all this was going on, other men were rolling drums of gasoline down the hillside into the valley. Then they poured the gasoline over the papers and set off the bonfire.

At this point Millie proved her value again. One of the officers in charge of this official bit of incendiarism was a good friend of hers, and he explained the whole thing. These were the official Yugoslav state papers. Secret treaties, diplomatic reports, everything they had been able to salvage before the government fled from Belgrade. Simovich had decided that the war had now reached a point where everything should be destroyed. It would prevent some embarrassing moments for a lot of people who might fall into German hands when Yugoslavia fell. And it might even avoid a few executions.

Somehow that document-burning scene was one of the most depressing sights we had seen. The war had been going on for only five days, but already by this action Yugoslavia was admitting that the cause was hopeless; that there wasn't a chance of holding out for long in any corner of the country. It seemed like the death knell of a nation that had existed as a nation for only a quarter of a century. Only since it had been given the breath of life at the peace tables of Versailles. Almost a stillbirth, if you looked at it from the long historical point of view. As we stood there in a snow-filled road between Užice and Sarajevo, watching the Yugoslav government destroying its archives, we somehow sensed that this meant the end of Yugoslavia, even though Croatia, Serbia, Bosnia, and all the other sections of the country might someday live again as individual entities, or as parts of larger entities.

But watching that bonfire was a break for us. We had been figuring out, as we went along, that we didn't have nearly enough gasoline to get the two cars to Sarajevo, and we couldn't all jam into one car, and what were we going to do when one of the tanks ran dry? But Millie was making hay while the road was blocked and the fire was burning. Suddenly she ran over to us and said her officer friend had agreed that if there was any gasoline left in the drums after the papers had been burned we could have all we needed. We waited. There was some left. And so we got our two tanks filled to the brim. That was luck, because we had to crawl along most of the night in first or second, and eventually we used twice what we had figured we'd be needing.

The farther we went along that mountain road the tougher the driving conditions, the deeper the snow, the icier the surface, the tireder the drivers, and the more accidents. At every curve, where the road widened a little, we saw parked trucks, motor busses, and large private cars that had broken down and been abandoned. By morning at least half, and maybe two thirds, of the vehicles in the procession at the beginning were missing. They had either gone over the cliffs or had been left along the road somewhere. The British abandoned a good percentage of their cars. Several times we came on a big sedan or a sport coupé off in a ditch, up to its hubs in trouble, but with its Union Jack still proudly flying. We often stopped to help these British in distress, and sometimes, tired and exhausted though we were, we were able to lend them just the extra man power they needed to get back into the road. But more often we watched them switch all their belongings to some other car, drain the last drop of gas from the abandoned wreck; and leave it as a gift for whoever, some other day, might be able to make it run again.

It had been spring in Belgrade when we left there. Forsythia and violets and fruit trees had been in bloom, and we weren't prepared for mountain snowstorms. When we were deciding what to salvage from the wreckage of Belgrade, most of us had figured we could abandon our overcoats and winter clothes with impunity. Now we shivered and our teeth chattered and we regretted our foolishness. Now coldness was added to exhaustion and hunger. And we were in a situation where all our wits were needed. Darkness had closed in without the German bombers arriving, but time was precious, because we knew that if we didn't make Sarajevo by dawn we might still be in for it.

Brock drove the big Buick most of the night, while I played first mechanic and lookout, sitting with my head out the window, or standing on the running board. Hill was driving the Chevrolet, and we let him keep ahead of us, because there was more chance of his car breaking down, and we didn't want to lose him. Sometime during the night Hill went to sleep at the wheel. Fortunately he was only going twenty or thirty miles an hour, but it took us a long time to get the Chevrolet out of the ditch. Then Macatee ordered me to take over the driving of the little car.

I was glad, when dawn came, that I was having to stay awake, because otherwise I might have missed the most glorious sight in all Europe. We were about ten miles out of Sarajevo when we first saw the city. The road that circled around the rim of a mountain seemed to be miles above the houses and factories and churches down there in the bottom of the valley. The sun was just coming up, painting the whole scene with great rich streaks of red and yellow. There was a light snow falling, which made just the right kind of a filter or screen. Through the snow this fairyland in the cup of the mountains looked even more lovely than it really was. They had said Sarajevo would be a safe place for the government and the rest of us to hide. But from our first glimpse of it we began to doubt that boast. Planes would have to fly high to get over the mountains, but once above Sarajevo, the town was a perfect target.

We didn't worry much about things like that now. Sarajevo, to us, meant civilization again. Heat, food, dry warm clothing, and maybe a little rest. That's what we wanted the most. A little rest. We tried to count the days. It must be Friday. The bombing of Belgrade had been Sunday morning. Then this was the beginning of the fifth day. It seemed inconceivable. Four days. We felt as if we had been wandering around for months. Less than a hundred hours ago Brock and I were having breakfast on the little balcony of the Srpski Kralj Hotel and watching for the Nazi bombers. Less than a hundred hours ago Yugoslavia was at peace with the world.

Sarajevo! We were pretty tired and we were hard-boiled newspapermen to whom the things tourists go for never meant anything anyway, but we did get excited about arriving now in Sarajevo. We knew the last war had started here and we knew that this war might eventually center here. What we didn't know that morning was that here the new Balkan war would really end. Here the doom of Yugoslavia, and Greece too, would be sounded.

Sarajevo wasn't much of a city, but it had a lot of color and atmosphere. I know those are trite words, but wait and I'll tell you what I mean. The sky was faintly blue. The sky always seemed to be blue over Sarajevo, even through the snow. And up into the blue poked the slender white minarets of dozens of mosques. Sarajevo, the most Oriental city in all Europe. More Turkish, it seemed, than Istanbul itself. Here the women all hid their faces behind thick black veils, exposing only their dark flashing eyes, which seemed so bewitching and so inviting. Here the men all wore red fezzes. Turkey herself had banned both veils and fezzes, and few people ever go into Turkish mosques any more. Here they really were more Turkish than the Turks.

That Turkish influence was also a reminder. A historical sign-post. A reminder that what was happening now to Yugoslavia was nothing new. Centuries ago the Turks had swept through this land of quiet green hills and peaceful people, just as the Germans and Italians were sweeping through today. The Turks were finally driven out, but they left behind them the mosques and the fezzes and the veils and a lot of other vestigial reminders of their visit. We thought about those things that April morning as we drove into Sarajevo and we wondered what the Axis would leave behind if and when it was driven out.

Driven out? They weren't here yet. But what we saw when we went down the main street made us realize that the people of Sarajevo expected them soon. Most of the shopkeepers had locked their doors, pulled down the steel shutters over their plate-glass windows, and given up any idea of doing business any more. The streets were almost deserted. Those few people who were abroad had a strange look in their eyes. They looked at you suspiciously. Accusingly. Their eyes seemed to say, Why have you come here? Who are you anyway? Don't you realize you'll attract those things in the sky? What if Sarajevo is bombed? Who will be to blame? You! You! You! Their eyes seemed to shout out the accusations. We live today. Tomorrow we may be dead, all because of—YOU!

I couldn't look into the eyes of those people, because I felt that their silent accusations were well made. What business did we have here? We were just parasites. Just lightning attractors. Cowardly, fleeing foreigners who had no interest in anything but our own skins, and to hell with anyone else. I felt sorry for the people of Sarajevo, but I was too tired to do much thinking about it. I wanted, like the people in all these hundreds of other cars, just a little food and a place to rest my head.

We went to the one hotel, the Europa. After I got back, many weeks later, to New York, I told an artist friend about these things, and he drew his conception of the café of the Europa Hotel in Sarajevo. He made it look like an imitation of the

Stevens in Chicago or the Waldorf in New York. So let's get it straight now. The Europa was the leading hotel in that part of southeastern Europe, but it was about as fancy as a third-rate workmen's hotel near the railroad yards or the steel mills in some place like Gary, Indiana. Third class. Dirty. Drab. But still it was a hotel, and we went in and asked for rooms. The manager just shook his head. No rooms. Then we went into the café. It was a big place with maybe three hundred tables, iron legs, marble tops. Around those three hundred tables were about fifteen hundred people, not counting the hundreds who circulated in and out of the room. As far as food was concerned it was Užice all over again. All they had to offer was slivo or pale tea that tasted exactly like dishwater must taste. We had both. Tea and slivo. The slivo warmed us up anyway.

Then we looked around. Everyone we had ever known in Belgrade seemed to be here. Nicky came running over and whispered in my ear that Sonia was here. Sonia! Thank God! Then Dave Walker, with his famous overcoat that trailed the ground and his half-kindly, half-cynical smile, strode across the room. Good old Dave Walker, the best friend any man ever had. Dave Walker of Reuter's and the London *Daily Mirror*. Wars could come and armies could fall and cities could be bombed and the British could make mistakes, but Dave will always represent the very finest there is about the English race. He had all those qualities we like to think all Englishmen have. A Rock of Gibraltar. As loyal a man, to his country and to his friends, as ever lived.

Dave took me aside and said, "I've got bad news for you, Bob. Leon Kay of the United Press and Leigh White of Columbia Broadcasting went through here last night. They left Belgrade with Fortier. They all went to G.H.Q. Then they came on here. They've been working like dogs trying to get news out. Yesterday they got the Admiral of the Yugoslav fleet to send something out for them over the fleet's wireless. But there was a lot of doubt whether the message was ever picked up anywhere. And now they've gone to the Adriatic coast to buy a boat and push off for Greece so that they can be the first to file the complete story of what has happened in Yugoslavia."

That, to me, was the worst news of the war. And to Chinigo too. Because Kay was our big rival. As far as we knew we hadn't got a single story out ourselves. Except, of course, that hundred-word message we had sent by the British short-wave set. But we had addressed our message to the UP and Columbia, as well as to our own outfits. So even if those hundred words had actually reached America, Kay and White were one up on us if they managed to get a message of their own out.

Just then Maplebeck came through the door in his R.A.F. uniform, and we pounced on him. He was grinning, as usual, but underneath the grin he looked worn and haggard. We hated to bother him, we said, but how about our dispatch? Had it gone? His grin completely vanished. Yes, it had gone—as far as London. But apparently the British censor had held it up. He was sure it had never reached New York. That news, plus the report about Kay and White, plus exhaustion, hunger, and a lot of other things, put all of us in a black mood.

Then Sonia came striding across the room. We were practically strangers to each other, for after all we had had dinner once together and I had walked home with her through the then quiet streets of Belgrade, but we shocked a lot of people that morning in Sarajevo by throwing ourselves into each other's arms. I really was glad to see her. Maybe it was just because my conscience had been plaguing me so much about having left her in Belgrade. Words tumbled from Sonia's lips in a torrent. I never did get exactly straight just what had happened to her. I do remember she said she hunted around Belgrade for two days for that damned American newspaperman who was going to play Father Protector to her, and then she got a train out of town, and . . . Well, here she was. She skipped over a lot of details about machine-gunning and death. She would! But now we were together again, she said, and she clutched tightly onto my arm. And we aren't going to be separated, are we?

I said no, and I meant it. I promised her faithfully that morning that I would get her safely as far as the seacoast, by hook or by crook. From there on? Who knows?

Sonia and I sat down, and we each had a glass of slivo and a cup of that nauseating tea, and I said, "How about your champagne and Scotch?"

I didn't want to ask her about Belgrade and dead bodies. I wanted right now to talk about tall, cool bottles and other things that weren't important. My head was swimming. The slivo and the rotten tea and the lack of sleep and that drive over the mountains had made me lightheaded.

Sonia asked, "How did you expect me to bring champagne and Scotch when you deserted me and I didn't have a car, and . . ."

So we skipped that. Then I held her hand under the table and said, "Cheer up, I won't desert you this time."

She pressed my hand tighter and said, "Let's go shopping."

That was just like Sonia. Let's go shopping. Trying so hard to be normal and natural and to pretend nothing was happening. Trying to pretend that we weren't right on the edge of hell. That death wasn't closing in fast on all of us. That her own country wasn't all washed up. Her own country that she really did love, as only a European can love his country.

We went out of the Europa café, hand in hand, like a couple of school kids. The rest of them grinned, but we didn't care. Sonia insisted first on going to an apothecary shop and asking for a box of face powder. I forget the make, but she insisted on exactly the right shade of brunette and exactly such-and-such make. I kept thinking, Sonia, you idiot, it won't make a damned bit of difference whether you have powder on your face or not when the bomb hits you. But Sonia asked for face powder, brunette, such-and-such a make. They didn't have it. And so we tramped the streets looking for another shop that was open.

Finally we found it, and while she was handing the money to the clerk and he was counting the pieces of silver very, very carefully, I thought, what does it matter if Sonia gets the right kind of powder, or the clerk collects exactly seventy-eight dinars for it? Powder and dinars will be as important as dust tomorrow or next week. But still, I liked Sonia for that gesture. That thumbing of the nose at fate.

Our big problem on that shopping trip was money. Both of us had plenty of Yugoslav dinars, but we had almost run out of silver coins. About all we had were banknotes, mostly thousand-dinar notes, worth about ten dollars apiece. No one would change them. Paper money was no good any more. They wanted silver. They were suspicious of paper money. They were suspicious of everything and everybody. From that day on paper money was practically worthless. Then I thought of Kay, with his thousand dollars' worth of paper dinars. I was damned glad then that Sunday's slight disturbance in Belgrade had prevented my money man from keeping that appointment with me to change my good American banknotes into dinars.

We noticed something else curious. You could buy things like face powder but you couldn't get cigarettes, matches, or food for love, for silver money, or even for American dollars. Once, later, I saw a dollar bill offered for a penny box of matches—and refused. I found it's a rule of war that cigarettes disappear first, then matches, then food. But you can always buy face powder if you're crazy enough to want it at a time like that.

We were still wandering around shopping like a pair of tourists just come to town when the air-raid sirens went off. I was glad I had found Sonia when I did. She clutched my arm so tightly that it made a bruise where her fingers pressed into my flesh.

"I'll kill you," she said, "if you leave me now." She was much more panicky, of course, than she had been in Belgrade.

But I told her she couldn't get rid of me if she wanted to, and then we started running. Neither of us knew where the air-raid shelters were, so we just ran. Pretty soon we were in a bazaar, like the bazaars of Istanbul, with streets and streets full of stalls and stands from which the natives sold souvenirs, jewelry, clothing, and all manner of merchandise. But we took only a passing glance at their strange displays. We were looking for shelter now.

Down a crooked street, just ahead of us, we saw Brown and

Hill and Chinigo. They were hotfooting it for a big building of some kind off in the distance. But their way was blocked by gendarmes and soldiers who insisted that everyone take cover right where they were. The three newspapermen were arguing furiously with the officers when we sailed by them. We headed for a little mosque at the end of the street and ran into the courtyard. The courtyard where good Moslems are supposed to wash their feet before going in to pray. Sonia was trembling and looking up all the time at the big planes circling over the cup in the mountains. We got as far as the door of the mosque before a young Moslem stopped us. I could understand from his gestures that he was trying to tell us we couldn't go in, air raid or no air raid, because I didn't have a hat on my head and because we both did have shoes on our feet. I knew how strict the Moslems are about religious etiquette, and so I said to Sonia, "Let's stand here in the doorway. We're as safe here as anywhere."

We stood and talked to the young Moslem while the planes roared back and forth over our heads. The young man had a low, soothing voice, and we talked philosophy, and Sonia quieted down amazingly well. Then they finally blew the all-clear signal, and we went back to the Europa.

Sarajevo was a city of bleak desperation that day and the next. It was a city of lost people. A city standing blindfolded on the brink of its doom, without quite knowing it. Hopeless, helpless people milled through the streets now. People who had fled down through the corridors of Europe, from places like Czechoslovakia, Austria, Hungary, and Rumania. They had been fleeing for years, but up until now they had been fleeing rather leisurely. By slow stages. Just keeping ahead of the Germans they hated so much but feared so much more. For the last few days they had been fleeing hysterically, frantically. Now there was little place left for them to flee to. It began to look as if most of them were trapped at last.

The fate of little nations was being decided by the Nazi army, which, for all we knew, was right now coming over the mountains. Clattering through those same snow-filled passes we had

just negotiated. Bearing down on Sarajevo. Everyone agreed that
if and when the invaders got to Sarajevo the game was up.
But it wasn't just the fate of nations that hung in the balance
those days. The fate of thousands of individuals was resting on
such picayune decisions as whether to take this road or that;
whether to head for the sea or up into the hills; whether it was
possible to head anywhere.

In Sarajevo that Friday afternoon we got reports that Skoplje
had fallen. None of us believed it at first. Preposterous! The Germans could never get through that mountain pass leading over
from Bulgaria. Wasn't it an axiom that two men with rifles could
hold that pass against the world? And the Yugoslavs had at least
half a million men to throw into that pass! Besides, if there ever
was any danger of the Germans breaking through, all the Serbs
had to do was to set off a few truckloads of dynamite along the
road winding through that pass. That, our military friends had
told us, would hold up the Nazi tank columns for weeks. There
was just one road through that pass. It was deep down in a
narrow cut. Even a Boy Scout brigade could figure out how to
make it impassable for a hell of a long time to come. No, Skoplje
can't have fallen, we said out loud, but some of us were afraid the
news probably was true.

How they had done it we didn't know. But we remembered
France. And we remembered those nights in Bucharest when the
lights burned until dawn in the Ambassador Hotel while the
Nazi officers worked over their maps. We remembered all the
other signs we had seen of the cold, merciless efficiency of that
army of young men from the north. And then we remembered
those ox carts. Yes, Skoplje might have fallen all right, as inconceivable as it seemed. Then I suddenly remembered Paul. Paul
Vajda, the Hungarian Jew I had sent to Skoplje because I
wanted to keep him out of German hands. Because I thought he
would be so safe there. If the Germans really were in Skoplje,
Paul might by now have been put up against a stone wall. I
cursed myself for my own bungling. My own lack of vision. My
own failure to act on the knowledge I had about the strength of

the Germans. How could I ever face Paul's friends some day and say, Yes, I sent Paul to Skoplje and Skoplje was one of the first cities the Germans took.

But there wasn't anything to do about it now, and so I tried to forget it and I went on circulating around the city in the eternal hunt for some real news about what was going on, for some gasoline to fill our empty tank, and for some kind of communications.

A little later I got it fairly straight that not only had Skoplje been taken, but that the Italians in Albania and the Germans who had come through that mountain pass from Bulgaria had met. That meant the corridor from Yugoslavia south into Greece was cut off now. That meant poor Yugoslavia was now hemmed in on three sides. The necklace of steel was tightening. It also meant that the British with their three hundred thousand troops and the Greeks with all the help they were going to send to the Serbs were cut off from their new ally. And it meant that all these thousands of people in Sarajevo had only one way out now. The Adriatic!

Back in the Europa café I found Macatee and Brock and Brown and Hill and Chinigo in a heated conference. Hill wanted to head quickly for the Adriatic and try to get to Greece by boat. Brock, more Serbian still than the Serbs, laughed his deep-throated laugh and said Hill had gone panicky. Hill didn't know the Serbs. Hill hadn't read history. The war had only begun. Wait until those Serbs got into their mountains. The story about Skoplje was probably a fantastic rumor. Why, even Belgrade hadn't fallen yet! It would soon, of course, but then the Serbs would draw the Germans down into the mountains and the fun would really begin.

I took Hill's side. Brown and Chinigo straddled the fence. Macatee, being a diplomat, did a lot of on-the-one-hand-but-then-again-on-the-other-hand arguing.

Brock's final decision was that he was going to stay. He said we still didn't know for sure that Kay, of the United Press, had left the country. Then he pointed out that if he and Kay and

Brown and Chinigo all stayed, and Hill and I left, and the war lasted another six months, as he still thought it would, wouldn't the New York *Herald Tribune* and the AP be in one sweet position? Hill and I, who were supposed to be covering this Yugoslav war for those two outfits, would be off in Greece or floating around on the Adriatic while the rest of them would be filing powerful pieces to New York about battles that might mark the turning point in the whole war.

That argument worried both Hill and me, because Brock of the *Times* was Hill's big competitor, and Chinigo and Kay worked for the AP's rival news agencies. But then we remembered that we still hadn't sent a story off. Hill and I argued then that even if war did go on another six months, what good would there be in sticking around and not being able to send anything out? Chinigo had the answer. He said that just an hour ago he had found the new headquarters of the Yugoslav government press bureau. It was right down this same street. Chinigo had filed a joint dispatch for all of us. The press chief had assured him it would be sent out within half an hour. The chief refused to say how, of course. He wouldn't even talk about whether that knocked-down radio station had arrived and had been set up. But he did assure Chinigo that finally a way had been found to send dispatches out of the country. That put a different light on the situation. We all took turns listening to BBC, and when late in the evening and again the next day we heard the London announcer say no word had yet been received from either the American or British newspapermen in Yugoslavia, we were sure the press chief was just playing a game. Just trying to pacify the impatience and the anger of the foreign correspondents.

So, in spite of all their arguments, Hill and I decided it was futile to remain any longer in Yugoslavia. We were playing two hunches. One, that the war was about over and that if we didn't move soon we would probably find ourselves in the hands of the Germans. Second, that regardless of how long the war lasted, the communications situation would continue to be impossible and

newspapermen without communications are about as valuable to
their employers as soldiers without ammunition are to an army.

The first consideration was in some ways the more weighty.
Hill had been expelled from Berlin for a story like those that had
gotten me into trouble: a reference to the well-camouflaged but
deep-rooted conflict between the Nazis and the Reds. Hill didn't
relish what the Germans might do to him if they caught up with
him. I felt the same way, only more strongly. I remembered those
telegrams from Berlin addressed to propaganda chiefs in Bucharest, Sofia, and Belgrade demanding that St. John be ordered to
move along. I also knew that the Wilhelmstrasse hadn't been very
pleased over the way great strokes of luck had helped me to
squirm out of those situations. And so I was all for moving along,
especially now that we couldn't get any news out anyway.

In the course of that round-table argument someone suggested
that we put up ten dollars apiece and each write on a piece of
paper the date we expected the Balkan war to end, the pot to go
to the man who came the closest. I forget now what the guesses
were, but they ranged all the way up to the spring of 1942. The
thing that surprised us when we opened the guesses was that
Macatee was the most pessimistic of all of us. So Hill and I
started working on him. If he agreed that the show was about
over, wouldn't he start out for the Adriatic with us right away?
He shook his head. His duty was to remain with the government,
and the government, as far as he knew, was right here in Sarajevo. But he did agree that we could take his Chevrolet. He and
Brock and Chinigo and Brown would use the Buick for their next
move.

Yes, Brock said with a bellow that startled the people in the
café almost as much as if it were an air-raid siren, we'll use the
Buick to drive back to Belgrade when the Serbs recapture the city.

Macatee also said we could take whoever we wanted to in the
Chevrolet, but then he said, "Be sure to take Millie, because I
feel indebted to her for all she's done for us."

And of course I had to take Sonia. When we invited Millie to
go with us she said she'd decide later. She had just met a young

Serb soldier she knew, and she wanted to have a talk with him before she made up her mind. We asked Sonia if she would help us find some gasoline. That slivo and dishwater tea hadn't done much for the gnawing pains in our stomachs, but we knew we could keep going a while longer without food, whereas the Chevrolet would go completely dead after the gallon of fuel we had left was gone.

Gasoline! How worthless all these hundreds of thousands of dollars' worth of cars parked around the streets were without the stuff! All through Yugoslavia we had seen how precarious modern civilization really is. How, if something goes wrong at one of the many vital little spots, the whole structure crumbles. It was that way with the automobiles. Yugoslavia had little gasoline when the war started. Now transportation had broken down, and it was impossible to distribute what fuel they did have. And here in Sarajevo there were thousands of people who knew they were doomed to capture and possibly death because they didn't have anything to put in the fuel tanks of these beautiful big automobiles parked around the streets. And we knew that before long, if the war continued, there would be thousands of army vehicles, including the few tanks and planes the Yugoslavs had, that were also going to be worthless.

And so everyone that black Friday in April in Sarajevo was hunting gasoline. It was a battle of wits, with no tricks barred. Whenever we parked the Chevrolet anywhere, one of us had to stand guard to be sure some unscrupulous or hysterical refugee wouldn't break the lock on the gas tank and siphon out our last drop of fuel. And at times in the café of the Europa we were reminded of the New York Stock Exchange on a two-million-share trading day. Men would wave bundles of dinars, and even bundles of American banknotes, and ask who would take them in return for a few gallons of gasoline. But no one wanted money. You can't eat money. You can't put it into a gas tank. There isn't much you can do with money. We found that out. But some business was done with diamonds. A lot of those refugees had translated all their worldly wealth into diamonds, because you can carry a fortune that way easier than any other way. And now they were offering those diamonds for gasoline. I don't imagine gasoline has ever brought so many carats a gallon as it did that day in Sarajevo.

We didn't have diamonds, but we did have Sonia. At first Hill wasn't much interested in taking Sonia with us. But after Sonia went into action Friday afternoon Hill realized what an asset she was. First we went to the office of the *ban* of the district. Sonia knew his secretary. The secretary shook his head as soon as Sonia mentioned what we were looking for. Then she went to work. Al Jolson would have envied her. She did a mammy act that almost made the secretary break out in tears. As a result, we got a little note to an army officer. Then, off in another part of the city, the army officer gave us a document ordering the local manager of an American oil company to pour fifty liters into our tank. The local manager was a Serb, but he was working for an American company, and because we were Americans he treated us well. We got the fifty liters without much trouble.

Then Sonia went to work again. Finally he broke down and cheated to the extent of adding another ten. That made about fifteen American gallons. Not nearly enough to get us to the Dalmatian coast, but it was fifteen gallons more than anyone else had been able to get that day.

Just as we were leaving the big flat field with its ill-disguised mounds of oil drums we heard the scream of sirens back in the city. And then we saw the planes coming. They were flying low. They were approaching Sarajevo in such a way that they would be going right over our heads. We were in a tough spot. Hill and I wanted to race down the road and get away from all those thousands of gallons of gasoline before the bombs started falling. But gendarmes who sprang out into the road with lowered rifles didn't approve. They forced our car over to the side of the road. And then they put the needle points of their bayonets an inch or two from our spines and made us run over into a field and hide.

Suddenly, a mile off across the field, a machine gun hidden in a cluster of houses let go at them. One of the planes circled around and dropped a stick of bombs into the settlement. In an instant the little wooden houses were all in flames. Then the planes flew right over our field. They were so low we could see the Nazi markings. Sonia and I were in a ditch near the road. She was clinging onto me like a person does when you're trying to save him from drowning. I could hardly breathe because of her grip. The closer the planes came the more she dug her fingernails into me. I wasn't half so much afraid of the planes as I was that I'd be strangled by Sonia. Then, just as the bombers got over our heads, all hell seemed to break loose. We hadn't noticed it before, but the field was crisscrossed with wide trenches about two feet deep. The trenches were full of soldiers who were lying on their backs now, blazing away at the bombing planes with rifles. For some reason the pilots didn't answer. I guess they were probably too amused. Ox carts against tanks, and now muskets against bombing planes! This surely was a musical-comedy war, except that people were being killed and houses were being burned to the ground and cities were being ravaged, and it really wasn't comedy for anyone except a few newspapermen. Newspapermen could laugh, but it wasn't any laughing matter for these poor Serbs with their pathetically futile muskets. They were doing the best they knew how. Only war wasn't what they had been taught war was supposed to be. They were fighting something this time that terrorized them; something they didn't understand. They were fighting machines that sailed right on in spite of all their rifle bullets.

Now those machines were flying over Sarajevo. We could hear a few ack-ack guns blasting away at them, but we could also hear the deep-throated sounds that meant bombs were being dropped and buildings were being destroyed and people were being killed in Sarajevo. We tried to get back to the car while the planes were off over the city, but the gendarmes seemed to mean business. One of them even pulled a shell from his cartridge belt and slipped it into his rifle and then started shouting short Serb words at us. Sonia translated. She said we'd better stay in our ditch. The gendarme was going to kill us if we didn't. I didn't mind staying there so much, even though we were still so close to all that gasoline that we'd certainly get a nice hot bath if the planes came back and bombed the dump. What did make me angry was that in all the raids in Yugoslavia, and later in Greece, the soldiers and gendarmes never would let us talk. Not even in whispers. It was just one more example of their ignorance of modern war. They seemed to think that even if we were hidden from sight, the Nazi pilots would be able to hear us if we as much as whispered. So we just lay there in the ditch and waited for the planes to come back.

Now we knew they were overhead without looking because we could hear the rifles going off again. But once more we were in luck. The pilots were saving their remaining bombs for more important things than gas dumps. They sailed right over our heads and on to the west. This time they were so high that no rifle bullets could possibly have hit them, but when two of the planes got a little beyond us and started down in a slow glide, the Yugoslav soldiers jumped out of their trenches and started cheering and waving their rifles. Some of them even fired shots blindly into the air in the most fantastic celebration I have ever seen. I asked Sonia what it was they were shouting, and she said, "They think the planes are falling. They think they shot them down."

I watched those planes closely while the Serb soldiers were still dancing around and slapping one another on the back. The planes glided down to a few hundred feet and disappeared behind a hill on the horizon. Then I saw what the Serbs didn't see and didn't want to see. I saw clouds of smoke go up and I heard the unmistakable sound bombs make when they hit buildings. I knew that behind the hill was the little resort town of Ilidže, which was where the government was hiding. The Germans also must have known the government was there, because those two planes gave the place a hell of a bombing. Those two planes the Serb soldiers were so sure they had shot down. Then in a few minutes I saw something else. I saw the planes come up again and disappear in the west. But the Serb soldiers were still celebrating. And if there had been such a thing as a real Yugoslav war communiqué, it probably would have announced that night that two Nazi planes had been shot down. That's one reason you can't believe all you read in the papers about the war.

When we got back to Sarajevo we found a lot of the streets full of debris and pieces of bombed buildings. A number of people had been killed. We never were able to find out just how many. But one thing we did find out. The press bureau, which had been pretending to send dispatches for us, was packing up and moving to unknown parts. In fact, there never was a press office in Yugoslavia after that air raid, because one of the bombs landed so close that the whole staff decided their lives were worth more than trying to fool the foreign correspondents any longer.

We went straight to the Europa. The hotel hadn't been hit this time. But in the café those thousands of refugees were more panicky than ever. Word had spread around already that Hill and I were going to leave in the Chevrolet, and a lot of people had found out, in some mysterious way, that we had gotten some gasoline. We were hounded everywhere we went by men and women who begged to be taken along. We could have filled a hundred automobiles with all of those poor benighted souls who told us why their fate was going to be worse than the fate of anyone else. Why we had to pick them, rather than anyone else, to go with us.

The most pathetic case was the old man with the shaggy white hair who started talking to us in English and then in his excitement switched to German, then to Polish, then to French, and finally to Hungarian and Serbian. But we understood most of his story. He was a Polish playwright. You know, THE Polish playwright. The greatest playwright Poland ever had. See! This ring proves it! This ring, they gave it to me on the stage in Vienna in 1931. Because in 1931 I was the greatest playwright in all Europe. Did you hear? All Europe! Now! This letter. It is from Mrs. Roosevelt. She is the wife of your President, *n'est-ce pas?* She says she hopes I get to America. And this book! Look! I carry it with me to show who I am and why I must be saved. This book is about what happened in my country. What the

Germans did to my Poland! I write this book in three languages.
The Germans know about this book. I run and run and run from
the Germans because they know about this book. If they catch me
now . . . Oh, Monsieur, you must save me. You must!

Well, what are you going to do when hundreds of people with
stories all as pathetic as that one demand places in your car?
What answer are you going to make to your soul for refusing
them, for lying to them, for saying maybe. For saying, we'll see.
For saying, tomorrow we'll tell you.

You can't take them all. You may not be able to take any of
them. But you know they are telling the truth about what will
happen to them if you desert them. You know that if you get out
alive yourself and someone ten or twenty or thirty years from
now says Sarajevo to you, things will tighten up inside your brain
and your heart will start skipping beats and you'll think of people
like that playwright with the letter from Mrs. Roosevelt and the
book he wrote in three languages and the ring he got because he
was the best in all Europe in 1931.

It was like a three-ring circus in the Europa café that Friday
afternoon. We kept bumping into people we knew, like the
English newspaperman, Edwards, and his wife, and the Yugoslav
Jewish journalist, Aroeti. We had left them behind in Užice because we hadn't been able to find them. Now they were here. But
why had we abandoned them? Where were the suitcases they had
left in our car? Would we take them on with us when we left
Sarajevo? The accusations and the questions tumble from their
lips, but before we can answer them here is Ruth Mitchell, still in
her crazy looking Comitaji uniform, still without her horse, but
eager now to tell the story of how she had been on a train that
was bombed and machine-gunned, and please didn't some of us
have a few thousand dinars she could borrow? While Macatee
is coming to the rescue, others see his bankroll and also want help
from the Americans, because all Americans are rich, aren't they?
And then someone says, did you notice all these Yugoslav pilots
sitting around the café? They're all fighter pilots and they're just
sitting in cafés now because all their planes have been destroyed

and they have nothing to do but just sit and wait for the end of the war.

And then we notice one pilot with a wild look in his eyes. We recognize him. He was a clerk in an office in Belgrade, only now he's in a blue flying corps uniform. He sits alone at a little table staring straight ahead with a crazy look in his eyes. We go over and sit beside him. We try to be jovial. To buck up his spirits. But he still stares off into space, and between his teeth he says, "I just got news from Belgrade. I got news they killed my mother and my sister. Those God-damned Germans. They dropped bombs on my house. They killed my mother—my sister."

It isn't pleasant to listen to the way he says it. He says it like a madman. He says it as if in another second his brain will burst and fly in pieces. Then he looks into space again for a minute, and finally he talks quieter, slower, calmer, but still between his teeth.

"I am a fighter pilot," he says, "but I tell you what I do tonight. Tonight I steal a bomber plane. A Yugoslav bomber plane. I steal some bombs too. Just like the bombs they dropped on my mother and my sister in Belgrade. I fly the plane to Sofia. Sofia is not far. The Germans are in Sofia. Tonight I bomb those bastards in Sofia."

Before we can say anything he picks up his little glass of slivo, drains the last drop, crushes the glass in his hand, throws the pieces onto the floor, and goes out. The waiter just stares at him. When the door closes, the waiter shakes his head and tears up the unpaid bill for the glass of slivo.

Then Dave Walker comes in and says, "The Croats are in rebellion all over the country. They're trying to set up an independent government in Zagreb. The flimsy structure the great men of Versailles created out of a hodgepodge of little nations begins to crumble fast. But more important than that, the Croats are stirring up revolution all along the Dalmatian coast. If anyone's going to try to get to the sea he'd better get fast."

Dave says he and Peter Brown, of Reuter's, are going to make a dash for it through Mostar. That's the shortest way to the coast. They've got a full tank of gasoline. Just about enough to get there. If we've got twenty or thirty gallons why don't we try it too? But we have less than fifteen gallons now, and that would get us stuck right in the area where the Croat trouble is supposed to be breaking out. We tell Dave we're sorry but we're still working on the gas problem. Maybe we'll be able to follow him tomorrow.

Then another Englishman comes along and says, "Good-by, maybe we'll never see each other again, because tonight I start off on foot for the hills. I'm going to go native. I haven't any way of escaping from the country. No car. No gas. So I'm going off into the wildest part of the mountains I can find. Someday, if I ever hear that England has won the war, I'll come back to civilization. In the meantime I don't think those God-damned Germans will ever be able to find me. I can live on roots of trees if I have to. But I'll live. I'm afraid a lot of the rest of you won't even be doing that in a few days."

Then newsboys come rushing in with an extra paper. It's the first paper we've seen since Brock and I were eating breakfast on Sunday morning and dropped the coffee cups onto the sidewalk in front of the Srpski Kralj Hotel and frightened the man with copies of *Politika* under his arm. The Sarajevo paper has a Yugoslav official announcement in big black type on the first of its four pages. It says that some general has been promoted because his army has retaken Skoplje. The important thing to us is that this is an official admission that Skoplje had fallen. As for it having been retaken, the details in the communiqué make us suspect it.

There's also some reference to great Yugoslav victories in Albania. But while we're still arguing about it the newsboys come back, only now there are gendarmes with them. The gendarmes say it's an order from the War Office that all those extra papers have to be given up. There's something wrong in them. Here are copies of a later edition. Someone made a mistake, they explain. The first paper is all wrong. What this new paper says is all right. We grab the new paper. The war communiqué is still on page one in big black type. The same communiqué, only this time it doesn't say Skoplje had been retaken. It just says fierce fighting is still going on in an attempt to retake Skoplje.

I think we had an egg apiece for supper that night. And maybe a chunk of black bread. All I remember is that we spent two or three hours in the dining room of the Europa shouting and begging and trying to bribe the waiters, who were rushing around explaining to everyone that there wasn't any use ordering or shouting, because there wasn't any food left. But more important than food was a place to sleep. Macatee thought he had it fixed up so he and Brock could sleep out at Ilidže, where the government was and where temporary British and Greek legations had been set up. They took the Buick and drove away. The next morning we found out that they had to sleep in the car. But at least they slept.

Then Millie took Hill aside and whispered something to him, and the two of them went off in the Chevrolet. The next morning we learned that Millie had found some friend of the family who got her a room in one of the summer hotels the government had taken over. But Hill had to spend the night in the Chevrolet. Anyway, he slept too. I don't remember where Brown and Chinigo went, but they both looked a little less seedy in the morning. That left me alone with Sonia, which was all right, because I wanted to try to calm her down before I left her and started hunting a corner where I could curl up for the night.

It had been a touch day and Sonia had already been through a lot more than the rest of us had, because she had stayed for two extra days in Belgrade. She said the city was on fire when she left, and her estimate of the dead was twenty thousand, a figure which American Minister Lane later told Washington was probably pretty accurate. Twenty thousand! Twenty thousand out of a population of three hundred thousand! One out of every fifteen killed! And God only knows how many of the other fourteen had been injured. Had lost legs or arms or other pieces of their bodies. One out of fifteen dead. Just as if half a million people were to be killed in New York City in a two-day raid. Or two hundred and twenty thousand in Chicago. Or a hundred thousand in Los Angeles, or nearly six hundred thousand in London in two days. And London thought it knew something about air raids! London hadn't lost that many in the whole war. But Belgrade had seen one out of fifteen killed. Sonia told me that night as we sat in the café enough about what she had seen in Belgrade to make me realize that she had done well to come out of it as sane as she had.

Sonia also brought the bad news that Lane's house had come in for a terrific bombing. It was a mass of ruins now. No one had been killed. The Minister and all the other Americans had been out in someone's suburban home when it happened. But buried down in that air-raid shelter we had constructed for them, buried down under tons of debris, were all the things we had salvaged from the Srpski Kralj. All our suitcases. All our manuscripts. Everything we owned but the few essentials we had carted along with us.

An English girl who had been in Sarajevo for several days had doubled up with a friend so that Sonia could have her little room, which was just about big enough for the one narrow iron bed and a chair, Sonia said. It was on the top floor, and after we both got so drowsy we couldn't even hear what the other one was saying, Sonia asked me to walk up with her, because the elevators weren't running, and it was against the law to have any lights on in the building except the candles the waiters kept putting on the marble tables in the café and a big candle on the manager's desk in the lobby. I walked up the five or six flights with her while she held onto my arm just as she had done that first night, ages and ages ago, back in the Srpski Kralj dining room in Belgrade.

My feeling for Sonia was a purely protective one. She seemed like such a helpless child, despite her age and intelligence. As I was holding her hand and saying good night she suddenly started to cry, hysterically. She said, "If there's an air raid during the night, I know I'll die of fright. This room is on the top floor. What if bombs land on the roof, as they landed on the roof of the Srpski Kralj?"

She said she didn't want to stay up in this damned little room all alone. She'd rather go down and spend the night in the café. We could put our heads on a couple of those marble-topped tables. But I knew they locked up the café at night, and I also knew that if we could both stretch out and get a few hours of sleep our heads would be clearer the next day to fight the battle of gasoline and transportation and everything else we would have to contend with.

And so I took one of the two blankets and rolled up on the floor. The room was so small that I was half under the bed. I was too tired even to take off my shoes, and I was asleep almost the instant my head touched the floor. But I remember feeling someone trying hard to take off those crazy Serbian peasant sandals I was still wearing. They were so caked with mud that they were almost welded to my foolish-looking Serbian socks. Finally I guess Sonia gave it up, because I still had them on when I woke up. I also remember that we lay there all night, Sonia on the edge of the narrow bed and I on the floor, with her right hand locked tightly around my left hand. She told me when she woke up that that made her brave. I said, "You crazy child, what makes you so afraid of the dark?" She answered, "I never was until this war started. But now the darkness gives me terrible thoughts. I almost think I'm insane sometimes."

It was just getting light when we woke up. I think maybe it was hunger that kept us from sleeping any longer. Or maybe it was because her right arm and my left arm were pretty stiff from that hand-holding. Anyway, she got dressed and we went downstairs, hoping to round up some food before the mob arrived. But the mob had had the same idea. The café and the dining room were both jammed. We had the same choice we had had the day before: dishwater tea or slivo. We made the same choice as we did the day before: both, please!

My head was a little clearer than it had been for days, and I began to worry seriously about all this dallying around. Kay and White now had a two-day start on us. Minutes are important in this newspaper game. Hours can mean you're a great journalist or a bum. Days! What if the opposition laid down this story of

Yugoslavia two *days* ahead of the AP? I'd have a lot of explaining
to do and I'd have to hang my head for a long, long time. So I
said, "Sonia, let's go into action today! Let's get out of Sarajevo!
You and I between us ought to be smart enough to beat this
gasoline game."

Sonia's eyes sparkled, and I liked her more than ever for the
way she snapped out the one phrase all European girls learn
these days before they learn any other English: Okay, baby!

We found Hill and borrowed the car from him and drove right
out to the gasoline dump. The Serbian manager was on duty
already, and Sonia started in on him. She began by a tear-jerking
act that would have brought down any house, but before she
really got going the Serb held up his hand in a commanding
gesture. Sonia, thinking she was losing her audience, just became
more intense. Finally the Serb manager put his fingers in his ears
and began shouting himself. When Sonia stopped for breath she
heard what he was trying to say. He was trying to tell her she
didn't have to act, because we could have all the gas we wanted.
When things quieted down he explained why. Late yesterday
afternoon German reconnaissance planes had flown over his gasoline dumps and taken photographs. That meant, he said, the
bombers· would be here any minute now to give the place the
works. So he'd much rather see the gasoline go to us than go up
in flames. How much could we carry? Well, first, we filled the
tank to the brim. Then we got some fifteen-liter cans and filled
those. I guess we must have taken twenty of them. That made
about seventy-five gallons, besides what we had in the tank.

"My God, Sonia," I yelled at her as she superintended the
loading, "where in hell do you think we're going? We can't drive
any farther than the coast, and that's only three or four hundred
miles."

"Shut up, you fool," she snapped back at me. "We'll need gas
for a boat when we get one, won't we? And besides, we can buy
our way into heaven or hell with whatever we don't need."

The Serb manager also wanted to give us lubricating oil, and
brake fluid, and stuff to clean the windshield, and cans of every-

thing he had in the place. I kept turning it down, but Sonia, being a practical woman, took the cans and put them in the back seat as fast as I tried to hand them back to the Serb manager.

Then we went to the hotel to find Hill and tell him about our luck. He and Millie were having a serious discussion. It seemed that Millie had had another long conversation with her soldier boy. He was a youngster from Belgrade she had known in school, and he had given her some fatherly advice. Up until that moment I didn't know anything about Millie and her motives for flight, but now it all tumbled out. She admitted it was just one big adventure. She had been chasing along with us just for the excitement. But her soldier boy knew she was a member of an outfit of reserve ambulance drivers, and he told her she was a traitor to her country and a slacker and perhaps even worse than that unless she turned right around and headed back into the thick of the fight, where she at least could tie bandages around wounded soldiers' heads even if she couldn't find an ambulance to drive. Millie said, "I know he's right, so good-by, and have a good trip. I'm going to be a good soldier. I've got my feet on the ground now. I guess I've got a job to do, only I'd forgotten about it."

The last we saw of Millie, she and her soldier boy were walking away grinning.

That morning a dozen people asked us if we had seen Macatee, because there was a cable for him. It's difficult to explain what happened inside our heads when people kept saying that. It was as if we had been for years on a desert island a million miles from civilization, and then suddenly someone had said, out of a clear sky, Sir, you're wanted on the telephone.

We finally discovered that by a freak of luck the little British short-wave set had picked out of the air a message that was being relayed from Secretary of State Hull in Washington to Macatee in Sarajevo. Just how Washington found out that Macatee was in Sarajevo we never did discover. But the important thing was that here was the first murmur from the outside world in nearly a week. For all we knew Hitler might have been assassinated;

America might have declared war; anything might have happened in all these days we had been cut off from the rest of civilization. And so we rushed around and found Macatee, and then we rushed around and found the cable, and then we waited, tense with excitement, for him to tell us what it said. It was marked "urgent" and "important," but I don't know to this day what it said. Macatee's face was a complete blank when he finished reading it. Then he handed it to us. It was just a lot of figures. The whole dispatch was in one of the American diplomatic codes. And Macatee, of course, didn't have the code book with him. The code book was back in Belgrade, if it hadn't already been destroyed. And there weren't any communication lines open to Belgrade. So there we were, with a long and urgent message from Washington, but with no way in the world to find out what it said.

That same morning Dave Walker returned. Poor Dave was as exhausted as any man can ever be and still move his feet and his tongue. He explained to us slowly that he had gotten almost to Mostar, which is halfway to the coast, and then had discovered that the Croat rebellion was so serious that it was impossible to get through. The fighting between the two factions was going on right in the highways. It would have been plain suicide to have tried to press forward. Then, on the return trip, their car had gone bad on them. I think they walked part of the way back to Sarajevo.

It was lucky for us that Dave came along just then, because we were about to set out on that same Mostar route ourselves. But now, Dave said, the British Legation was getting worried about the rapid progress the Germans were making toward Sarajevo, and also about the air raids, and so a caravan was being organized. It would leave for the coast by another route tonight. He saw no reason why we shouldn't add our Chevrolet to the procession. He told us to be out at Ilidže at nightfall, after the danger of air raids was over for the day.

Then a new figure appeared on the scene. Pappas the Greek!

We didn't know then, of course, that his story about the three hundred thousand British soldiers and all the planes in Greece was slightly wrong. It was a long time before we found that out. And anyway, we liked Pappas. He was a journalist of the old school, of the European school. Cultured, well-mannered, superficially a gentleman. But now he looked like a cornered wildcat. His eyes moved quickly, as if he expected that someone were going to pounce on him from a dark corner. He talked nervously. He had, he said, been on his way from Greece to Belgrade when war broke out. He was with Sam Brewer, of the Chicago *Tribune*. On Monday they got within twenty or thirty miles of Belgrade. Then their train was stopped. They could see the smoke and fire of the burning city. He and Brewer had somehow gotten separated. He didn't know where Brewer was now, but here he was. And please, for God's sake, would we take him with us! As I said, I didn't know then what I do now about the story of the three hundred thousand men, and so I still thought I owed Pappas a debt for having given me exclusive American rights to the information. And besides, Hill and I talked it over together and decided that Pappas would be a great asset to us. Sonia could do the translating and the arguing until we got out of Yugoslavia, but when we got to Greece she wouldn't be of much help, not knowing the language. But then, if we had Pappas with us, he could take over. Not only was he a Greek but he was an important Greek, and he probably could take care of some of our troubles, such as the fact that we wouldn't have any Greek visas in our passports or any Greek military passes. We told Pappas we would guarantee him a place in the Chevrolet and that we expected to leave tonight.

That afternoon they were shooting suspected spies in Sarajevo. While the roundup was going on, some of the newspaper boys got on a trolley car and were arrested as agents of the enemy. A policeman boasted that he had killed forty-nine men himself already today, and now was looking for Number Fifty. He was more suspicious of Dave Walker than anyone else. The rest of us couldn't figure out just why, because Dave didn't look like any spy I ever saw in real life or in the movies either. But the officer made Dave put his hands above his head and keep them there for about ten minutes while he searched every one of Dave's pockets and examined his British passport, backwards and forwards and upside down, although of course he couldn't read a word of it. All trolley traffic in the city was jammed up while that little party was going on. Then the officer took Dave to the police station.

We fully expected that maybe the fiftieth execution was taking place after all. But while the rest of us were trying to save him by bringing some kind of diplomatic pressure to bear on the police, Dave walked into the Europa. He wore a big grin, but we could tell that it hid a lot of nervousness. Later he admitted it was about the closest call he had ever had. The dangers of those arrests and and public cross-examinations are greater than you might think. First, everyone is always suspicious of you, because you talk a foreign gibberish and don't speak their language. That's one strike on you to begin with. Then, worst of all, even if you convince the official of your innocence, the mob is likely to get worked up and take over your case, which means just what mob action means in any country. We all had experiences there in Yugoslavia and later in Greece that made us fear this spy-caught-by-cop drama more than anything else, even bombs. You can't reason with a bomb, but neither can you reason with a mob that speaks a strange language and sees spies everywhere it goes.

That same afternoon I spotted the pilot with the crazy look in his eyes sitting in the Europa café again with another little glass of slivo. I slapped him good-naturedly on the shoulder and asked, "Well, did you make your little journey to Sofia?" I tried to say it casually, as if I were talking about a motor trip over a holiday week end. He wheeled around and looked me straight in the eye with a glassy stare I've never seen before except in the eyes of insane asylum inmates.

"Yes," he said, "I went." He paused; then he added bitterly, "And I came back, too. But I left a few souvenirs in Sofia. All of them landed in the railroad yards. They made a nice fire. I kept thinking of my mother and my sister when I dropped them. And tonight—tonight I think maybe I go to Budapest. They have big railroad yards in Budapest!"

I don't know if he ever bombed Budapest, but I think so, because after I got back to America I looked up the newspapers for those days and I found that the Axis war communiqués mentioned first the bombing of Sofia and the next night the bombing of Budapest. Of course the papers didn't say that both raids had been made by a crazy air pirate who had stolen one of his own country's bombers because his mother and sister had been killed. They didn't know that in America, and they didn't know it in Sofia or in Budapest either. No one knew it except the crazy pilot himself and a few of his friends. It didn't do me any good to know it, because I still hadn't found any way to send news to America.

As soon as it got dark, Sonia and Pappas and Hill and I wedged ourselves into the Chevrolet with all the cans of gasoline and brake fluid and other paraphernalia. We said good-by to the rest of the boys and started out, we thought, for the seacoast. We didn't have any trouble getting to the government headquarters and the British Legation in suburban Ilidže, but we found a lot of confusion there. Everyone seemed to be running around in circles. It was almost midnight before the British finally told us the caravan couldn't start tonight, because there was still some question about which was the best route to take. Go back to Sarajevo, they said, and get here right after daylight in the morning. Then maybe we'll know something.

Hill and I were wild. That meant Kay and White would have twelve hours more of a jump on us, if they really had started out on the Adriatic. We could never catch up with them now, unless they broke a leg or got bombed. But there wasn't anything else to do about it, and so we turned around and drove the twenty or thirty miles back into town.

We had just gotten into the Europa when the sirens went off. Hundreds of hysterical men and women ran for the only door leading out of the café. Then someone yelled, "There's an air-raid shelter down in the cellar."

As it turned out it wasn't an air-raid shelter at all. It was just a deep basement. The darkest, dampest, most morbid place I have ever been in. The atmosphere didn't bother me, but Sonia kept saying it made her feel as if she were being buried alive. It made her think of stories by that American writer—what was his name —something Poe.

We didn't have any light except from two candles. Pretty soon they burned out. After that the cellar was an eerie place. Pappas, who had trailed along right behind us, didn't help matters much. He kept talking about how we would probably all be entombed down there, if the hotel were hit, and why had we been so foolish as to come underground, and didn't we know that most of the casualties in Belgrade had been people who had been in underground shelters? He kept it up until suddenly Sonia dug her nails into my arm and started to scream. Not a delicate parlor scream, but a blood-curdling, Lady Macbeth kind of a scream. That set everybody's nerves on edge. I grabbed her by the shoulders and talked fast and evenly to her. I tried to talk sternly but quietly. I told her I'd leave her to fend for herself if she didn't muster up some self-control. I tried to talk to her like a father, even though she was nearly as old as I was.

It worked, because she finally quieted down, but then she whispered that she hated Pappas. It wasn't only what he said, but it was something about his voice. He did as much, she said, to un-nerve her as I did to keep her calm. Please, she begged, couldn't we get rid of Pappas? I felt sorry for both of them. I liked Pappas. And I liked Sonia. So I whispered to Pappas that Sonia was almost a mental case and he'd have to help me with her by keeping quiet. Then I took Sonia's arm and walked off to another corner of the cellar with her.

After the raid was over we went upstairs and began to think about how hungry we were. Damned hungry. Too damned hungry to drink dishwater tea and slivo any longer. We went into the dining room, and I tried slipping one of the waiters a handful of Yugoslav dinars. He took the money, and we waited an hour and nothing happened. When I spoke to him about it he said I must have made a mistake. I hadn't given him any money, and besides there just wasn't any food to be had. No, not even for English money or American money or any other kind of money.

I turned around to tell Sonia what I thought of him, but she was gone. I just saw the back of her red skirt sailing through the door into the kitchen. I knew her well enough by then to know she was up to something. It was about ten minutes before she came back. She had something under her arm wrapped in a newspaper and she winked at us, so we followed her out to the street. When we got safely inside the car she unwrapped the package. It was a can of cherries. One of those cans that sell all over America for ten cents. There was only about a spoonful of cherries apiece for each of us, but it was food. Real honest-to-God food. I was telling Sonia how smart she was when I noticed that her heavy leather jacket was missing. I asked what happened to it. She just grinned. Then I knew. She finally admitted it. She had given the jacket to the chef out in the kitchen in trade for the ten-cent can of cherries. You can't understand just what that meant because you don't know how cold it was up in those Bosnian mountains in April.

I wish we had never gone back into the Europa that night, because we were trailed and hounded and harried everywhere we went. Pappas was the worst of all of them. From the moment of that little unpleasantness down in the cellar he became a leech. He seemed afraid that under Sonia's influence we'd try to go back on our promise of transportation. I know he was unnerved by what he had seen in Belgrade and that he was terrified at the idea of being captured by the enemy. He was a Greek, of course. A belligerent. I tried to make all those allowances for him, but he was also a man, after all, and what if we had never agreed to take him in the first place? What would he have done then? And besides, I had no idea of going back on the promise. Only I was too damned tired to have a big six-foot Greek chasing at my heels and hurling questions at me every second about where I was going and what I was going to do. Furthermore, he did most of his talking in French and my brain wasn't up to the mental gymnastics that I always had to go through to understand French the way Pappas spoke it.

There were a lot of others for whom I ordinarily would have felt very sorry, but it all seemed so futile now. With our typewriters and our few pieces of essential luggage and all those extra cans of petroleum products there was hardly room in the car for the four of us. We couldn't possibly jam another person in. Yet here they were by the dozens, whining and begging and pleading and offering us money and jewelry if we would only take them with us. There was an attractive young red-haired Swedish woman who didn't know a word of any language except English and Swedish. How she got to Sarajevo, who she was, where she wanted to go, and why she was so terrified I don't know. But she cried that she couldn't make anyone else understand her but the handful of English and Americans. And soon we would all be gone, and what would she do then?

I honestly tried to help her. I tried to find someone else to accommodate her. But she insisted she was going with us. Then, when we refused flatly, she started exercising her feminine wiles. Well, I was in no condition to give in to feminine wiles and neither was I in any condition to resist them, and so I just ran away from her. At the same time I was trying to shake myself loose from Pappas. I finally took refuge in the men's washroom. At least the redhead couldn't follow me there, but Pappas stood outside the door waiting. Then I noticed that there was a door leading out of the washroom into the kitchen and I ducked out that way. On my way through the kitchen I grabbed two hard rolls off a plate some careless person had left on the table and stuffed them into my pockets. Then I ducked through the café, which was closed by now, and went out to the car, where Sonia and Hill were waiting for me.

Sonia said, "Where do we sleep? That friend of mine has given her room on the top floor to someone else tonight."

I suggested that she take the back seat of the Chevrolet and Hill the front seat while I tried to find some corner of the hotel lobby to curl up in. But Sonia said, "No, I've got a better idea than that. You boys wait here. I'm going to get a hotel room for us, with beds.and clean sheets and all that sort of thing."

Before we could ask her how she was going to work it she was gone.

"That girl's crazy," Hill said. "A person couldn't rent a room in that hotel tonight for a hundred dollars."

"Yes, she's crazy all right, Russell," I told him. "Just about as crazy as a fox. There wasn't any food, but she got us a can of cherries, didn't she?"

In a little while Sonia was back. She slipped into the seat beside me and dropped something cold into my hand. It was a key on a chain with a metal tag attached to it. I still remember what that tag said—Chambre 201.

"How did you do it?" Hill asked. He was really impressed.

"Easy," Sonia said, with a rich laugh that made us forget planes and bombs and death for a second. "On the law of averages," she went on, "out of two or three hundred people in a hotel you'd expect to find one or two who'd be careless, even in an emergency. So I ran up to the top floor and started working down. I looked in every door to see if anyone had gone off and carelessly left his key in the lock. Finally, on the second floor, I found this. I peeked in the room. I think it's the bridal chamber or the bedroom they save for the king. Anyway it's the biggest room in town. But we'd better get up and lock ourselves in before the real tenant shows up."

So we left the car and paid a fellow to watch it and started for Chambre 201. Pappas was waiting for us in the lobby. He asked where were we sleeping, and when we told him we had a room he said, "Quite frankly, I'm not going to let you out of my sight. I'll just come in and share the room with you if you don't mind."

I felt a tug at my arm. It was Sonia. She took me aside and said that if I let Pappas in the room she'd probably strangle him, and besides it was her room and she surely had a right to pick her own guests if she wanted to. So we compromised by telling Pappas he'd have to find a corner out in the hall where he could keep an eye on our door if he wanted to. Then Hill and Sonia and I locked ourselves in and left the key turned halfway in the lock so no one could push it out from the other side with a skeleton key. I guess I wasn't quite so tired as I was the night before, because I managed to pry the Serbian peasant sandals off my swollen feet before I fell asleep. It must have been an hour or two later when I woke up. It wasn't the noise that startled me. It was Sonia shaking my shoulder.

I whispered, "What's the matter?" But before she could answer there was a heavy pounding on the door. I laughed and said to Sonia under my breath, "I hope our host had a good night's sleep last night."

And then I went to sleep again.

CHAPTER SIX

Too Late for Help

———◆●◆———

I GUESS it was the church bells that woke me up. It was just dawn. I rubbed my eyes and tried to figure out where I was, and what day it was, and why church bells were ringing. Finally I remembered. I wish I hadn't remembered, because otherwise I might have been able to get to sleep again. We had been in bed only three or four hours, and it was the first bit of real, untroubled sleep in a full week.

But now thought killed sleep. One week. Then this must be Sunday. Easter Sunday. So that was why the church bells were ringing so early in the morning. Easter! Christ on a cross. Christ risen from the dead. Peace on earth, good will to men. All so beautiful, until Christians abandon their Christianity and go to war. As ye do unto them, so will I do unto you. A lot of words from the Bible tumbled through my head as I lay there listening to the church bells. They were ringing out a futile call. When savage instincts get the upper hand, no one pays much attention to what the church bells say.

Then I remembered a service flag that used to hang in a big

134

church out in Oak Park, Illinois. I used to be proud that there was a star on that flag for me, because I had been over in France in the last war, a boy crusader. I was religious then. I thought I was fighting in a holy crusade. But that war killed religion for a lot of us. I wasn't proud when I remembered how a man used to step up into a pulpit in that church in Oak Park, Illinois, and preach, instead of Christianity, propaganda that sent young boys like me rushing to enlist in a holy crusade. Now I had seen what that holy crusade had done to a lot of Europe. Big chunks of territory grabbed from this country and given to that country without rhyme or reason, until, in sections like the Balkans, they all hated one another. Which was just what a lot of people wanted. Because then they could play one little country against another little country and keep them busy and make them pawns in the big chess game.

Maybe you can reconcile international politics and Christianity. Maybe you can reconcile war and Christianity. But as I lay there in a stolen bed in the Europa Hotel in Sarajevo, which was so soon to be almost obliterated by bombs on Easter Sunday, I couldn't make sense out of it. I wondered where God was, anyway. I wondered how Christians on both sides—because there are Christians on both sides—reconciled these things.

I remembered talking to young German officers in Bucharest, and young British officers in London. The young German officers said, "We probably don't know as much as you do about National Socialism and Hitler and Jewish persecutions and things like that. We aren't really fighting about these things. We're fighting for our survival. We remember when we were boys back after the last war, and how we had to take bushel baskets of paper marks down to the store to get a loaf of bread. We went hungry in those days, and we were told it was because our enemies of the last war were trying to snuff out Germany. We were told that if we were ever to live again as decent human beings we had to fight a holy crusade for our right to a place in the sun. That's why we're fighting. Sure, we're for Hitler. We're for Hitler because he gave us food, even while we were working to get ready for this war. More food than we had back in the twenties, when France and England were trying to starve us. Hitler gave us hope, even though he may be the horrible creature you say he is."

That was their argument. I know there are plenty of answers. I know what the answers are. But I'm just telling you what they told me.

Then the Englishmen had a good argument. They were also fighting a holy crusade. Always it was a holy crusade. Both sides called it a holy crusade, just like last time. The Englishmen said they were fighting this time for the liberty of individuals, for peace in Europe, for the freedom of little nations, for democracy.

Then I remembered how another Englishman, James Hilton, had written a little book just a couple of years ago in which he said you can never fight a war to make the world safe for democracy, because all wars kill democracy, and you can't fight a war to end all wars, because each war begets a new war. Only that book wasn't as popular as *Good-bye, Mister Chips* because—well, because we were all about to fight another war for democracy and peace.

Those were the things I thought of as I lay in a stolen bed in Sarajevo on Easter Sunday, the day of peace. But I promised to tell you only what I heard and saw and smelled in Europe. I'll stick to my promise from now on, but I couldn't help thinking, just that once. It was all so peaceful at dawn on Easter Sunday, and I had a strange feeling that this would be the last peace for a lot of us for a long, long time.

I got dressed quietly in order not to wake up Hill and Sonia. I sneaked out into the cold of the early morning and wandered down to the garage on the edge of the city where we had left the Chevrolet so that it wouldn't be wrecked if the city were bombed during the night. The radiator was frozen and the starter wouldn't work and the man who had promised to sell us a pair of chains so we could get through the snow-filled mountains that lay between us and the sea had changed his mind. He didn't talk anything but Serbian.

I didn't get the chains, but I finally got the car started and drove up in front of the Europa just in time to give Dave Walker some help. His car was frozen too, and his starter was also broken. We tied the two cars together with a rope, and I started towing his piece of wreckage around the streets. We were right beside a big government building when the sirens went off and the planes started coming over. We could hear their roar above the church bells, which were still ringing out their message of peace on earth, good will to men. The fellow at the wheel of Dave's car got excited and put on his brakes quickly. The rope broke.

I knew the big government building would probably be one of today's targets, because the Nazi planes had been concentrating on government buildings, and so I couldn't leave the other car stranded there. I got out and tried to tie the ends of rope together, but just then the planes came right overhead, and I decided to push the other car instead. After a couple of blocks the other engine started all right, and the driver raced away, waving a thank-you. But that final effort had been too much for the Chevrolet. Now its engine died.

I was right in the middle of a street in a very vulnerable part of the city. The starter was still refusing to work, and I couldn't use a crank because the front of the Chevrolet had been mashed in during one of our frequent accidents coming over the mountains from Užice. There were a few cars tearing around the streets, but I couldn't ask them for help, because they were all ambulances or trucks being used as ambulances to haul the raid victims to hospitals. And so I sat on the running board and waited. I was beginning to get fatalistic about air raids anyway. I remembered what Brock had said under the piano in the Srpski Kralj dining room—either it's got your number on it or it hasn't. Of course that's a lot of foolish fatalism, but it's good psychology to adopt when you're in a corner and you can't do anything about it. It's next best to being religious and praying to God to spare you.

After a while Dave's car came back. The driver had missed me. Now he pushed the Chevrolet. Our bumpers got locked, and even after the engine of the Chevrolet began to turn over by itself we couldn't get separated. We drove tandem fashion up to the Europa, where everybody was waiting for us. A dozen strong men yanked the cars apart, and then the refugee rush began. Of course everyone wanted to get out of town.

I locked the doors of the Chevrolet and ran up to Room 201. Hill was still asleep. Sonia was taking a bath in a washbowl. (Even bridal suites in Yugoslavia don't have private bathrooms.) I told her to get ready in a hurry because we had to get out of town before the streets got so filled up with debris we couldn't drive through them. Then I yanked Hill out of bed. While they were dressing I threw what few worldly possessions I owned into a knapsack I had just bought from a street hawker in front of the hotel. He was doing a land-office business with refugees like myself who finally were getting wise about trying to haul suitcases around. Then I packed up the huge knapsack Sonia had carried on her back all the way from Belgrade. It must have weighed fifty pounds, and Sonia was no truck horse of a woman either. In fact she was slim, almost frail. While I was looking around to be sure we weren't leaving anything I opened the doors of a wardrobe.

"My God," I yelled. "Look!"

There was a whole shelf of canned goods. Ten cans of goulash, four small cans of pheasant paste, eighteen of sardines, and twelve of anchovies, besides a big bag of cookies. When I saw the pheasant paste and the cookies I knew we had stolen the room of some Englishman. No one but an Englishman would be hauling delicate tea cookies and pheasant paste around.

"Put them in that big paper bag," Sonia commanded. "We need them as much as anyone else does."

Out in front of the hotel we found the British caravan getting organized. It was in charge of a handsome, curly-haired fellow they called Major Simmons. He had been the British military attaché at Budapest. He took a fancy to Sonia the minute he saw her, and Sonia, always the politician and diplomat, did nothing to discourage him. She knew, as Hill and I did, too, that we were going to string along in this British caravan only by courtesy of Major Simmons. And most English diplomatic and military men, we had long since discovered, have an ingrained antipathy for newspapermen, their own as well as American. We always felt we had one strike on us the minute we announced our profession. Besides, it was true that we were horning in on their caravan without much claim to a place in the line of cars. Sonia knew all that, and so she played up to the handsome major. They were getting along perfectly within a few minutes. He was telling Sonia all his troubles. He had, it seemed, been locked out of his room last night. And a jolly good room it had been, too. Someone, it seemed, had procured the key somehow. He nearly broke the door down, but it did no good. So he finally had to spend the night in the lobby. Beastly nuisance. Clothes all wrinkled. No place to shave. No . . .

Just then Hill came along, loaded down with the cans of goulash and sardines and anchovies and pheasant paste. The major pounced on him. Sonia tried to play peacemaker. She told him quite frankly that we were the ones who had stolen his room. There was nothing we could do about that now. But as for the food, we would be perfectly willing to divide it with him. Fifty-fifty. Wouldn't that be all right?

Well, since not even a hard-boiled British army major could have said no to Sonia, Hill and I took our twenty-two cans and dumped the other twenty-two in Simmons' car. Then we got started. We had to drive all the way out to Ilidže first, even though it wasn't on our way, in order to get final instructions from the British Legation. That cost us some precious hours, and it was afternoon before we headed for Sarajevo again on our way south through the mountains of Bosnia and Montenegro toward the Dalmatian coast.

As we approached the city a furious air raid was going on. The Germans were celebrating the sacred holiday by dropping Easter eggs on Sarajevo. On the outskirts we saw four or five huge bombers going up and down a little valley, only a few hundred feet off the ground. We couldn't figure out what it meant until we noticed that they all bore Yugoslav markings. Well, Hill said, that proves the Serbs have learned one thing from this war anyway.

So many of their airfields and hangars had been bombed and so many of their planes had been destroyed on the ground that they now had sense enough to get their bombers into the air the minute the Nazis roared out of the clouds. The Yugoslav bombers of course didn't dare go up and do battle with the German machines, because the German machines were so much faster and the pilots so much more expert at dogfighting, but by hiding just over a valley this way they hoped to escape destruction. By this time I don't think the Yugoslavs had a single fighter plane left. All through that short war we never saw a real battle in the air between German and opposition planes. And we never saw a single British plane anywhere in all of Yugoslavia. Or a single British soldier either. Little Yugoslavia was taking it on the chin, all alone.

Sarajevo got it that day, and she had to take it lying down. There wasn't anything to be done but to fire off the anti-aircraft guns occasionally, although, of course, hundreds of soldiers still wasted thousands of shells shooting their rifles into the air.

We could see before we ever got into Sarajevo that we were in for trouble. But there was no way out of it, because the roads all go right through the heart of the city. We held a conference on the edge of Sarajevo. All of us, except Pappas, voted to make the dash. We agreed that if gendarmes tried to stop us we'd sail right by them. We might pick up a few rifle bullets that way, but if we had to stop every time planes came overhead we'd probably never get away.

Pappas was beginning to be a problem. Several times we had stopped out in the suburbs, when the planes came close, and each time Pappas had been the first to find shelter. Even before the wheels stopped he was hurtling over Sonia and making a dash for a safe place. Of course Sonia was roughing it and asking for no special consideration because she was a woman, but still the

Pappas hysteria when there was any danger around somehow went against our American sense of etiquette.

We voted Pappas down and agreed with Simmons, who was tough as nails, that we'd roar right through Sarajevo, despite everything. Hill was at the wheel of the Chevrolet and Pappas was sitting beside him. Sonia and I, by special arrangement, were wedged in the back seat with all the gasoline. As long as I didn't have to worry about driving I could hold her hand and keep her calm. Just holding her hand in a viselike grip seemed to help her retain a good degree of self-control.

We had to drive along the edge of a canal in Sarajevo, and that was where most of the bombs were falling because that was where the big government buildings and hospitals and barracks were. We did a lot of detouring, because the streets were filling up with bricks, stone, glass, pieces of roofs. Even where the bombs weren't falling, balconies and cornices were breaking loose from damaged buildings.

Then we saw that water was going to be a big problem for Sarajevo if and when the raids finally ended. A lot of the water mains had broken. There wouldn't be any way to put out the fires. And furthermore, that city in a cup of the mountains was in for a real flood, because the water was roaring in torrents through the streets.

We were passing a big factory right after it had been hit by a sizable bomb. Our car was at the end of the caravan. Just as we reached the building two men came out carrying something that had once been a man. Now he was just a mass of broken bones, bloody flesh, tatters of clothing. The two men hailed us. Hill slowed down. The two men yelled the Serbian word for hospital. Hill pulled up the hand brake. I jumped out to help them put the man in the back seat. Sonia bit her lips and looked the other way, but she raised no objection. Just then Pappas began shouting in three different languages. "Don't stop. We'll lose the rest of the caravan. Keep going. The man's probably dead anyway."

Hill paid no attention to him. He was already out of his side of the car helping to get the dying man into the back seat. But

Pappas jumped over behind the wheel. Suddenly the car started forward. We were on a slight hill. Pappas had taken off the hand brake. Now he was trying to find the starter button with his foot.

I think that's the only time in my life I ever saw red. I never even understood what the expression meant until that Easter Sunday in Sarajevo. I couldn't control myself. I dropped the legs of the wounded man and jumped onto the running board. First I yanked up the emergency brake. Then I grabbed Pappas by the neck. I thank God now that I was too tired to be very strong. Otherwise I probably would have killed him. There wasn't any sense to what I did, I suppose. But I was almost insane. I dragged Pappas from behind the wheel and pounded him with my one free hand. Then I sent him flying into the street. Sonia told me later I yelled things at him she hadn't ever heard in English before. I called him a yellow son of a bitch and a bastard and a rat and a lot of other things I hardly know how to spell. Sonia in the meantime had jumped out and was helping Hill and the two other men to get the injured man into the car. I got behind the wheel and we started toward the hospital. Pappas just managed to grab onto the door handle by the tips of his fingers and pull himself onto the running board. A few blocks down the street we saw stretcher-bearers coming out of a dressing station. We hailed them and they took the victim off our hands.

By that time I was a little calmer, but I was still angry. Sonia was wiping the blood off the back seat. I told her to come up in front with me. Then I told Pappas to get in back, if he wanted to, but that if he as much as opened his mouth on the rest of the trip I'd knock his head off. He didn't say a word.

We got started again. Of course we were all twisted up now. None of us knew much about the geography of the city. We had lost Simmons and the caravan. Bombs were still falling all around us. But I was so hot under the collar that I just put the accelerator down to the floor and headed in what looked like the right general direction.

"What if we do lose the caravan?" I asked Hill. "What if we get nipped by a piece of shrapnel? At least we've got a clear conscience. We did what we could for that poor bastard who was all torn to pieces. Maybe it was foolish heroics. Maybe he's already dead. But if we live we've got to live with our own consciences, don't we?"

I was sure Hill felt the same way, because he was the one who had stopped the car in the first place. But the person I admired the most was Sonia. I knew the sight of all that torn flesh had made her ill. Yet she had helped to lift the man into the car. Sonia had come through with flying colors in the moment of crisis.

We got through the rest of the city without much trouble. Then, where the houses stopped and the country highway began, we caught up with Simmons and the caravan. Soldiers with machine guns had stopped them. All the cars were under a tunnel bored through the side of a mountain. When we stopped, our front wheels were in the tunnel, but all the rest of the car was exposed. There were a lot of planes roaring around in the sky. The soldiers said it was dangerous to go on, because the bombers were concentrating on a fort right above us on the top of the mountain. We were still sitting in the Chevrolet when the bombs landed. They must have hit the side of the mountain, because tons of boulders and rock broke loose and came cascading down onto the road just behind us. We threw ourselves onto the floor of the car. We were lucky. A few medium-sized rocks hit the top of the Chevrolet and one broke a window, but that was all.

"I guess we've still got horseshoes around our necks," Hill said with a nervous laugh.

Sonia laughed too. She was getting hardened a little now. "God's looking after his sinners," she said. Pappas didn't open his mouth.

Even after the soldiers said they thought the raid was over and we could go on, we couldn't get started because ahead of us the road was full of boulders and big bomb craters. So we took off our coats and got to work. I don't know how long it took us to make that road passable. It seemed like hours. But finally the Anglo-American caravan was under way again.

We turned around occasionally to look at burning Sarajevo. In some ways I think that that Easter raid on the Bosnian capital must have been much worse than the Palm Sunday raid on Belgrade. The poor little city! It hadn't wanted anything. Just to be let alone. But now it had joined the land of silent people. The land of people who were either physically dead and dying, or spiritually dead and dying.

Late in the afternoon we started around a tortuous mountain road. Hill was driving. He went into the curve too fast, then he slapped on his brakes, did some fancy skidding, and ended up with the car at right angles to the road. The front wheels were half over a precipice. It looked like miles down to the bottom of the gorge. We crawled out of the car gingerly, in order not to give it any excuse to take the plunge. We were still at the tail end of the caravan, and so we had to work out our own salvation. It took us quite a time. We didn't dare use the engine, but Hill and I were both New Englanders by adoption, and we got the car back where it belonged by using small trees as levers and pries, just as a Vermont farmer would have done.

A little farther on we caught up with the caravan. It was stopped because Walker's car had broken an axle on a narrow bridge. We pushed the wreckage off into a ditch, and then we presented it to a white-bearded Serb peasant. Somebody made a long presentation speech in English, not one word of which the Serb understood of course. We talked about the *entente cordiale,* and how we were all allies, and how this gift was an Anglo-American tribute to Serb bravery. I wish I had a copy of that speech. And I wish the old man could have understood it. I would have liked to see his facial reaction.

We each took some of the baggage and passengers from the wrecked car. Our share, by request, was Walker and two suitcases. To get them in we had to get rid of some of our gasoline cans, and so we treated the other cars to fuel.

The next time we stopped, the major and Sonia had a whispered conversation. Then the major suggested that he and Pappas change places for a while. Pappas, with his long legs, must be cramped in our small car. He'd have more leg room in the major's sedan. I think the poor Greek was glad to get away from us. And furthermore, we had been talking about how we were going to buy or steal a small fishing boat when we got to the Dalmatian coast, and I don't think that appealed to him. He kept saying, why didn't we all go right on with the British, because they would, of course, be taken off by a British warship. We shook hands with Pappas when he left our car, and everyone was happy, especially Sonia.

It was late in the night when we got to Plevlje, a town where we had decided to make our headquarters until dawn. By this time the Chevrolet had outstripped all the other cars in the caravan. Plevlje was just a country town in the mountains of Montenegro. The only place where there seemed to be any life was a dirty, bleak, down-at-the-heel cafana filled with men who sat around tables drinking slivo and talking in whispers. There was a candle on each table, but no other light. The five of us stumbled through the door pretty well exhausted. We stood in the center of the room. No one paid any obvious attention to us, although all the men kept looking suspiciously at us from under their hat brims. Finally an army officer made room for us at a table. We thanked him in French, English, and finally Serbian, by courtesy of Sonia.

But as it turned out it was no act of courtesy. As soon as we were seated he demanded our military passes. Well, that was something the American military attaché back in Belgrade eight days ago had told us we'd get when the necessity arose, but of course we never had gotten any. We produced our passports instead. That cross-examination went on for an hour. Half a dozen army officers took part in it. They never did get to my passport and Sonia's and the major's. They spent the whole hour studying Walker's and Hill's. None of them could read English, and half the time they had the passports upside down. But they were certainly thorough!

They wanted to know such things as why Walker had two passports stapled together. That looked suspicious. It did no good to explain that that was regular British passport procedure, to hitch an old passport to a new one. Then they wanted to know why Hill's Greek visa was issued before his Yugoslav visa. And a lot of other foolish questions. By the time they got through with us it was too late to get any real food. All we got were two miniature pork chops, which had to be divided among the five of us, and one slice of bread apiece. Then we asked about a place to sleep. There must have been a hundred men in the place, but no one volunteered any suggestions.

We went off into the night and were just getting ready to sit up in the car and try to amuse one another with stories when a dignified little man came up and started talking to us in Serbian. He and Sonia held a long conversation, and then she translated it all for us. He was, he explained, the headmaster of the local school. He had a big classroom. He would spread mattresses for us on the floor. And he had some blankets, too. Nothing very fancy, you understand, but better than sitting up in the car.

Simmons told him there were about twenty others in our party who ought to be coming along sometime during the night. The headmaster beamed. He would be delighted to accommodate them too. We went to the trim little schoolhouse, and the headmaster started spreading mattresses. He even sent word down to the cafana so that the rest of the caravan would be guided up to where we were. We were all too tired to take off our clothes, except Simmons. He was an English gentleman under all circumstances. He even folded his trousers neatly and put them under the mattress so that they would be pressed by morning. Sonia lay on a mattress between Hill and me.

"I don't think there'll be any bombs here, do you?" she whispered.

I told her I was sure we'd have one night's vacation from them anyway.

A vivid sunrise woke us up. The major had already dressed and left. He later explained that he had dispensed with an hour's sleep in order to get a shoe shine and a shave.

"I guess that explains something about the strength of the

British Empire," I said to Hill. And I didn't mean it sarcastically either.

Out of the roomful of mattresses only five of them had been slept on, which meant that the rest of the caravan hadn't arrived. When we tried to settle with the headmaster for the night's lodging he was insulted. There was nothing commercial about it. He wouldn't even let us tip his servants. Then he explained to Sonia, very hesitantly, that he had been in the cafana while we were being cross-examined on the suspicion of being foreign spies. He had felt ashamed, he said, for his countrymen because of the way they had treated us. He himself was a man of education. He could tell that we were honest, respectable people and not spies. So this was his little way of making amends for the ordeal we had gone through.

It was a neat little speech, spoken with great sincerity. We wanted to do something to show our appreciation. So we asked the headmaster if we could take the youngest of his three children for a little walk around town. He was delighted. The child was just able to walk. We took her into the only real shop in Plevlje, except places that sold liquor. We bought everything the youngster took a fancy to. I think our total bill came to about a dollar and ninety-eight cents, translated into American money, but I'm sure the headmaster's children never had such a Christmas as they did that day.

When we found the major he was talking with a Greek diplomat who had been with the rest of the caravan and had just arrived in town. He had been given a lift by a Serbian truck driver. He brought the news that the other cars were all stuck on top of a mountain some miles out because of flat tires, engine trouble, and other difficulties.

We were sitting in the same dirty cafana discussing what we should do when Sonia noticed an army officer with his head swathed in bandages and one arm in a sling. His uniform was torn and dirty. He looked as if he had spent a month in front line trenches somewhere. It was impossible to tell his rank because his epaulets were ripped off.

"I know him," Sonia whispered excitedly. "That's Captain Obrad Obradovic. He's aide-de-camp to General Simovich. What a break for us!"

So Sonia stepped up and shook hands with him and then brought him over to our table. We had a long talk. He spoke French as well as he did Serbian. He talked like a man who had just come back from the fringes of hell. He spoke slowly, deliberately, meditatively, with the restraint of a hardened army officer. He had been badly wounded in the bombing of Belgrade while he was trying to get some important documents out of the War Office, which, as we all knew, was the first target of the Nazi planes. Now he was going in the same general direction we were. He was on an important mission for the General. He was leaving town in a few minutes. We couldn't follow behind him because his car would be racing ahead much faster than our Chevrolet could go. But this was the best route. And he drew it for us on one of our maps.

Then I remembered something that had been worrying Sonia for days. She had no visa in her passport giving her the right to leave the country. She was afraid she might get into trouble without it. So Obrad Obradovic pulled out a pen and wrote her out a visa. Only he insisted on knowing how she was leaving the country, and when she said she might be leaving with me in a boat that we expected to buy or steal, he wrote in her passport: "Permitted to leave Yugoslavia only if in the company of Robert St. John, American journalist."

I never have figured out just why he did that. But anyway Sonia was happy. She acted five years younger. She finally had a visa.

Then Obradovic wrote out a military pass for each of us, and finally he looked us straight in the eyes and said, "I've done a lot for you and now I'm going to ask you to do something for me." He bent forward while he talked.

"You know who I am. You know the fix Yugoslavia is in. We haven't had a bit of help from either the British or the Greeks. We're going to go under soon if we don't get it. We need planes and tanks and gasoline. And we have to have them in a hurry. We've got to have real help if they expect us to hold out. We were told the British had three hundred thousand men and plenty of planes down in Greece. We can't understand why they haven't done anything for us. We can't seem to get in communication with them any more. I want to start out from the Dalmatian coast tomorrow for Greece by power boat and see how quickly I can get in touch with the British. I've got to let them know how desperate our situation really is. There will be a certain advantage if you Americans are with me. And there will be a certain advantage for you if I'm along. I'll bring six good soldiers armed with machine guns. I think I know where we can get a fast boat. But I've got a job to do in the meantime. I'll be in Podgarica about dark. I'll meet you near the bridge. If we miss each other there, go on to Danilovgrod. I'll be in the big cafana right on the edge of town."

Hill and Walker and Sonia were as excited and as enthusiastic as I was. We didn't really have any plans of our own. None of us knew the Dalmatian coast. And we all had hidden worries that we might get stuck there without finding a boat. This Obradovic scheme sounded good. Of course we didn't see what value we were going to be to him, but there certainly was plenty of advantage for us.

Obradovic stood up. He leaned on a cane with one hand and with the other he saluted us like a good soldier. He said he wanted this to be a solemn agreement that both sides would feel bound to keep, so let's shake on it. It was a dramatic little scene, the five of us standing there in the center of the dirty cafana with our five right hands locked in a huge handshake. It was the sealing of a solemn war pact that might affect the fate of nations. At least it would affect the fate of five human beings, some of whom sought personal safety, or communications so they could send stories to America, or, in Obradovic's case, aid for a beleaguered little country that was almost breathing its last.

The major wasn't around when we made our deal with Obradovic. But we found him at the gendarme headquarters, where he was leaving instructions for the rest of the convoy to follow us on to Podgarica. Then we got under way.

At noon we stopped in the rural town of Sahovici. There wasn't much to the place except another dirty cafana, like the one in Plevlje where we had had such an unpleasant reception the night before. But everything was different in Sahovici. We couldn't understand much of what that roomful of people said, but as soon as they found that we were Americans and Britishers they insisted on buying us all the slivo we could drink. We toasted Yugoslavia and sang "Oi, Serbia," and then they toasted America and England and Greece. It was pathetic to hear them talk of victory and what the Serbs were going to do to the Germans and then to have them ask how long would it be before the United States would pitch in and help the little countries? We in America were friends of Yugoslavia, weren't we? Sure! Of course! Well, if we wrote anything be sure to explain to the people in America that the Serbs were counting on American assistance.

We told them that President Roosevelt had promised to send help to Yugoslavia as soon as she entered the war. They cheered when Sonia translated that to them, and then they bought us another drink. Of course we omitted telling them that we didn't think any help would arrive in time. And we didn't tell them what we knew about the fall of Skoplje and how the corridor from Greece up to Yugoslavia was cut off now. We didn't have the heart to put any damper on what they called their victory celebration.

"Let them be happy as long as they can," I whispered to Dave.

Most of this time Sonia was out in the kitchen helping a woman beat up eggs and make us an omelet. Finally, when we started on our way again, Sonia produced a dirty newspaper package. Sweetbreads. Pounds and pounds of sweetbreads, which Sonia said we would get someone to cook for us tonight. The patron's wife back in the cafana had given them to her for the Amerikanskis.

Planes were flying over Podgarica when we got there. But they were Italian planes. Italian planes that had been trying for days without success to hit the big concrete bridge over the river. It was the only bridge that automobiles going toward the sea could use, and so it was an important military objective. We could see what poor marksmen the Italian pilots were, because there were bomb craters scattered for two miles around the bridge and yet not one of them was closer than two or three hundred yards to the target. When we saw the low-flying planes we had Sonia ask a native where we should hide. He said if we really wanted to be safe we should drive our car right on the bridge and wait there until the raid was over. We did. We weren't hit. Neither was the bridge.

Darkness settled down over Podgarica and still there was no sign of Obradovic. I noticed Sonia and the major in several little tête-à-têtes, and finally she said she thought we ought to go on to Cetinje. Cetinje is due east of Podgarica. And just a little distance farther east from Cetinje is the sea. The shortest distance from Podgarica to the sea is naturally by way of Cetinje. Danilovgrod, where we had promised to meet Obradovic, is north from Podgarica. Miles and miles off the route to the sea. But we had promised Obradovic to go on to Danilovgrod if we missed him in Podgarica. It was a solemn pledge we had made to him. I reminded Sonia of that, and I reminded her that she had joined the rest of us in making it, and also that she had accepted favors from the captain and ought to feel just as much indebted to him as we did, pledge or no pledge. She argued that he had failed to keep his date at the Podgarica bridge and maybe something had happened to him. He might even have been killed in an air raid. We couldn't risk not getting out of the country ourselves, she said. I could see it was the major's doing. He wanted to go straight on to Cetinje and then on to Cattaro, the seaport where the British expected to be evacuated by the navy. The major apparently had invited Sonia to go along with him and be evacuated too. But he hadn't extended the invitation to the rest of us, so we didn't have any choice. We had to shift for ourselves.

Hill was just as insistent as I was that we had to keep our

promise to Obradovic. But we finally worked out a compromise. Sonia and the major agreed to go on to Danilovgrod with us on the understanding that if we didn't find any trace of Obradovic we would turn back and head immediately for Cetinje.

It was a miserable drive. There wasn't any moon. There weren't any stars. The road was patrolled by soldiers who wouldn't allow us to show a single pinhole of light. They even shouted at us when we tried to light cigarettes. The road was jammed with oxen and peasant carts and other automobiles and big army trucks, because this was G.H.Q. for the Serbian army, which Cy Sulzberger and a lot of other people had thought was going to sweep down through Albania and drive the Italians back where they came from. Only instead of driving the Italians back, the Serbs were being driven back themselves.

Hill and I took turns at the wheel. After about ten minutes of peering out into the shadows we began to see cows where there were no cows, and we saw nothing where there really were groups of poor peasants who went sailing into the ditch when our fenders brushed them. There were several suggestions that we turn back, but Hill and I took turns at the wheel because we were determined that no one should ever be able to say that a couple of Americans had gone back on their word. And what was more, we wanted to get out of Yugoslavia as fast as we could. We didn't mind the danger. Speed was what we were after. In a fast power boat we might even catch up with Kay and White.

We finally got to Danilovgrod. We were promptly arrested and taken before a group of Yugoslav General Staff officers. No, they hadn't seen Obradovic. But they did want to talk to us. They were quite friendly. They wanted to know just how badly things were going in the rest of the country. They didn't say so, but it was obvious that they had had no communication with Simovich or the government or the five other Yugoslav armies.

Most of the generals spoke French and a few of them spoke English, and so we got along quite well. They warmed up to the conversation about the war. They turned aside from their maps and opened some canned food for us and even dug up a tin of butter. It was late in the night before we could get away. We enjoyed those few hours of relaxation, but I kept thinking of Bucharest.

The army these Yugoslavs were fighting was the army I had seen in Bucharest. It's the army the British had to fight a few weeks later in Crete, and the army that went after the Russians in July, and the army that—well, who knows where it may spring up tomorrow? I kept thinking, as these Yugoslav generals calmly chatted over nonessentials with a few refugee newspapermen, how unconcerned they seemed to be about what was happening to their own Yugoslavia. Hill and Walker and I had a hunch that it was only a matter of days now before little Yugoslavia would fold up. Then the big slaughter would begin. Then this bastard child of Versailles would be cut up and the pieces distributed among the winners. It would be Versailles in reverse. And here in Danilovgrod, just thirty miles from the Albanian frontier, members of the Yugoslav General Staff, on the eve of a great military debacle, were spreading butter on salted biscuits and talking about things that didn't matter and never had mattered and never would matter.

There were red pins in their map on the wall. The red pins represented fast German motorized units. I had seen those units in Bucharest. I had seen their generals at work. I knew those generals never idled away their time talking nonsense with any-one, not even in those days when the Balkan war was still weeks off. They were doing a job. They were like shop foremen in a Ford factory. They were running a complicated piece of machinery, half steel, half human. It ran with the efficiency of a Ford factory simply because the Germans were all taking their job of making war as seriously as an American manufacturer takes his job of making automobiles. And the reason they were succeeding so well was because the opposition was still, after nearly two years of it, playing soldiers.

Several times during the night Hill or I went out and searched the cafanas for Obradovic. We left word with the gendarmes to be on the lookout for him. We had the General Staff officers telephone everywhere they could think of, but there wasn't a trace of him.

Finally we all got very tired, and Sonia and the major agreed with us that we might just as well spend the night here in Danilovgrod. A man who had once lived in America and spoke faltering English said he had a room. There were two single beds in it, and he could put three mattresses on the floor. In that way we got a little sleep again.

I woke up early and decided to make one more stab at trying to find Obradovic. I routed out Hill and Sonia, and we got away without disturbing the major and Walker. We had had a tip that the government had left Ilidže, near Sarajevo, the same day we pulled out, on Easter Sunday, and that they had been heading for Nikšic, a town thirty miles north of where we were. So the three of us raced up to Nikšic. We asked everywhere for Obradovic, and a lot of people said yes, he had been there during the night, but he had vanished this morning. They didn't know where he had gone. And the government? Yes, Simovich and most of his Ministers had also been in Nikšic during the night. But they, too, had disappeared.

We knew there was an airport in Nikšic. We knew that a whole fleet of big planes had recently been flown to the Nikšic airport. Now we discovered that the planes were no longer at the airport. Yes, Simovich and his Ministers, and probably Obradovic too, had disappeared all right. While we hunted them in the streets and cafanas of Nikšic they were flying through the clouds toward Greece. It was too late now for Obradovic to ask the British why they weren't sending help to Yugoslavia. It was too late for him to steer a power boat toward Greece and beg for tanks and planes and gasoline. The government had fled. Yugoslavia was through. It was all over now except the carving up.

CHAPTER SEVEN

Farewell

———————◆◆◆◆◆———————

Sonia and Walker and Hill and I stood in a rocky, barren graveyard on the edge of Podgarica, looking down at a plain white cross, which bore the words:

RALPH W. BARNES
American War Correspondent
18. 11. 40

Nobody spoke. The cross didn't mean anything to Sonia, but she knew what it meant to the rest of us, because we had been talking about Ralph all day. We had told her how Ralph had been one of us. And Russell had told her how they were expelled together from Berlin. And I had told her about the last time I saw him in Bucharest. He had just bought a white linen suit and he came into the Athenee Palace as proud as punch, until we asked him what girl had bitten him on the leg. He looked down. There on his leg were two perfect red lip marks. It was a great mystery until Ralph remembered that he had just come from a tea shop, where the Rumanian girls, after they make up, wipe off the surplus lipstick on the leg of a chair. Ralph obviously had rubbed his white trousers against one of those depositories for surplus lipstick. Russell and I had also pointed out the big mountain behind Podgarica and had told Sonia how one nasty winter night a British bombing plane in which Ralph was taking a ride got lost and hit the side of the mountain.

But when we got to the grave nobody said anything, because we were all thinking, tough luck, Ralph, you were a grand newspaperman. As good as they come. We'll miss you when we gather around some day to talk over what happened back in the forties. But we'll raise a glass to you anyway.

And then we looked around for some flowers, because that's the way we felt, but all we could find were some little blue star flowers; and when we put them on top of all the stones that covered the grave you couldn't even see them, but we felt better for having done it. We felt that we had paid some kind of a tribute to a man who loved getting a story enough to die for it.

Then we took a quick look at the smashed airport hangar just behind Ralph's grave. It had met the same fate as nearly all the other hangars in Yugoslavia. It and all the planes that were housed inside had been destroyed by Nazi bombs before most Serbs even realized a war was on. We knew that was why the enemy had had the sky over Yugoslavia to themselves all these days.

We had to hurry now, because any minute the Italians and Germans might be closing in on us. We went back into the city and found the major. He said he was going to wait right there in Podgarica for the rest of the caravan, which hadn't yet put in an appearance. Then he asked Sonia for the last time if she didn't want to go along with the British to Cattaro. But Sonia had made up her mind. She was going to stick with the Americans, she said. I was glad, because we had gone through a lot together already, and she was having just as good an effect on my morale as I seemed to be having on hers. We left the major, but we took Walker along with us, because he still hadn't made up his mind what he was going to do.

The four of us had the happiest hours of the whole trip that day. We were all beginning to get hardened to two or three hours' sleep a night and a little food whenever we could get it. So on the way to Cetinje we sang and told stories and tried to forget all we had seen during the last ten days. It was whistling in the dark, but it worked for a while. We even stopped several times to admire the wild mountain scenery. And once we talked about how there was no reason why the four of us, if we couldn't get out of the country, shouldn't find ourselves a shack up in the hills somewhere and hide out for the duration.

But when we reached Cetinje we lost our spirit. We got quick confirmation that the government had fled by plane the day before; but worse than that, some renegade army general had signed an armistice with the Axis, and within twenty-four hours the Germans and Italians were expected to complete their occupation of every corner of Yugoslavia.

Early in the evening I was standing in the lobby of the Grand Hotel in Cetinje waiting for Sonia. While I was waiting I got into conversation with a young Englishman, and he said, "Are those other three newspapermen eating dinner in the dining room in your party?"

"No, who are they?" I asked him.

"Well," he said, "I know one of them is called Kay and . . ."

I didn't wait to hear any more. I went bounding down the hall and into the dining room like a wild heifer let loose. I slapped Kay on the back twice as hard as I did Leigh White, who was with him, because, while I knew White much better and had worked with him all over the Balkans, he was with CBS and wasn't a rival of mine. But finding Kay still in Yugoslavia lifted one of the blackest clouds that had hung over us for days. Hill was almost as happy as I was that we were all in the same fix again. The score was still even. White and Kay hadn't been able to get a word out of the country, and neither had we.

They had come down here to Cetinje with Terence Atherton, of the London *Daily Mail*, who was about my own age, which meant that he was considerably older than the rest of them.

Atherton had provided the transportation, a little four-cylinder Opal. They had wasted several days wandering around the coast, but tomorrow they were going to head for the little town of Budva, the nearest seaport to Cetinje. They knew as well as we did that every hour was precious now. They asked us if we would like to join forces with them. Six might make out better than three. We agreed. We had to go out hunting for rooms, because the Grand Hotel, where they were staying, was full, and so we said we would meet them at five in the morning.

We found enough rooms to accommodate the four of us, and we parked our knapsacks there and went out looking for a place to eat. We saw lights across the street and went into a sordid-looking place where half a dozen people crowded around a big table were having an uproarious time. The celebrators turned out to be some of our fellow travelers in the British caravan. One car had finally gotten to Podgarica, picked up the major, and come on to Cetinje, and here they were, eating a four-course dinner and drinking some of the finest champagne any of us had tasted since the second world war began. We joined their party and we ordered up a few more bottles of champagne and we all had a party. The trip from Belgrade to the sea was about over. Nobody knew what lay in store for us tomorrow, or next week, or next month. But we had escaped the bombs over Belgrade and the bombs over Sarajevo and—well, drink it down, boys, because we're alive today and who the hell cares about tomorrow anyway? We stayed there until the patron said he was sorry, but we had used up the last bottle of champagne he owned. We couldn't pour raw slivo on top of that magnificent champagne, and so we went to bed.

Dave and Russell and Sonia and I went up to our rooms feeling pretty gay. But there was one serious question to be decided. What was Walker going to do? He had been on the Gestapo's black list for a long time. He had written a book based on a trip through Germany before the war. It was well done but hardly pleasing to the Wilhelmstrasse. Then he had covered every move the Germans had made since the Czechoslovakian crisis for one

London paper or another. Most of his stories were so caustic and some of them so vitriolic that the name Dave Walker had come to be a synonym to the Germans for everything they hated about the British press. If they could get their hands on Dave they might even think that was reward enough for a lot of the fighting their soldiers had gone through here in the Balkans. And if they got their hands on him, there wasn't much doubt about what they would do with him.

But the situation was a difficult one. He had two choices. He could come with us, we told him, and we would take every conceivable risk to see that he didn't fall into enemy hands. Or he could branch off from us here at Cetinje and head with the rest of the British for Cattaro, where all of them might or might not be evacuated by the British navy. I knew a human life was at stake, and the life of a good friend. I hated to say anything that would tip the scales either way. I listed all the advantages and all the risks on each side. We might fall into the hands of the Italian navy. Or if he went to Cattaro the British might not be able to get a destroyer up to save him and the others.

Dave finally told us to go to bed and try to catch an hour's sleep. He'd lie awake and think the thing out. By the time we got ready to leave he'd have an answer. At four-thirty I went in to wake up Hill and to say good-by to Dave, because I had a hunch what Dave would have decided. He was sound asleep. I hated to disturb him, but I shook his shoulder.

He grinned and said, "I think I ought to go with the British."

I knew what he meant. He hadn't decided on the basis of personal safety. He felt that a certain intangible thing called duty or loyalty to his own countrymen required that he not take what some of the others might consider an easy way out. The British do stick together. Nearly all of them have a fine sense of patriotism and loyalty.

I shook hands with Dave, and I wondered whether I'd ever see him again. But all I said was, "Happy sailing!"

We got to Budva by midmorning. Budva is a place I want to visit again some day, if peace and reason ever return to Europe.

It's a walled city, with a fortress on the edge of the sea, and quaint, narrow streets lined with trim little shops. The people in Budva are the cream of the Balkans. Many of them had been to America and had stayed long enough to learn a little English and get a taste of the West, yet not long enough to lose their natural charm and foreign grace.

Budva on that historic day in April was something to put a lump in your throat. The second we stopped our two cars, swarms of dazed, bewildered people clustered around us and asked questions. When they saw the American flag on the fender of the Chevrolet they asked their questions in broken English. What had happened? Was the war really over? Simovich hadn't really fled the country, had he? Who had betrayed Yugoslavia? The war couldn't possibly be over after only ten days, could it? Where was the Yugoslav army? Were the Germans closing in? Would the Italians be here soon? The questions flowed out in a cascade of confusion. Men and women in peasant dress, soldiers in ragged uniforms, sleek-looking army officers, city people in clothes like you and I wear, refugees who spoke a babel of languages—all of them pressed around our cars.

We were afraid to answer any of the questions. We knew that here in Yugoslavia, just as in France, wild rumors had been manufactured and spread into every corner of the country by the enemy in an attempt to create confusion. We didn't want to do anything to make the plight of these poor people any worse. Also there was still grave danger of being shot on the spot as fifth columnists or foreign agents by overzealous patriots, especially by gendarmes and army men, if they thought we were trying to spread panic. They wouldn't need much evidence. Just the fact that a crowd had gathered around us might be enough, even if we didn't open our mouths.

We kept moving the car. Every time we stopped again, another crowd gathered. We had come from the interior. We were the latest arrivals. We must know something. What was going to happen to Yugoslavia? Tell us, tell us, tell us! They begged and shouted and pleaded with us. They were hungry for news. There was terror in their minds and there was terror on their faces. But we didn't dare tell them. We didn't have the heart to tell them. We just shrugged our shoulders. I guess they thought we were rather stupid.

Some of them even thought we were the advance guard of the enemy, a reconnaissance party. That put us in a delicate position. But most of them were kind. Unbelievably kind, when you consider the fix they were in, and what was going to happen to them so soon. One old man ran off to his home and came back with a bottle of a pure white liquid about as potent as vodka. We refused it, because we were afraid he was trying to trap us into talking. But the old man only wanted to be friendly, to do something for the "Amerikanskis." He had been in Cleveland once. That was thirty years ago. America, it is wonderful! But please have a drink! It is not bad. I made it myself. It is like your whisky, only not black but white.

We had a drink and we toasted Yugoslavia. The crowd around the car cheered. We told Sonia to tell them, Yugoslavia will always live. The crowd cheered again, but I was sick down inside because I knew that Yugoslavia was already dead and that there might never be a resurrection.

Since time was precious, we split up. Atherton, White, and Kay went off to try to buy a boat. They suggested that Hill, Sonia, and I start accumulating supplies. There was an open market place near the water front, but about all they had for sale were bunches of lettuce and some strange root vegetables. Then an old woman came up and tried to sell us a smoked ham. It hadn't been cooked and it was a filthy-looking object, but Sonia said we'd better buy it. She insisted on paying for it. It weighed eight kilos, nearly twenty pounds.

White came back and said Atherton was negotiating for a boat, but he and Atherton and Kay wanted to talk to me privately about Sonia. They all were suspicious of her. They were sure she was a Nazi agent. Could I prove that she wasn't? Who was she anyway? How long had I known her? Did I know any of her connections? She was a Croat, not a Serb, and all the Croats were pro-Nazi. Why was she so anxious to get out of Yugoslavia? If I could convince them they were wrong, Sonia could come along, but otherwise she'd have to stay behind.

I didn't know all the answers. I didn't know much about Sonia's history, but I thought I understood her. I tried to explain to White, but he said, "Talk to her and accuse her of being a Nazi agent and see what she says."

It was sheer cruelty, but Hill voiced a faint suspicion too, and so with four against one I had to talk it over with Sonia. So we went off for a walk and I told her quite bluntly what White had said. First she was furiously angry; then she asked if we couldn't sit down in the Chevrolet. She started to cry. Softly at first, and then hysterically. She said she didn't blame them for having suspicions, but she never thought I'd lose faith in her. I said I hadn't, but after all, I didn't know anything precise about her. I didn't know the answers to all those questions. Why, for example, was she so anxious to get out of the country? At first she insisted it was because she had so many English friends that she was afraid her name would be on the German black list. She told me of public dinner parties given by the British that she had gone to. She told me how she had written articles for Atherton's paper. She said all of the diplomatic corps in Belgrade was aware of her pro-British sentiments.

But I knew it was even more than that. I knew by now something about her psychological make-up. I knew she had a strange terror in her soul. Darkness, noises, soldiers, even the tramp of marching feet did something to her. Of course I didn't know her case history. We had never discussed it. I didn't know what planted those seeds of fear within her. It might have been something back in her childhood. Maybe it was the atrocity stories of the last war, because once she asked me if I thought the German soldiers really would rape all the young women in Yugoslavia after they took over the country. I had been asked that question often in Europe by women who feared rape by the military. I suppose one has to be a young woman living in Europe where such things do happen to understand what a fear like that can do to the mind.

Anyway, as Sonia sat there in the Chevrolet with her head on my shoulder crying her heart out because she had been misunderstood, I felt like a fool. I was disgusted with myself for having put her through this new ordeal. So I told her to dry her eyes and cheer up, because I'd convince those suspicious idiots that she was all right. But suddenly she took a new line. She wouldn't go, even if they agreed. I couldn't clear up their doubts with a few words. They would always be suspicious, and the situation would be unbearable. I felt that she was telling the truth. I knew White and Kay. Even if they did agree to let her go, it would be with reluctance. She would always be a Nazi spy to them. And they would be subconsciously looking for proof in everything she said or did. But I didn't tell Sonia that. I left her sitting in the car and told her she was going with us, regardless of what she said and what they said. I was going off to make that announcement to the rest of them.

I found them down on the beach. They had just completed the big deal. They had swapped Atherton's little Opal for a twenty-foot sardine boat, complete with a one-cylinder outboard engine, a sail, which the owner said was whole and all right, and four oars. I took one look at that boat, and then I knew that Sonia wasn't going to go with us. There was hardly room for six people in the boat. There surely wasn't room for six people if we had to do any rowing. Six men might get somewhere, but five men and a woman? No, it was impossible. When we had talked about a boat I had had visions of a cabin launch of some kind, with a couple of bunks and a bathroom and a real engine. A boat in which we could live for days or even weeks, if need be, like civilized human beings. We had two or three thousand dollars in American money between us. And we had two automobiles. Surely we ought to be able to afford something better than this dirty rowboat! But Atherton and White and Kay said they had searched the coast for days, and there weren't any boats of any kind to be had. It was great luck that they had stumbled on this sardine boat. And then they said, of course, that girl can't possibly come along in a boat like this, even if she isn't a Nazi.

I stood looking for a long time at the *Makedonka,* as the owner called her. I didn't say anything, but I did a lot of thinking. In a few hours we would be tossing around on the sea in that frail, insufficient little boat. Five men who knew nothing about the sea and a woman who had often said she was afraid of the sea. We would probably have to do most of our traveling by night, and Sonia was terrified of the dark. Five men whose nerves were already on edge, and a woman who four of them were sure was a Nazi spy. After days of hardship, God alone knows what state our minds might be in. We were all newspapermen, which meant we were too individualistic for our own good. We might be out on that dark sea for days, maybe weeks. There would be little food. We might even get to the point of eating shoe leather. We would have to be primitive about performing some of the duties of nature. What a situation for a lone woman to be in! One woman and five men. Three of them disliked her. The fourth was almost as suspicious of her as the others. And while I neither disliked her nor was suspicious of her, I knew Sonia. I knew she had been a good sport so far. She had taken the hardships of these ten days of war like a man. She had done her share of physical labor and her share of the work.

But Sonia was a psychological case. Up to now I had been able to help her get through the ordeal. By talking quietly when the planes were overhead and by holding tightly onto her hand when the danger was great I had kept her calm. But my own nerves were beginning to get frazzled.

I didn't care for the sea very much myself, because I had one indelible memory of it. That trip back from France, when I was just sixteen. The transport we were on ran into a storm. We were lost at sea for days. It was an experience that had left a black scar on my mind. No, I'd have my own fears out there on the Adriatic in the little *Makedonka,* and Sonia might be more of a problem than I could handle.

I finally went back to the Chevrolet and sat down beside the girl who had seldom been away from my side throughout this long, grim week. She was powdering her nose and grinned at me. Her eyes were still red, but they were bright now.

"I've made up my mind," she said. "I'm coming with you. I don't care what happens. I'm coming with you!"

I'm afraid I groaned. She noticed it. "That's what you want me to do, isn't it?" she asked.

I tried to tell her about the boat. She kept shaking her head. No, I've made up my mind. I know now what I want to do.

I could see it was going to be difficult, and so I asked her to walk over and look at the boat. When we got there, White and Kay looked at us with ill-disguised feelings and walked away. Sonia noticed it, but she just bit her lips. I tried to point out the lack of accommodations.

"Imagine," I said. "You and I and four other men in that boat. There are going to be dangers and hardships you've never dreamed of. For you, the gamble isn't worth it. I know you want to get out of the country. I know you're afraid to stay here. I know I promised to get you this far if I could, and then out of the country if it was possible. But Sonia, it isn't possible! You'd never survive a trip in that boat. And anyway, it isn't worth the gamble. You won't be in any great danger here. You're one of millions of Yugoslav women. You won't be bothered. In a year or two the whole picture may change. The tide of battle may turn. The Germans and Italians may be forced to leave. You will have the courage to put up with hardships for a year or two. If you did go with us, and we all did survive and get to Greece, what then? You'd be in a strange country among people speaking a strange language, and I know you'd be unhappy."

But I was talking to a block of stone. She kept shaking her head and she kept whispering softly, no, her mind was made up. I finally said, "If you are determined to leave Yugoslavia you can go out with the British. They invited you. And it still isn't too late to catch them up at Cattaro. Cattaro is only about fifty miles up the coast. I'll drive you up there now."

She still shook her head.

Then I remembered a Church of England clergyman and his wife who had been playing the father-mother role to Sonia when I found her in Sarajevo. They were in the British caravan. I knew they would realize the impossibility of Sonia going in an open boat with five men and I suggested that we ask their advice. I agreed that I would abide by whatever decision they made. Only I didn't know what I would do if they approved of Sonia going with us. Sonia, still as stubborn as ever, said, all right, she was willing to drive to Cattaro and ask them, but she was sure she could persuade them that she was right.

I left Sonia and hunted for the rest of the newspapermen. I told them I was taking Sonia to Cattaro; that I couldn't just abandon her. I didn't tell them that she thought she was coming back and sail away on the *Makedonka* with us. They seemed greatly relieved that the woman problem was solved, but they said that if I wasn't back in three hours they would leave without me. I figured I could make the fifty miles there and the fifty miles back in three hours all right, and so I agreed.

"If I'm not back in three hours, just forget me."

On the way to Cattaro Sonia snuggled close to me, linked her arm through mine, and said she was very happy, because she had her mind made up. She was looking forward to the trip in the *Makedonka,* no matter what the hardships were going to be. I felt like a rat, because I knew she couldn't go. I knew what Kay and White had said about refusing to take her. And after all, they had bought the boat. I was going to pay my share, somehow, but it really was their boat.

Halfway to Cattaro the Chevrolet refused to run in high gear. I didn't have time to try to find out why. I just raced along in second as fast as the engine would go. Half of my three hours were up when we got to Cattaro. And none of the British had arrived yet. They apparently were still waiting in Cetinje for the stragglers in the caravan. That complicated the situation. But then Sonia ran into a brother-in-law and we asked his advice. Since he spoke nothing but Serbian, Sonia had to translate and I didn't have much of a chance to present my side of the case.

He finally listed all the disadvantages of Sonia going on the *Makedonka*. He mentioned that no British destroyer had appeared yet and maybe none would. Then he told Sonia what he thought life for her would be like if she had to stay in Yugoslavia. We finally left him and went back and sat in the Chevrolet.

"Sonia," I began in a final argument on which both our futures hinged, "I like you a lot. You've been a good sport. You've been a great companion."

It was then that she threw her arms around my neck in a burst of emotion that stunned me.

"I was waiting for you to say it," she said. "We're in love, aren't we?"

That wasn't what I meant at all. I wasn't in love with Sonia. I liked her immensely, but I wasn't in love with her.

"And that's why I refuse to leave you now," she went on, her eyes as bright as diamonds. "I want to go with you to Athens and then to Cairo and then to New York. Think of the fun we'll have!"

"But Sonia," I said as softly as I could, "there's someone waiting for me in Athens or Cairo. I don't know which, but either in Athens or Cairo. I'm not alone, you see. That complicates things, doesn't it? That's why you can't go to Athens and Cairo and New York with me. See?"

I didn't want to hurt Sonia, but I couldn't hurt Eda either. Eda had left Belgrade just before the bombing. She was now in Istanbul. Eda and I of course would meet in Athens when I got there, or in Cairo, or somewhere else as soon as a reunion was possible. It would be difficult to explain Sonia to Eda. Eda might not understand this strange relationship with Sonia. Sonia, who had done so much to make this escape from Yugoslavia possible for all of us. Sonia, with whom I had never once discussed things like love. We had all been living in a sort of vacuum for nearly two weeks. Someone who hadn't been through all those bombings and the strain of those terrible days might never be able to understand how everything had gotten out of focus. But now Sonia, by talking about life away from this land of death and destruction, by talking about a future we had never mentioned before, was changing the focus, trying to see through the glasses something that it wasn't possible to see.

I looked at my watch. In exactly one hour White and Kay and Hill and Atherton would be shoving off in the *Makedonka*. One hour to make fifty miles with a car that wouldn't run in high.

Sonia finally spoke. She was amazingly calm. Calmer than I had ever seen her.

"I understand," she said. "I know we haven't been—that we haven't ever discussed things like this before. And it's pretty late to talk about them now. I guess the only reason I was so anxious to leave the country was because you and I got along so well together. You made me so calm and gave me such strength, just by little things like holding my hand. I can see now that it couldn't last forever. But I've got a lot of strength stored up from this week we've been together. I'm going to be so strong after you leave that you'll be proud of me. There really isn't much danger here for me. I can go with my sister and her husband and be safe all right. I'm not a coward. But no one has ever believed it until you did. Now I really believe it myself. And I'm going to prove it."

I held her hand tightly, just as I did under the table that night we met in the Srpski Kralj Hotel in Belgrade. Her fingers tightened around mine. She was quiet for a minute when she finished the long speech, and then she said, like an explosion, "But you will come back to Yugoslavia some day, won't you? Promise to come back some day and take me on another automobile ride when there aren't any bombs or any planes."

I promised her I would. Then she said she would take a room in the hotel here in Cattaro, and after I left she'd find her brother-in-law and ask him to make some plans for her. I carried her knapsack into the hotel. As we started to say good-by she suddenly said, "I'm going part way to Budva with you. I'll ride the first few miles just as if we were going off on a trip together somewhere, and then I'll walk back."

The harbor of Cattaro is a beautiful thing to see from the road that winds from the water up into the green Dalmatian hills. It looked especially beautiful that April afternoon as Sonia and I sat side by side in the car, while I drove with my left hand and held her fingers with my right hand. We were both happy, for different reasons maybe, but principally because a human problem had been solved and I had promised her that some day I would come back to Yugoslavia again and we would take another trip in an automobile through the mountains.

I left Yugoslavia that night with a lot of pictures indelibly stamped on my mind: pictures of dead bodies in Terrazia and mangled bodies in Sarajevo and crowds of bewildered people in Budva and the white cross over the grave of Ralph Barnes; but one of the clearest pictures was the picture of Sonia. Sonia standing in the middle of a road in the foothills of the Dalmatian mountains waving a little red handkerchief. Sonia, strong, smiling.

CHAPTER EIGHT

Escape

———◄•●•►———

I HAD THIRTY MINUTES to make the fifty miles back to Budva. And suddenly the Chevrolet refused to run even in second. How much longer first gear would hold out I didn't know. The road from Cattaro to Budva is all hills. That was lucky, because I could disengage the clutch and keep my foot off the brake going down hills and hit a speed that didn't even register on the speedometer. That gave me enough power to climb the next grade. It also helped me on the fuel consumption, which was important, because the tank was nearly dry.

On that winding mountain road I saw something that belongs in the pages of history. The saga of World War II isn't complete without it. You can't understand that Balkan campaign and why it failed unless you know that on April 16, 1941, after the war had ended, after Yugoslavia had capitulated, after the government had flown away by plane and an armistice had been signed, common soldiers, ignorant of what had happened, were finally building tank traps on the road from Cattaro to Budva. I saw them building them as I drove back to Budva. Traps to stop

German mechanized forces that already had reduced Yugoslavia to a vassal state. Tank traps, which should have been built months, years before. Tank traps no one had thought of until it was too late. Until the war was definitely over.

Farther on, the road was full of soldiers. Not neat columns of well-trained soldiers on the march, but ragged groups of men. These were soldiers who had heard that the war was over and had deserted their units and taken all the rifles and ammunition they could get their hands on and were going off into the mountains. You can call it desertion if you want to, but it really was patriotism of the highest degree, because these men were going to continue the war no matter what papers were signed by renegade generals and what claims of victory were made by the Axis. They were going to hide in the mountains and harass the enemy by guerrilla tactics which they understood better than any other soldiers in this part of the world.

I didn't dare slow down to give them a chance to get out of the road. So I drove with my right hand on the button of the horn and I prayed I wouldn't have a flat tire, because if those soldiers I sent flying off into the ditches ever caught up with me, God help me. One group after another tried to stop the car. I didn't know what they wanted. They might have only wanted a lift, but more likely they wanted to question me to see if I were an enemy agent. I didn't have time for cross-examination. I had thirty minutes to make fifty miles in a car that was pretty close to worthless except for coasting.

There were plenty of curves on those down grades, and if anything had been coming from the other direction it would have been soft music for all of us, because I had to stick to the center of the road to get around the bends without slowing down. But one curve was so sharp that I did have to use the brakes. That meant I had difficulty climbing the next upgrade. And that was how I got arrested. Hundreds of soldiers swarmed around the car. They all shook their fists and said things I was glad I didn't understand. There didn't seem to be an officer among them, and no one talked anything but Serbian. They forced me out of the car, and one soldier got behind the wheel and tried to drive the Chevrolet away, but he fortunately didn't know much about automobiles and he kept stalling it. It was a tough spot, because they wouldn't even let me reach into my pocket for my American passport. I guess they were afraid I was reaching for a gun. Each time I made a move with my right hand, someone slapped it down.

Fortunately an argument broke out among them. Apparently it was about what they were going to do with me. While they were still arguing, a colonel appeared on horseback. He was of the old school. His uniform was spick and span. His waxed mustache was neatly twisted. His boots had been freshly shined. The soldiers instinctively backed away from me and stood about half at attention. They had deserted their units, and had thumbed their nose at army discipline, and didn't have much use for their officers any more because they figured a lot of them were traitors, but instinctively they groveled before the handsome colonel.

The colonel spoke some French and he gave me a real third degree. Whose car was it? Did I have the registration papers? Where had I been? Who was the girl I had taken to Cattaro? Where was I going now? Why was I trying to flee from the country? It went on for only ten minutes, but those ten minutes seemed like hours. Finally he let me go, and I roared off in first gear with a thunderous noise that seemed to terrify the soldiers, who had been cheated of their prey by a colonel who spoke a language they didn't understand.

I was very late getting in to Budva, but the rest of them had been too busy working on the boat to notice the time. I told them, well, I'm free of all encumbrances and now I'll do my full share of the labor. There was obvious relief that I had come back without Sonia. Hill said the first thing was to get rid of the Chevrolet. We went to the little cubicle they called the mayor's office and met Joko Boreta. That was a pleasant interlude.

Mayor Boreta was a gentleman as well as a politician. Like so many of his constituents he had once been in Cleveland and he remembered every word of English he had ever learned. Of course he wanted to help the Americans. He would be glad to take Macatee's Chevrolet off our hands. It would cost us just ten dinars for the legal documents. Then he started to work on the documents. He had an old Oliver typewriter, which he must have gotten twenty years ago when he was in Cleveland. He punched a key with a finger on his right hand, and when it stuck, as it always did, he pulled it back into place with the fingers of his left hand. He apparently had been typewriting that way for years, because he had a smooth technique. The document he finally turned out was only eight lines long, but it took him nearly an hour to type it. Painfully, one letter at a time. Then he had to look for his rubber stamp, because nothing is legal or even worth reading in the Balkans unless it's got a rubber stamp on it. When he found the stamp he couldn't find the ink pad, and so he just breathed on the stamp and pressed it against the paper. Then he translated the document. It said that he, Joko Boreta, Mayor of Budva, in the name of this community had. assumed full responsibility for one Sevreley and that the community of Budva would guard said Sevreley with all diligence, but . . . the community of Bulva could not be responsible if any harm comes to said Sevreley at the hands of forces not now within our midst.

We watched the Chevrolet being stored in a fireproof garage, and I wondered how soon it would be before the Italians would be using it.

Then the mayor insisted that we go back to his office to meet a lot of the distinguished citizens of Budva.

Many, he said, have been, like me, in your handsome country.

It was a pathetic scene. Here was the helpless little town of Budva about to be seized by Italian and German troops that were, at this very moment, not many miles away. But we and most of the distinguished citizens of that walled city on the sea sat in the mayor's office talking about Cleveland and the American way of life and how much they all wanted, some day, to go back to the United States, the land of the free and the home of the brave.

Finally we left them, with many handshakes and many wishes for happiness and success.

White had assumed the role of skipper of the *Makedonka*. I could see that that was going to cause trouble. He and Kay were having a bitter argument when Hill and I got back from the mayor's office. We tried to act as peacemakers, but the feeling seemed to be strong between them. It all started over some minor point such as where the sail should be stored. Kay had done some yachting on the Great Lakes. White had read a book or two about sailing. Each had his own positive ideas about how things should be done. It looked as if we might be in for trouble of a variety we hadn't thought of.

White didn't know about the ham Sonia had bought for us, and so he had bought another twenty-pound chunk of the raw, smoke-blackened meat. We put both of them in gunny sacks in the bottom of the boat. Then we stored away what was left of the canned goods we had appropriated from the major's hotel room in Sarajevo.

Someone had sold Atherton two big wicker-covered demijohns. The larger held twenty-five liters, and we filled it partly full of fresh water. The other held twenty-three liters. We half-filled that one with potent Serb red wine. Then we went out on a final search for food. For some reason we never could comprehend, they were willing to sell us all the liquor we wanted, and we bought a lot of slivo and brandy and rum. But when it came to food they just shook their heads grimly and positively. We flashed rolls of American dollars, but they were wise. They still shook their heads. They knew that soon they were going to be in a position where money, even good American money, wouldn't help them to exist. We couldn't even get a square meal that day in Budva, in spite of all the friends we had made during the few hours we had been there. But we did manage to round up ten loaves of black peasant bread. It was made without any white flour, under the new Yugoslav wartime rationing law. It was hard and tasteless and unpalatable even when it was fresh. But the ten loaves we bought were stale. So stale they made a noise like rocks when we threw them into a burlap bag, which we put safely away underneath the foot-square deck in the bow.

Part of the boat-car deal was that Atherton retained title to all the gas in his Opal. Of course we drained the last drop out of the Chevrolet when we turned it over to Mayor Boreta. Then there were several cans left from the supply that had been forced on us by the man in Sarajevo. Altogether we figured we had fifty-one liters, about thirteen gallons.

"You boys may have hated Sonia," I told them with some bitterness while we were loading in the cans of gas, "and that was your privilege, but if we ever get anywhere in the *Makedonka,* you can thank her for it."

Since none of them except Hill knew what I meant, I told them how she had wangled the gasoline for us. They didn't do any cheering. They just kept on loading the cans into the boat, which was filling up rapidly, what with the sail, which looked as if it was going to be constantly in the way, lying as it did across the seats, and the two big demijohns, and the sacks of food, and our typewriters and knapsacks.

Kay wanted to know if we had a compass and sea charts. We had already asked Mayor Boreta and a lot of other people about things like that. They just laughed. In the first place, Serbian fishermen never use compasses or sea charts; and in the second place the mayor, just to prove his point, had sent his office boy scouting all over town. The boy had come back shaking his head. There was no compass in Budva. And no one even knew what a sea chart was. But we had some good automobile road maps that showed the shore line and the islands in the Adriatic, and we thought we would be all right.

Someone said, "We've got to get out of here today, and if we fool around looking for things like a compass we may be overtaken and put in a place where we won't need a compass or a boat or anything but someone to draw up a will for us."

We still had a few little jobs left to do when the sun set, about seven o'clock. But just then we heard the cracking of rifles, not only in the town but also off in the hills. We didn't know what it meant, but we didn't want to stay to find out. It might be an advance guard of the Italians and Germans arriving, or it might be the first shots in a revolution. Whichever it was, we knew we had tempted the gods long enough, and it was time to weigh anchor and get along.

The anchor was a lot of scrap iron tied onto a heavy rope. We were just pulling it up and getting ready to shove off when Kay announced that he was staying behind. We asked him why and he said:

"Because you don't have any compass or any charts, and you're damn fools to start out now. It'll be dark in half an hour. You don't know anything about sailing, or running a gasoline engine, or even about rowing. You don't know anything about the geography out there on the Adriatic. You don't know anything about where the Yugoslav and Italian mine fields are, or how to get through them. Even if you get down off the Albanian coast you'll probably be picked up by the Italian fleet. You haven't enough food to last, and there won't be any discipline because you haven't even appointed a skipper. And anyway, not one of you knows enough about what you're doing to take charge. So, good-by, and have a good time and I'll write your obits. Happy sailing!"

None of us knew Kay very well. He had worked as a lone wolf in Belgrade. He never attended the almost nightly farewell and welcome-home parties we used to give for the newspaper boys as they drifted in to the Srpski Kralj from far corners of Europe or as they left for New York, London, Athens, Beirut, or Cairo. But we had been counting on Kay's two hundred or two hundred and ten pounds. We knew that weight behind an oar some night on the Adriatic might just mean the difference between making or not making land. But I could see there was no use arguing. It wasn't really a matter of compass or sea charts. It was human friction between two tired, nerve-worn men, one at least ten years older than the other. There would be friction enough among the rest of us. No two of us were alike in any way. And when the going got tough, there would be some real problems besides the problems of motor and sails and oars. Therefore I didn't argue with Kay. I just shook hands with him and smiled in what I hoped he would realize was an understanding way.

Kay was lumbering up the road leading to the town when White yanked the rope that started the one-cylinder engine. The putt-putt sounded like machine-gun fire. But the engine was running, and that was consoling. The noise, echoing out over the water and hitting the rocky hills and bouncing back and forth, brought a lot of people running to the shore.

There were black clouds in the sky. Some of them were daubed faintly with little streaks of red from the sun, which had gone down in a blaze of fire. I remembered a childhood rhyme about red sky at night, sailors' delight; red sky in morning, sailors take warning. That was about the extent of my nautical knowledge. I wondered then whether it was a safe axiom to follow. The black clouds seemed to contradict it.

A mist was coming in from the sea. It looked as if it were raining, off in the distance. Kay might be right. We were probably in for it all right, but we were all four of us happy right then. We were leaving Yugoslavia, with its dead bodies, ruined cities, and desolate villages. We were sailing out on the clean, blue water where we wouldn't see things like blood and the wreckage of human beings. We were in our own boat. We weren't complete masters of it, but right now the engine was running smoothly and we felt confident. We were heading for Greece, a place where we could sit down at a typewriter and pound out a story and then go to a cable office and send it off to America. We could go to the Grand Bretagne Hotel in Athens and get a good meal and go to sleep between clean white sheets.

The crowd on the beach were waving. I remembered the little American flag I had broken out of its fastenings on the fender of Macatee's Chevrolet before we turned it over to Mayor Boreta. I rummaged around in my knapsack for it and then waved it to the people on shore. They were quickly becoming just black dots, but suddenly we heard a cheer echo over the water. Just a faint medley of voices. But we could distinguish the one word "Amerikanskis." A lump came in my throat. I said, half to myself and half aloud, "Those poor bastards! They stand there cheering us, as if they didn't have a worry in the world. I wonder how many of them will be alive a week from now. Or a month from now."

Hill said, "I only hope the Italians occupy Budva instead of the Germans."

I told him I did too. The Italians will understand a little better than the Germans that those people only wanted to be let alone. To live and be let alone. To live and let live. That's all we want right now, too, isn't it? Yes, and that's all most of the world wants.

Half an hour out from Budva it began to pour rain. That for the red-sky-at-night jingle! We didn't mind it much. We didn't mind that we were getting soaked to the skin and that water was pouring over our typewriters and our knapsacks and probably ruining a lot of things. But what did give us our first fright was that the outboard engine suddenly stopped. Leigh White, whose knowledge of internal combustion engines was about equal to that of the average American youth in his twenties who used to have an old Ford when he was in school, was playing engineer when it happened. He yanked the piece of rope that was supposed to start the motor. He kept yanking it until his arm was tired, and then the rest of us tried it, but we couldn't get a single kick out of the motor. Atherton pointed out in his mild British way that he had noticed the rain water pouring from Leigh's hat down onto the motor and that maybe the water had short-circuited whatever it was that was supposed to supply the spark.

Hill said, "What we need is an umbrella for someone to hold over the motor."

But White wasn't in any mood for joking. He was working like a dog trying to dry the magneto and the spark plug, but now the rain was beating down with a real fury. A stiff wind was beginning to blow. It was pitch dark, and the boat was being tossed around like a peanut shell.

Atherton asked, "How about the sail?"

But the rest of us, landlubbers though we were, knew we couldn't possibly put a sail up in a wind like this. The sea seemed to get rougher each minute. Now the *Makedonka* was tossing so badly that we were beginning to ship water and somebody had to start bailing.

We had been told that the outboard engine only weighed about a hundred pounds, but when we tried to lift it out of its brackets in order to put the big wooden tiller in place, it seemed to weigh a ton or two. Every time we had it raised almost the six inches that would free it from its fastenings, a wave would strike the boat and we would all go flat on our faces and the motor would drop back into its brackets. But we knew we were in for real trouble unless we could steer, and since you can't steer with the motor in place unless it's running, we kept at it. Finally, between rolls, we got the piece of useless machinery into the boat and slipped the wooden tiller in place. We didn't know how to drain out the gasoline, and so we lost the whole tankful, and by bad luck it spilled all over our ten loaves of bread.

White said we had better get the oars working. It didn't matter about getting up any speed with the oars, but if we didn't keep them working, the *Makedonka* was going to capsize. So White sat at the tiller straining his eyes to keep the shore in sight and yet not get so close that we might hit the rocks that dotted the water. Hill worked with the bucket, bailing out dirty bilge water. The only trouble was that about two out of every three times he tried to throw a bucket of water over the side, the wind, which seemed to be blowing at us from all directions, threw the water right back in our faces. And there was gasoline mixed with the water. Gasoline isn't much fun to get in your eyes.

Atherton and I unlashed two of the oars and got to work. And it was work. It was work to keep the waves from yanking the oars right out of our hands. Those oars were designed for stronger men than we were. They were about twenty feet long. Sixteen of those twenty feet were over the side of the boat. And they were made of the heaviest wood I had ever seen since I tried to cut down an ironwood tree on my farm in New Hampshire back in the days before I ever dreamed of covering a war in Europe and going rowboating on the Adriatic.

Thinking of that ironwood tree and New Hampshire made me wish we had a couple of husky New England farmers like Rex Wheet and his brother here in the *Makedonka* now. I had seen Rex Wheet, who had the farm next to mine, take the front wheels of a Ford and lift them right off the ground. That's what we needed in the *Makedonka* that night. Brute strength. And instead we had four worn-out newspapermen who were hungry, tired, thirsty, and sleepy, and who had less strength left than four healthy high-school girls would have had. When Atherton got tired, Hill took his place. When I got tired Atherton took my place. And so it went all night. Two men at the oars, bending their backs, straining every weary muscle, often standing up in the boat in order to put their full weight into trying to pull the oars through the water.

The Serbs had never heard of the American kind of oarlocks. Instead, they tied a piece of rope loosely around the oar and then looped this rope over a peg of wood in the gunwale. Normally those ropes probably don't break very often, but while we battled the storm that night the rope oarlocks broke every ten or fifteen minutes. When the break came, it generally landed the oarsman flat on his back on the bottom of the boat. Then the *Makedonka* would go into a wild dance, bobbing around on the waves, out of control because there was only one oar to make her behave. The man who was "resting" and bailing had to get busy and find more rope and fashion a new oarlock. And then we'd start all over again.

There isn't much sense trying to describe that night. If you've ever been tossed about for nine or ten hours at sea in a storm in an open boat during a gale and rainstorm without knowing anything about the water and without the strength to do real battle with the elements, you know all about it. I realized for the first time in my life that night what sheer exhaustion really means. Several times the combined force of the wind and waves tore the oars from our hands, and we had to risk drowning to grab them as they flew through the air and landed on the water. And I remember once that I leaned back and just quit rowing. Hill was sleeping for a minute. Sleeping as he lay on the bottom of the boat in a foot of water, soaked from head to toe, but too worn out to care. Atherton was the Rock of Gibraltar. He was displaying all those qualities that have made the British a great race. He was gritting his teeth, forgetting his own suffering, and pulling on his oar with a strength he himself didn't know he possessed. But that was just the trouble. He was on the starboard oar. I was on the port oar. He was doing such a good job that the boat was going almost in circles. I couldn't keep up with him. And White kept shouting from the stern, "Stronger on the port oar. Stronger on the port oar. What's the matter, Bob? Stronger on the port oar!"

But I couldn't go any stronger on the port oar. I couldn't keep the port oar in the water. I kept thinking, it isn't worth it. Life itself isn't worth it. I can't go stronger on the port oar. I guess the vodka I drank in Istanbul, and the barack in Budapest and the tsuica in Bucharest and the slivo in Yugoslavia were beginning to show. That and the lack of sleep and food. I was tired. I was too tired to go on. I didn't give a God damn. I didn't care whether we got to Greece or not.

Greece! Why were we going to Greece? So we could send a story to the papers in America, which a few million people riding in subways and trolley cars would read on the way home and then forget the next minute. Why should I go through all this just to give them a few paragraphs to read on their way home? What did I care about them? What did I care about reputation and job and—yes, what did I care about life itself? Life wasn't worth this.

I hadn't minded the bombs in Belgrade and the bombs in Sarajevo. That was a gamble. You had a chance. But out here on the black Adriatic we didn't have a chance. We were fooling ourselves. I felt just as I had felt the morning of the earthquake in Bucharest when buildings started to tumble around us and the world seemed to be doing a dance of death. You can battle other men, but when the elements are lined up against you, what's the use? You can't win when the dice are loaded. The dice are loaded against us tonight. I feel so God-damned tired. I can't pull that oar another single stroke. To hell with it! To hell with trying to live when it's such a tough fight. To hell . . . with . . . I'm sleepy. I guess I'll just go to sleep. The water will cover me over pretty soon. Soft water. Water will feel good, lapping against tired muscles. I guess . . . I'll go . . . to sleep.

I heard White yelling, "What's the matter with the port oar?"

But I didn't care about the port oar any more. I was going to sleep. Sleep. Sleep.

It was Atherton who kept me from falling out of the boat. And it was Atherton, the Rock of Gibraltar, who slapped my face so hard that I really woke up and got mad and said, "God damn it, what are you doing?"

And he said, "Get to work on that oar, you bloody idiot, do you want to drown all of us?"

And so I picked up the oar and started rowing again.

It was like that all night. Sometimes, when I quit and Hill relieved me at the port oar, I bailed until I saw that the more I threw over the side, the deeper the water in the boat seemed to get, and then I lay on the bottom of the boat in the water and went to sleep.

And then we'd switch places. And that was a job too, because we kept banging our hands on the outboard motor that took up so much of the twenty feet of space in the boat. Several times we got deep cuts from crashing into the blades of the propeller, but it was dark and we just felt a warm sensation where the cuts were, and since we couldn't see the blood, it didn't make any difference.

It was Leigh White who got us through that night alive. He did much of the rowing. He kept his head better than any of us. He never seemed to get sleepy.

It rained and it stormed all night, but when it got light we discovered we were just barely within sight of land. We strained our eyes and we all agreed that we could see a cove of some kind. We took a vote about what we ought to do. The chances were

ninety-nine out of a hundred that the Italians had occupied this
area, because we had been going south all night toward the
Albanian frontier. Even if we hadn't made much distance, we
knew that the Italians, when we left Budva, hadn't been far
away.

We all agreed that we couldn't face any more of the sea until
we had rested and gotten the motor dried out. Atherton, the
Englishman, and White, who had a Spanish loyalist wife waiting
for him in Athens, and Hill and I, who were on the Axis black
list, all agreed that nothing, not even a German concentration
camp, could be worse than what we had gone through the last
eight or ten hours.

So we started heading in for the shore. We rowed and rowed.
We put the last ounce of strength we had left into trying to push
that boat through the water. But the shore seemed to stay right
where it was when we first saw it. I think it took us about three
hours to make it. There wasn't a soul in sight. The coast line was
rocky, but we spotted a place where there was some sand. We
tried to head straight in, but as we got close a breaker swirled the
Makedonka around, and before we could collect our wits the little
sardine boat was being pounded to pieces on the rocks. I jumped
out with a rope into water that was chest high. While I pulled,
the others got out and tried to point the boat in. We were
all struggling around in the water when a Serbian fisherman
came running down from his house and took charge. He got a
block and tackle.

After an hour's work he had the *Makedonka* beached. But the
strain of that last hour had been too much. The *Makedonka* was
beginning to go to pieces. The bow had pulled away from the
rest of the boat. Seams had opened up. The *Makedonka* had
gotten us safely through the night, but it looked now as if she were
through. We didn't care.

We asked the fisherman where we could sleep. He said, "Who
are you?" Atherton, who spoke perfect Serbian, told him. The
fisherman looked frightened. He was frightened for us, he said.
This town was Petrovacz na Mare. The Italians last night had

formally occupied the town. They had stayed a few hours and then gone on. They had stayed just long enough, he said, to buy up everything in sight. They had given the Petrovacz shopkeepers Italian lire for what they bought. The fisherman said it with disgust. Italian lire! It was just as if he had said counterfeit money. Yes, and they had called all the people "Our brothers," which made all the people very angry, but none of the people dared say anything. Then all the Italian trucks and motorcycles had gone on. On toward Budva. But they said they would be back. They would be back sometime today.

"And so," said the Serbian fisherman, "I think you better not stay in Petrovacz na Mare."

"Look at that boat!" we said. "Can we go on in that?"

He admitted that we could not. Then he brightened up. "We will hide you," he said. "The people of Petrovacz na Mare are fine people. They like Americans." Then he looked at Atherton, who had explained his own nationality. "Yes, they like the English too. The English have promised to save us. We think some day the Americans will help save us too. So we will hide you—you men who are allies of Yugoslavia. We will hide you from the Italians. They shall never know you are here, even when they come back. Now follow me, this way. It is my own house I take you to. It is a hotel. A fine hotel. We have four rooms for rent. Only two are occupied. You shall have the other two. If you have no money I charge you nothing. Not one dinar."

CHAPTER NINE

Adriatic Odyssey

————◆•◆————

I DON'T KNOW how long we had been sleeping. It wasn't more than a few hours. I remember that when I woke up and found Kay shaking my shoulder I thought I was dreaming. I'd been tossing around the bed in the fisherman's house in Petrovacz na Mare, living over again that night at sea. I could tell from the condition of the bed that I had probably been rowing for my life, making the oars go like mad, while I should have been resting. But sometimes you can't shut things out of your mind and make your body behave, even if you do fall asleep. So I didn't feel very rested after those few hours in bed, and I didn't like Kay standing there laughing.

Kay said that shortly after daylight a motorboat had arrived in Budva from Petrovacz. The boatman told a story about some crazy Americans who had been shipwrecked. The story spread around town. Like all stories that travel by word of mouth it got exaggerated with each telling. Kay picked it up about an hour later, fifth or tenth hand. By that time the Americans had all been killed. So Kay got the motorboat to bring him down to Petrovacz so that he could write our obits. He laughed because we said we weren't dead at all. Just dead tired.

Kay told us what had happened in Budva after we left. There had been some shooting, and practically all the army units in Budva had gone off into the hills to carry on the war. The city was expecting the Italians any minute now.

We got the idea that the real reason Kay had come to Petrovacz was because he had changed his mind about going along with us. But he didn't say anything, and neither did we. He sat down with us in the dining room, and we all had bowls of water-thin soup and some black bread. After that we went into the kitchen and looked over our shoes and clothes. The fisherman's wife was trying to dry them, but it was going to be an impossible job. Then we went shopping. The Italians had cleaned the stores out of almost everything we wanted, but we did get a few provisions for the next lap of the voyage. One onion, one orange, two lemons, five bars of "Turkish Delight," six bars of chocolate, a pound or so of raisins, ten boxes of matches, five hard-boiled eggs, twenty cigars, and about a hundred cigarettes. It wasn't a very imposing array of food and tobacco for a trip that might last for weeks, but it was all we could find.

Then we looked all over town for a compass. Most of the fishermen didn't know what we were talking about. We decided not to even ask about sea charts. We wanted more sleep, but we had taken the edge off our weariness, and the Italians might be coming back any time now, and there were things to be done. We went down and looked over the *Makedonka*. It wasn't much of a job to dry out the engine, but the boat itself was in bad shape. Our host, the proprietor of the four-room hotel, said he knew a good carpenter, Milan Francisikovicz. Milan had worked for years in America, especially around some Philadelphia shipyard. He was about sixty years old, but the fisherman said he was a bearcat at fixing a boat. So we sent for Milan Francisikovicz.

We took a liking to Mike the minute we saw him. Over in America, he explained, he went as Mike Francisco, because Milan Francisikovicz was too foreign-sounding and too hard for most people to say. So he asked us to call him Mike, because that would make him think he was back there where he had been so happy. Mike spoke English with a decided Irish accent. We never were able to figure out why, because he said he had never known any Irishmen. Mike was about five feet tall, but he had hands like a baseball catcher's glove, covered with callouses and as brown as a Negro's. While Mike worked on the boat we talked to him. We asked him if he knew anything about the Adriatic. Sure, he said, I know it like a book. I used to be a fisherman on the Adriatic before I went to America. I know the Adriatic like a book.

We held a whispered conference and then we asked Mike how he felt about the Italians. He said he hated them. We said, "Well, you're going to have to live with them now, aren't you?"

He looked up quickly. Then he went on sawing a slit in the tiller of the *Makedonka* so that it would fit better.

I may leave here myself, Mike said slowly, half under his breath.

Well, one of us said, how would you like to leave with us?

Mike didn't jump at it. He'd been in America and he wasn't a fool. But finally he said he was all for it, except that some provision had to be made for his wife. We asked him how much he felt he ought to leave her. Mike thought a long time and then he blurted out, "Eight hundred dollars in American money."

We could tell the way he said it that he didn't really expect anything like that. Eight hundred dollars was just his asking price. Just the place to begin bargaining. So we bargained. Finally we struck a deal. Mike would come along with us to show us the best way down the Adriatic to Greece. In return we would turn the *Makedonka* over to him when we reached port, or we would guarantee to get him a job at sea with the Greeks or the British, or on some American boat if we could find one. And besides that we would give him a hundred dollars in American money for his wife. Mike insisted on shaking hands with each one of us to bind the deal. He nearly mashed my hand into a pulp when he grabbed it and shook it the way you shake an apple tree when you're trying to knock down a stubborn apple up on the very top branch. I said to myself, "That's the kind of a hand a man needs to operate those damned heavy oars!"

It was almost dark when Mike pronounced the *Makedonka* seaworthy again. If we treated her gently. Then we held a weather conference. Someone said the barometer up in the mayor's house—the mayor had the only barometer and the only radio in town—was still dropping. The sky was still filled with black clouds, and the Italians hadn't come back yet. And so, although we were impatient to get going, we decided to wait until daylight. We gave Mike his hundred dollars and told him to be back in the morning.

We couldn't get to bed early that night because the town of Petrovacz na Mare wanted to talk. It was a community secret by now that some American newspapermen were hiding in that hotel with four rooms run by the fisherman. Everyone wanted to have a look at the foreigners, and then to have a word with them.

While the fisherman's wife was serving us a frugal supper she kept mumbling something under her breath in Serbian. Every time she put a plate down in front of one of us she'd say the same collection of words. Atherton finally cleared up the mystery. What she was mumbling was, why didn't America help us before it was too late? Why didn't America help us before it was too late? She kept repeating it like a litany. We decided it would be a little too complicated to try to answer, and so we went on ignoring her It was over soon because there wasn't much to eat.

After supper a tall, handsome Serb in his twenties came to call on us. He was in civilian clothes, but he said he had been in the Yugoslav army. His eyes flashed while he talked, and there was such a sincerity and honesty about his whole manner that we all believed he was telling the truth. He told us that most of the young men of Petrovacz, after hearing about the Americans who were soon to push off for Greece, had gathered and discussed the Yugoslav situation. They had appointed him their spokesman. They had instructed him to see us and say that they wanted to fight on against the Italians and the Germans. They knew this guerrilla warfare in the mountains wouldn't amount to much. It wouldn't have any more effect on the Axis armies than a mosquito bite on an elephant. A mosquito bite on an elephant. Those were his words. The young men of Petrovacz wanted to do something more than that. Most of them had been in the army. They were good soldiers, if they had the right kind of leadership and half a chance. He repeated that phrase several times. If we had only half a chance.

We listened patiently. We wondered where we came in. We found out before long. We were Americans. He said it like all those Balkan people used to say it. As if we were half gods. As if just being Americans made us all-powerful. As he said it, I kept thinking of those three Americans out on the Adriatic last night, and how completely helpless they had been. Anyway we were Americans and we must help the young men of Petrovacz na Mare who wanted to fight on and show the damned Germans and Italians. We must work out a plan for them. We must find some way for them to get to Greece and join up with the British and keep fighting until the last German and the last Italian had been driven out of the Balkans.

Well, what would you have said to the young man with the black hair and the flashing eyes and the zeal of a holy crusader? He talked about several hundred young men who wanted to go to Greece, and we had a twenty-foot sardine boat with too many men in it already. We finally suggested that they organize a fleet of small fishing boats and try to follow us down the Adriatic. We couldn't, we said, do much for them except that if we all got to Greece we would see that they were put in touch with the proper British authorities. The young soldier seemed disappointed. I don't know why. I don't know what he expected us to do. But he went off saying he would report back to his comrades. When he shuffled out through the door that was the last we ever saw of him.

We talked to a lot of other people in Petrovacz who flocked to see us. They all wanted to know what we thought about the future of Yugoslavia. They put the questions to us flatly, coldly. There wasn't much of a chance to dodge them. But we couldn't tell them the truth; any more than you can tell a man on his death bed that you don't believe in an afterlife, when you know that that's what he wants so very much to believe. So we said, wait. Be patient. The war has only begun. The first inning or two has gone to Germany. But just wait until the United States gets into this war. Then see what happens. Ask Milan Francisikovicz about the United States. It's a country full of factories and machines. When they start making airplanes in the United States, the sky will be black with them. Tens and tens of thousands of planes. All Europe can't make as many planes in a week as we'll be making soon in America in a single day. Be patient. Just wait. It won't be long before the United States enters the war and then it won't be long before the Germans will be driven right off the face of Europe. Then Yugoslavia will live again.

That's what we told those poor people in Petrovacz because that's what we knew they wanted to hear. The younger people brightened up and kept whispering to each other. We could hear the word Amerikanski being used in almost every sentence. But the older men didn't look very happy. One of them made a little speech. Atherton translated it very carefully, word for word.

"All that," he said, "is fine. Fine for the young people. But what about us old men? We'll never live to see that happen. We have only a few more years left to us. We'll be dead and Yugoslavia will still be a slave. Yugoslavia will still be starving. Yugoslavia will still be in chains. Yugoslavia will never be free again while we live."

I remember that speech almost word for word. And those are almost the exact words the little old man used as we stood looking out over the dark Adriatic that April night when Yugoslavia was breathing her last. There were tears in the old man's eyes when he finished. And the other old men with thin white hair and weather-beaten faces kept wagging their heads in silent agreement.

Christ! I mumbled to myself. That was all. Just, Christ! I don't know if I said it religiously or profanely. I guess I said it like Amy Lowell did in that poem that goes: Christ! what are patterns for? Religiously and profanely, both at the same time. My emotions were begining to get pretty raw. I was beginning to feel like the hero in that old melodrama, *Alias Jimmy Valentine,* when he sandpapers his finger tips down to the raw nerves so that they'll be sensitive enough for him to do one more safe-opening job. All our nerves were raw, like the nerves in Jimmy Valentine's finger tips. It was a little more than I could stand to see this circle of old men wagging their heads so tragically and some of them with tears in their eyes. So I just said, Christ! And then I walked down to the *Makedonka* and pretended to see if she was leaking.

The next morning we all tumbled out of bed as soon as it was light. Kay came in and said, "Well, I've tossed a coin and I'm not going with you this time either. I tossed a coin to see whether I'd risk my life for fame."

We all said in chorus that that sounded like a dirty crack.

Kay grinned and said, "The coin came up tails, and so I'm going back to Budva and let the Italians get me and see what happens. I'm not in any danger like the rest of you. Nobody's ever expelled me or even thought about it."

I couldn't help having a last dig at good-natured Kay. I said, "By the way, you laughed at me the day before the Belgrade bombing because your money man got a thousand dollars' worth of dinars for you, and my money man failed to show up with my thousand dollars' worth. Now who's the joke on?"

He laughed and said, "Do you want to buy a few dinars, huh?"

I said, "No, charge your thousand dollars' worth to the UP on your expense account and then paper your living room with them some day."

But Kay wasn't the only one who got stuck with worthless Balkan money. Hill and White had rolls of dinars, too. And of course I didn't say anything to Kay about all the Bulgarian leva and the Rumanian lei I had in my own wallet that I'd never be able to turn into real cash. We were all in the same fix.

While we were loading up the *Makedonka* and getting ready

to push out, an Italian bomber flew low over the little harbor of Petrovacz. We hid under the wreckage of a rowboat on the beach, and the plane went right over us without anything happening.

When we finally got ready to go we looked around for Mike. No one had seen him all morning. He had gone out last night to give his wife the hundred dollars and hadn't been back since. His home was about five miles out of Petrovacz, and no one wanted to go out there, because they had heard the Italians were arresting anyone who went down the highway. So we just waited. The fisherman-hotelkeeper said he was sure Mike wouldn't fail us. Late in the afternoon Mike finally came puffing down to the beach. The Italians had taken over his house and had found a hidden supply of guns and ammunition. They were waiting there for him to return so that they could give him the third degree and perhaps lock him up on suspicion of being a dangerous character. But Mike had fooled them. He had sneaked up to a neighbor's house and sent a message to his wife, and they said their good-bys at a meeting place in the woods. Mike said his wife was quite pleased with the American banknotes. "And now," Mike finished, "I'm rarin' to go!"

Just then a boy came running down from the home of the mayor of Petrovacz. He said the mayor wanted to tell us that his little barometer was rising and he had just listened to the radio and from what he heard he thought we had better get under way in a hurry.

The entire town was down on the wharf to see us off. They said that if the Italians asked them anything about us they'd say we had gone to Bath. Bath was the next Yugoslav town down the coast. The natives thought that would save us from being chased all the way down the Adriatic and also that it would be a good joke on the Italians. They laughed and pounded one another on the back at the idea of the Italians chasing all around Bath looking for the American newspapermen who wouldn't be there at all.

Then we dug out the American flag and put it in the bow. There was a lot of handclapping when those Serb fisherfolk realized what flag it was. Kay sat on the dock grinning and puffing on his pipe. I'm sure he thought we were as foolish as children. But there was nothing foolish or childish about it to us. We were putting our necks right into a noose. We weren't fully aware of the trouble that lay ahead of us, but we had a good hunch that it wasn't going to be any picnic. Anyway, we were rested now, and things were assuming their proper proportion, and we knew that we were doing the right thing. We were avoiding the risk of falling into the hands of the Italians, who of course would turn us over to the Germans, who might make life very unpleasant for us for a long time to come. More important than that, from a professional point of view, we were doing our job. We were trying to get away from this communications-locked country to some place where we could tell the world about the tragedy of Yugoslavia.

You should have seen Mike when we turned over the motor and started out from that wharf. He was the proudest little man I ever saw. He was the hero of Petrovacz na Mare. This was the one big moment of his life. Out of all the hundreds of citizens of that small town Mike had been chosen to go off with the Americans. Off to Greece. Maybe off to the United States again. Anyway, off to freedom and liberty. Of course he didn't know then that he was sailing off to his death. And a miserable death at that. But neither did we. If we had known it we wouldn't have taken him.

The people of Petrovacz didn't know Mike was sailing off to his death either. But they cheered him and waved to him, and I know from all the things they had been saying the last twenty-four hours that they envied Mike and that Mike knew they envied him and that this really was the climax of Mike's life. I like to think of that scene as we sailed away and of how happy Mike was, because it helps me to forget what happened afterwards. I like to think of Mike, the hero of Petrovacz na Mare. Mike sailing away on his one grand adventure, to the cheers of his friends and his fellow townsmen.

As we pulled out to sea we noticed a line of army trucks racing down the hill into the little fishing village of Petrovacz na Mare.

We had slipped away just in time. The Italians were back. The people on the wharf noticed them too. We watched that cluster of figures racing for cover. Just like frightened mice. From now on they were going to be living constantly in fear. That was our last glimpse of crucified Yugoslavia. That picture of frightened people running to cover because the army of the invader had arrived in town again.

It didn't take long to get out of sight of Petrovacz. Then we settled down to business. We would only have a few more hours of light. We must profit by the experience we had had coming from Budva to Petrovacz.

The other men decided that I, being the oldest, had better take over the job of rationing out the food. I was to be undisputed master in that field. Also, I was going to keep the ship's log and a chart of the course we followed and try to figure out the gas consumption so that we could tell whether we could afford to use the engine or whether we had to sail and row occasionally.

We avoided the delicate question of appointing anyone skipper of our twenty-foot ship, because that might raise many questions about age, ability, experience, capabilities, and all that sort of thing. But we agreed that Mike would be navigator, and White would be engineer in charge of the outboard motor, and Hill and Atherton would man the sail when and if we could use it. We had our food stored where it wouldn't get wet in case of storm. Everything was shipshape.

At 16:40, about an hour and a half before sunset, Mike shouted out that we were passing Sutomore. Mike knew Sutomore all right. But it was the only piece of navigation information he volunteered on the whole trip that wasn't vehemently questioned and debated. Sutomore was nine kilometers. That wasn't bad. An average speed of about ten kilometers an hour. The rest of them began to figure that we might make the island of Corfu, which was the nearest Greek soil, in a couple of days. But I was figuring out rations with pencil and paper. My plan, which they agreed not to dispute, was to count on a maximum of ten days at sea. If the motor held out, we might make it in two. But if we had to row, it might take us at least a couple of weeks. Ten days was a fair average. That meant a loaf of bread a day among the five of us. Plus a few cookies and a handful of raisins and a can of something.

The one thing we could have all we wanted of would be ham. We had about forty pounds of it. But Sonia had warned us about the ham. It wasn't cooked. Just smoked. She had said she didn't think we'd care a great deal for it. But after we passed Sutomore I dug out a loaf of bread and hacked off a few slices and then went to work carving chunks off one of the hams. They all ate the bread, but no one could do much with the chunks of raw ham. If tougher meat is ever grown, the Serbs will probably grow it. That ham was just like pure muscle or gristle. We all had good teeth, but no one could make an impression on it. The rest of them wanted to forego the ham until necessity drove us to it, but we compromised by just sucking out what little juice there was in it and not trying to swallow the meat itself.

By sunset we had gone twenty-five kilometers. Then the engine stopped. We were worried until we found we had run out of gas. But that was bad news too. Twenty-five kilometers on three liters. We had a total of less than fifty liters. We could go, then, only four hundred kilometers by motor. And Corfu was farther than that, even if we went on a fairly straight course. We agreed that from now on we would have to experiment with the sail, unless we wanted to do a lot of rowing at the tail end of the journey, when we wouldn't feel much like rowing.

We were averaging only about eight kilometers a liter. And the original owner of the *Makedonka* had guaranteed ten kilometers to a liter. We laughed. Somebody ought to go back to Budva and tell him he was just like the average American automobile salesman with his gas-consumption claims.

From Sutomore on, Mike began to express certain perplexity about just what this or that promontory or cove or headland really was. That surprised us, because he still wasn't many miles from his home town and he was, he had told us, an old Adriatic fisherman. But gradually the whole sad truth came out. First, Mike's eyesight was very bad. He should have had glasses, but he had never owned a pair. Next, he hadn't been down the Adriatic from Petrovacz in twenty years. And Mike's memory wasn't very good. In the third place, all the fishing he had done had been either in the immediate vicinity of Petrovacz or to the north. Mike turned out to be a complete loss as a navigator, and that job was divided among the rest of us. But even after we found that Mike knew little about sails and less about motors and nothing about navigation we still never regretted our deal with him. He had an amazing repertoire of stories that kept us awake when we otherwise might have fallen asleep over our jobs. And he was a sterling character, unselfish, honest, and loyal to all of us, collectively and individually, which of course put a great strain on his diplomatic ability during the days that followed, when we were all in such nasty moods that we kept at one another's throats night and day.

Mike talked to us often about America. He could forget hunger, sleeplessness, broken masts, torn sails, hard work, anything at all just as long as we let him talk about America. He wished now that he had never come back. But he got homesick for the hills of Dalmatia and the beautiful blue Adriatic. He thought he would pay a visit to Yugoslavia. Then one complication after another prevented his return.

"But," Mike would say, "after this damned war's over I'm going to work my way back to Philly and nothing will ever pry me out of America again."

He talked that way for days, and he meant it. You could tell that by the way his face lighted up every time he got on the subject. He seemed to slough off ten or twenty years of his sixty when he talked about his younger days in America. From the way he talked about going back you would have thought he was just on the doorstep of life. Planning a long career.

We were all pleased with ourselves when dusk came and we

knew from the contour of the coast line on our automobile road maps that we were now leaving Yugoslavia and entering the territorial waters of Albania.

But that raised a new problem. Mines! The Adriatic was one of the most heavily mined bodies of water anywhere around the continent. We knew it because just a few days before the Balkan war started we had all written stories about the sinking of the biggest passenger ship anywhere in this part of the world. It was a Yugoslav excursion ship and it had been sailing up the Adriatic to hide away for the duration of the war, which by then everyone knew was coming. The captain apparently knew where the mine fields were, but he hadn't posted a lookout to watch for floating mines that might have broken loose from their anchors. The ship hit one of them and went to the bottom in a hurry. The captain and his crew had been rescued, but the next morning the captain's dead body was found on the shore. In a fit of despondency over his own carelessness he had thrown himself into the same water that had swallowed up his ship, the pride of the Yugoslav merchant marine.

We had all written that story and we were acutely conscious that we now faced the danger of floating mines. Not only Yugoslav mines but Italian mines too. And later British and Greek mines. The proverbial inefficiency of the Italians and all the Balkan people made the danger doubly great, for most of the mines probably hadn't been properly anchored, and the surface of the water might be covered tonight with floating death charges.

Knowing all this, we agreed that from dusk to dawn one man must lie on the foot-square deck in the bow with his head as close to the water's edge as possible and keep his eyes open for mines. If he saw one he was to shout the location to the man at the tiller, who would try to swing the *Makedonka* around in time to miss it. Besides the man at the tiller, another man must be on watch all the time to help navigate. That meant two of us could sleep until one of the men on watch got too tired to keep his eyes open any longer.

We were in the dark of the moon during that trip down the Adriatic, which meant that during the night the men on watch had to strain their eyes both to navigate and to watch for mines.

Now come up with me on the one-foot-square deck and lie on your belly and let's see how much fun that job was. The *Makedonka* is cutting through the water at eight kilometers an hour, which isn't fast, but it's fast enough to throw a salt water spray up into your face almost constantly, because the boat rides low in the sea. Now, with that burning water in your eyes, you've got to look twenty or thirty feet ahead and try to see if there's anything that looks like a mine floating on the water. Of course, since some of us had never seen a mine, we didn't even know what we were looking for. And besides, the water that first night was choppy enough so that every black wave looked as if it might be a mine.

Add to all that the distraction caused by the phosphorescence of the water. The Adriatic is one of the few seas that is phosphorescent, which means that when the bow of a boat or the oars or anything else cuts the water, there's a glow such as you get when you strike a kitchen match and it doesn't flame up but just gives off a strange phosphorescent light and then dies. The water that night looked as if people all around us were scratching matches that never quite burst into flame. Damned distracting if you're trying to look for mines!

And then you know what happens to your eyes in the night when you concentrate for any length of time on one spot. Pretty soon you start seeing things. That first night I saw everything out there on the water from the *Queen Mary* to Mussolini riding a surfboard. When it got too bad and I felt that the safety of all of us was being jeopardized by inability to keep my eyes functioning any longer, I'd call for a relief. Then Hill or Atherton would grunt and get up and stretch and agree that an hour's sleep is worse than none at all and come up on the miniature forecastle and try to see mines where there were no mines.

Now about the navigation. Remember, we were just as ignorant of nautical things as an average Iowa farmer. And although we had all had a fair degree of education, our minds were slightly fuzzy during this period. Our object was simple. We wanted to stay as far out to sea as possible, and still keep land within sight as a guide. We wanted to stay as much offshore as possible, because we knew that the mine fields were in close and that there were Italian warships anchored in all the harbors; it would be easier for lookouts to see us if we came in too close.

It was simple during the daylight hours. But at night, with no moon, it was a problem. Visibility dropped from eight or nine miles to almost zero. In order to keep the hills of Albania within sight at night we would have had to sail dangerously close to shore. So we solved the problem this way: At twilight, as we sailed along parallel with the shore but out eight or nine miles, we stopped trying to keep land in sight and went in for celestial navigation. It was very simple the way we did it. In our tired stupidity we just spotted a group of stars dead ahead. Then we reasoned that if we continued to sail straight for those same stars all night we'd still be eight or nine miles offshore in the morning. Of course we made some slight allowances for the fact that the shore line curved a bit this way or that. But we didn't remember one very important little scientific fact about stars. But that's getting ahead of the story. I'm just telling you now how we did our navigating that first night.

The man in the forecastle who was looking for mines and the man at the tiller doing the steering acted as checks on each other. If the helmsman dozed and the *Makedonka* no longer pointed toward those stars we were supposed to be steering by, the lookout would shout, "Off your course. Bear port," or, "Bear heavy to starboard." We were trying to make it all sound very nautical.

Often during that first night we saw flashes of fire off the port bow. Once, just to settle an argument, we cut off the engine and anchored awhile and listened. A few seconds after we saw the flashes we heard what we knew were the sounds of an artillery battle. Probably Greeks and Italians talking back to each other with heavy cannon.

It grew bitterly cold during the night, and we cursed ourselves for not having thought of blankets. When we had retrieved our clothes from the fisherman's wife at Petrovacz they were still wet and clammy. She hadn't thought of wringing them out before she hung them in front of her stove. Then when it got cold, we were really miserable.

"Holy Christopher," Hill said once during the night, when we were all shivering, "I'd give six months' salary right now for a good cup of coffee in Child's on Fifth Avenue!"

I didn't know what Hill's salary was, but I would have been willing to match his offer.

We were traveling, of course, without lights. We were even being careful about lighting cigarettes. But the noise of that motor gave us away, because suddenly, early in the evening, a searchlight from the shore picked us out. It must have been on a truck, because we could see the light going up into the mountains and then down near the shore again. The man who was focusing it knew his business. Regardless of where he was, the other end of the light was always on us. We both kept right opposite each other for hours. It was like suddenly putting a spotlight on a pair of lovers dancing a waltz on a darkened dance floor. We felt just that embarrassed. But what could we do about it? We kept expecting a visit from an Italian patrol boat all that night, but finally the searchlight went off and we stopped worrying.

Once during the night, when White was at the tiller and I was playing lookout, we saw the light of a ship. It was off our port side, which meant it was inshore from us. It might, of course, be heading in to Albania, or it might, God help us, be coming out and heading for Italy. We took a chance and steered far out to sea in an attempt to run around her. Gradually the light got dimmer, and we decided that she had been going toward Albania after all and that we had won our fifty-fifty gamble.

At dawn we found we were completely out of sight of land. For all we knew we were in the middle of the Adriatic. We might even be near the Italian shore. We couldn't figure out how it had happened, because we had followed that same group of stars religiously all night. Fortunately we knew that the land we wanted to be near was to the east and that that is where the sun rises, and so we pointed the *Makedonka* right at the sun until finally, after what seemed like hours, the mountains of Albania loomed up again.

"Tonight," White said, "we've got to follow those stars a whole lot more carefully."

The rest of us agreed.

At six I rationed out the breakfast. Someone had used the package of hard-boiled eggs during the night as a pillow and had smashed them pretty badly, and so I decided to get rid of them right away. There was just an egg apiece. Then a chunk of dark bread, some ham to suck on, and water. But that morning we made the sad discovery that during the stormy night on our way to Petrovacz the cork had bounced out of the water demijohn and salt water had splashed in, and the liquid in the demijohn was really too salty to drink. So from then on we had to concentrate on the red wine, the five bottles of brandy, the one bottle of rum, and the two liters of slivo. But now my rationing problem was more complicated. We had a lot of smoked ham and some anchovies and salty sardines. But if I gave them too much salty food they'd get thirsty. And if anyone drank too much wine, brandy, and slivo he wouldn't be much help watching for mines or straining to see land and Italian ships. So I had to hold back on the salty food.

We were just finishing breakfast when we spotted two cruisers heading across the Adriatic toward Italy. Italian cruisers, probably loaded with wounded soldiers. We cut the engine and dropped the anchor and waited. They were making good time, and after fifteen minutes we felt it was safe to go on.

Then White said he felt in good shape because he had been the last one to have a quick nap, so why didn't all the rest of us turn in and he would play combination navigator, engineer, and lookout for a while. We did. But in less than an hour White was shouting, "All hands on deck."

He had shut off the engine and was staring at something on the horizon dead ahead. It was an Italian convoy going toward Italy. But this time the ships were crossing at such an angle that they would surely come close to us. Since we couldn't turn the *Makedonka* around and try to get away from them, because they were coming at twice our maximum speed, we let out the anchor, pulled caps down over our faces, dangled pieces of rope in the water and pretended to be fishing. Atherton was the nervous one this time. He pulled all his documents and identification papers out of his pockets and began tearing them into little pieces and throwing them on the water. He even tore an English label from his suit. Then he said, "If we get picked up, remember I'm Bill Small and I'm an American working for the Chicago *Tribune.*"

"That's all right," someone replied, "but if you want anyone to think you came from Chicago you'd better pretend to be dumb, because that accent of yours isn't exactly Chicago."

We fished for one hour. There were three ships in the convoy. A destroyer, a big oil tanker, and a transport ship of about eight thousand tons. They came close, but I guess our fishing trick fooled them, because they didn't pay any attention to us.

There wasn't a dull moment from then on. We always seemed to be either dodging Italian ships or holding our breath while Italian seaplanes followed us. Sometimes they came down so low we were sure they were going to drop things on us. But all they did was to look us over and keep a close watch on our movements.

By midday we were off Durazzo. Durazzo is right around the corner from a big headland. We could see the city miles and miles before we got opposite it. Smoke was pouring up from a cluster of buildings, and it wasn't coming from chimneys either. Atherton was convinced that during the night or early morning someone had bombed Durazzo, which was the chief Albanian seaport. Of course there was an argument, but since there wasn't any way to settle it we finally dropped it. A little later we spotted at least a dozen Italian ships idling about the harbor with steam up. That frightened us. This Italian fleet might not be brave enough to go down into the Mediterranean and do battle with the British navy, but it probably wouldn't be terrified by a twenty-foot sardine boat. Therefore we turned the bow of the *Makedonka* toward the west and headed out until the Albanian shore line was just a dim gray streak in a dull gray sky. Then we changed our course and kept parallel to the coast for the next few hours.

It was just eleven forty-five when Mike suddenly shouted, "Look!"

We looked and saw what he had seen. Two slender black lines on the horizon. We cut the engine again and strained our eyes.

"Submarines!" White said.

Then we argued. We argued for half an hour. We argued about which way they were going and what they were and what we ought to do. No two of us agreed about anything. One man wanted just to anchor and wait. Another wanted to head out to sea. A third wanted to turn around and race back toward Yugoslavia. A fourth wanted to head in toward the Albanian shore. I was the fifth man, and I didn't dare express an opinion, because there wasn't any fifth choice, and if I had sided with any of the others there would have been trouble.

I argued on all sides, stalling for time in the hope that the two spots would disappear entirely or come closer, so that we could determine for sure what they were. They came closer all right. They were coming right at us. We finally voted to start the engine and try to outmaneuver them.

As we approached each other we realized that they weren't submarines after all. When we first spotted them they were so far over the horizon that all we saw was their masts. Now we could make out the shape of ships. And now we could tell they were Italian mine layers. They seemed to be going in circles. That made it difficult to plot a course to avoid them. But we knew they had seen us by now, so there was no use trying to run away.

One of the ships was ignoring us, but the other was bearing right down on us. We changed our course half a dozen times, but each time the Italian ship did too. We decided to parallel the coast line again and go right along our normal route and see what would happen. Now we could make out two guns in the bow. And then we saw men running down the deck. They were taking up their gun positions. They were stripping tarpaulins off the guns. They looked like large machine guns. The men were swinging the guns around. Now they had both of them trained on the *Makedonka*. I fumbled around and found the dirty old cotton American flag. The wooden staff had broken, but I lay on the forecastle and held the flag in its proper position. White was at the tiller. He knew that even if they didn't fire their guns we were going to be tossed around by the wake of the mine layer.

"Wave your caps," White said.

The Italian ship was almost within earshot of us by now. Some one of us hollered, "Viva il Duce, viva America." The others all waved their caps. I waved the American flag. We could almost see the expressions on the gunners' faces now. They didn't seem to know what to do. We could see an officer who looked as if he might be the skipper. He obviously didn't know what to do either. The mine layer had cut down her speed, but now we were getting her wash. The *Makedonka* was being tossed around like a dead leaf in a gale. Now we were even with the Italian's bow. Now we were out of range of her guns. They couldn't fire straight down at us. We did a lot more waving of caps and flag, and a lot of viva-shouting. And then the gunners relaxed and waved their own caps and shouted something we couldn't hear, and another crisis was over.

At 13:30 three Italian war planes flew low over us. They looked like bombers and they were heading from Italy toward the Vardar Valley. We guessed that they were probably going to mop up some Yugoslav holdouts. At 16:50 we were opposite Fieri, Albania, and another day at sea was nearly over. There was a little wind, and my calculations showed we were doing much less now than eight kilometers on a liter, and so we put up the sail. That may sound simple to you. It would have been simple if anyone had known anything about a sail. Mike, of course, had some ideas, but he hadn't ever seen a sail quite like this one of ours. And most of the rest of us hadn't ever seen a sail of any kind except in pictures. But we finally got the thing into place, and then suddenly the wind freshened and we went zooming across the water. I think "freshened" is the right word. Anyway I know that "zooming" is.

We sailed until three o'clock the next morning. By that time the ship's morale was very low. White and Hill and Atherton were grumbling constantly about being hungry. They said it was foolish to ration the food for ten days. And who did I think I was anyway? If the majority wanted more food, I had no right to hold out on it. So I opened up one of the cans of goulash. We had quite a few cans, and we hadn't touched any of them yet. It took half an hour with an old jackknife to get the can opened. And then we found that the fat and meat inside were green with age and smelled like dead fish. We threw that can overboard and spent another half hour opening another one. One by one we threw all those cans of goulash over the side.

Then I tried to give them a ration of "Turkish Delight." I hope you know what Turkish Delight is. It's a gummy, sticky, saccharine sweet candy. We bought it only because we couldn't get anything else. I forget who it was, but the first man who tried to eat it vomited, and so the others passed it up. Then we tried the sardines. They were all right, but so salty that everyone kept tipping up the demijohn of wine or the bottles of liquor. But I was through trying to be cautious and wise. If we all got drunk and the *Makedonka* capsized or ran into a mine, what the hell? So we had another can of sardines and then a can of anchovies. Then a lot of rum and slivo and wine. Then we sang some Comitaji songs and adopted the old fatalistic spirit. If the mine's got our number on it, we hit it. If it doesn't, we don't. So why worry?

But now the sea began to roll. The wind was whipping into the sail. The mast began to creak and groan. White was having difficulty holding onto the tiller. The *Makedonka* was shipping water again, and in a little while the bilge water was up to our ankles. Then above our ankles. No one had caught any sleep yet, and now there wasn't a dry place left to sleep. Then someone knocked over a can of gas, and we lost about fifteen liters of the little we had left. That brought on a lot of profanity from the others. Short, ugly words were tossed back and forth.

Someone said, "Who's running this boat anyway?" No one answered. Then an oar got knocked over the side and someone nearly got drowned trying to grab it out of the water. That caused more bitterness. Then we got into a five-cornered argument because someone said we weren't steering by the same group of stars we had started out to follow when it got dark. Then someone remembered that by now we were passing through the Straits of Otranto, where Italy and Albania come within forty-five miles of meeting, and if we weren't careful and didn't navigate just right we'd probably run into the tip of Italy and then all the risks we had taken would come to nothing, and hadn't White better bear to the port, regardless of what the stars said. But White reminded us that we either had to navigate by the stars or by something else; if we just headed blindly to the east we'd get into trouble, because we'd end up by running into Italian patrol boats off the Albanian shore.

It went like that all night. Feelings kept getting more and more intense. There were even several fights over possession of the tiller. For a couple of hours I was afraid we were all done for. I had an automatic in my pocket that the bodyguard of little King Peter had given Atherton as a souvenir when he and Peter flew off to Greece and he didn't think he'd have any more need of pistols to protect his boy king. I kept it in my trousers pocket, and several times when the fighting on board the *Makedonka* got really serious I fingered the automatic and wondered whether I could restore order by whipping it out and trying to intimidate the quarrelers. But if I did that it would look as if I wanted to assume charge, and that was the very last thing I did want. I knew less about who was right and what we should do and how to run a boat and how to hoist a sail than any of them. I tried not to enter into any of the arguments because of my sheer stupidity about nautical matters.

I couldn't help grinning to myself in the dark when I realized how stupid I was about the sea. I was the oldest. I had served a short hitch in the American navy during the last war. I had been in the crew of an American transport. I had been to France. And yet all I knew about nautical matters was how to swab down a deck with a holystone and water. I couldn't even tie a square knot without occasionally making a granny out of it by mistake. A veteran of the American navy, with an honorable discharge as a second-class seaman, yet I couldn't even swim. I was the last person in the world who should have gone off on the *Makedonka*. Often during that night of fighting and trouble I half wished that I had faced the possibility of a German concentration camp instead.

Then the mast block cracked. We were clipping along at a merry rate when we heard first a groaning, such as a human being makes when he's in pain, and then that unmistakable noise of wood splitting. The waves by then were at least five feet high. The *Makedonka* was riding them most of the time, but occasionally a big one would break over the bow and drench all of us and put us all to work with buckets bailing out the water. Then the mast block cracked. That meant we had to take down the sail and the mast too. Several times during the half hour it took us to do the job, Mike or Atherton or Hill or I nearly got knocked overboard. That mast was about twenty feet tall and very heavy. To take it down we had to lift it straight up into the air for about two feet, to get it out of its brackets, and then we had to lower it gently. It may sound simple, but try it sometime when the wind is blowing a gale and the waves are five feet high and you haven't had a good night's sleep in two weeks and not much to eat in all that time and you don't know much about how to do such things anyway. After all, most of us had spent most of our adult lives pounding typewriters in hotel rooms, which isn't very good training for playing with broken masts.

Well, we got it down finally and then White said, "We've got to get the outboard motor into place."

That was no simple job either. The motor had two little prongs that had to be dropped into two eyelets. If you want to know what that job was like, have someone drive a model T Ford as fast as it will go along the roughest country road you can find and you sit in the back seat and try to thread a needle. But after half an hour of smashed fingers and cursing and many futile attempts, the two prongs and the two eyelets suddenly met. Then we got under way. By that time none of us, except maybe Mike, gave a damn whether we ever made land or not. When it began to get light we found out that, just like the morning before, we were out of sight of the shore. There never will be any way to prove it, but I think we actually must have been closer to Italy than to Albania. It was weeks later, when we finally had had plenty of rest and food, before we realized why our amateur celestial navigation hadn't worked. We were telling someone how we had always been far out from shore in the morning, and this someone said, "Of course you remembered that stars move, just like the sun and moon. You allowed for that, didn't you?"

But of course we hadn't. Each night we had steered religiously toward the stars we had picked for a guide. And each night those stars, as they moved through the sky, had pulled us right out to sea. Right toward Italy and away from the shore we were trying to follow.

This second morning we headed due east again, when daylight came, and finally saw what we figured out must be the Point of Palermo, Albania. That meant we had passed safely through the Straits of Otranto and were getting close to Corfu.

Then a brilliant sun popped over the horizon and the water calmed down a bit and the wind eased off and life began to look just a little brighter.

Suddenly White yelled, "Look! Islands dead ahead! Islands! They must be those islands just off Corfu!"

We grabbed our maps, and Hill, who was a very precise map-reader, started making measurements and figuring out directions from the sun and the shore line, and finally he announced that White was right. That first island must be Erikusi and there was another to the west and a third behind it. Just like the map showed. When we got along a little farther we would be able to see Corfu itself!

Well, something happened to the morale on the *Makedonka* just then. Five men who had been at one another's throats during the night danced around in that little sardine boat as much as space allowed. We slapped one another on the back. We sang and shouted until tears came into our eyes.

We're going to make it, boys! The good old *Makedonka!* Land! Corfu! Greek land! On Corfu there will be hotels and beds and clean sheets, and cable offices and a place to sit down and write a story and . . .

Now for Christ's sake, St. John, dish out some food for us, will you?

And so we had a feast that Sunday morning as we sailed into a red, red sun that put a rosy glow over everything and showed us the land we had been heading for for so long. I took the one orange and peeled it and handed each man his two little slices. That was the Waldorf-Astoria touch to the meal. Slices of fresh orange! How plutocratic! How very, very swank! Oranges for breakfast! Then I took the rusty jackknife and opened up the two cans of pheasant paste. Every mealtime the others had said, how about the pheasant paste? But there wasn't enough in the two cans to ease anyone's hunger. The pheasant paste was just a gesture. I had been saving it for a party, for a celebration, and this surely was the time to celebrate. So we had pheasant paste on our black peasant bread that morning. Only I had to hunt around for the day's loaf of bread, because we had been using those loaves for strange purposes. Some had been used as pillows and some were so hard we had been using them as tools. A two-week-old loaf of Serbian peasant bread makes a perfect hammer, or a wedge to hold something in place, or it could even have been used as an anchor, only we happened to be well-supplied with anchors.

CHAPTER TEN

On Greek Soil

⚊⚊⚊⚊◆⚊⚊⚊⚊

Corfu! It probably means to you what it meant to us before we set foot there. An island of romance and glamour. An island they've written songs and poems and novels and plays about. Beautiful Corfu, where the Adriatic and the Ionian meet and lap the sandy shores of this little paradise of an island.

Well, Corfu wasn't any of those things. Corfu in April was an island of lost people. An island of terrified, panicky, fear-haunted people. I think I've used some of those same words before, about the Yugoslavs, but I can't help it. The people of Corfu were like that too. Only more so. The people of Corfu knew that any day now planes would start unloading their capsules of death over the island, and then steel-helmeted troops would come, and then life as they had known it would end. The people of Corfu were like people who knew they were about to die, but didn't want to die and were afraid to die. It was that kind of a fear.

But let's get back to the story. I want to tell you everything just as it happened.

It took us many hours after we first saw Corfu in the distance before we got there. Thank God Russell Hill and Leigh White both had a hobby of collecting maps. Because now we pulled one of their maps out of a knapsack and found a little cove that looked like just what we wanted. A little cove on the north side of the island of Corfu called Casopi. Therefore we headed for Casopi and we got there at one o'clock on the afternoon of Sunday, April 20. Easter Sunday, because Corfu is Greek, and the Greek Orthodox Easter is a week later than our Easter. Easter Sunday again.

As we got close to the cove we could see that a reception committee was waiting for us. And the reception committee was armed. There must have been a hundred wild-looking young men, each with a rifle in his hands. And every single one of those men seemed eager to use his rifle. They stood on the shore glaring at us. Looking at us with an antagonism and a distrust that really frightened us. We'd come hundreds of miles down through mine fields and Italian ships and storms to get to Greece, a friendly country, and now we were being greeted with rifles! It didn't seem right. But we headed in for the cove anyway.

We beached the *Makedonka* without wrecking her as we had done at Petrovacz na Mare. The men stood a few feet from the water's edge in a big semicircle, silent and waiting. I held up the American flag, and we all said a lot of things in English, but no one seemed to understand. Neither the flag nor what we said impressed them. But before we could do any more explaining an Italian bomber roared out of the clouds and came down at us. The men of Corfu made for a ravine, and someone pulled us along too. The men of Corfu lay in the ravine with their rifles aimed at the plane, but they were a little wiser than the Serbs. They held their fire, and the plane finally flew on after doing a few circles over our heads.

Then some of the men made us understand with gestures what the trouble was. They pointed to the disappearing plane and then to our boat and then to the sea. They were trying to tell us that we had attracted the plane. That we were bringing enemy planes and bad luck to Corfu. They were definitely antagonistic to us.

After we had made the *Makedonka* fast they marched us up a hill to the village of Casopi. We had to go ahead. They followed with their rifles in position for quick use. It wasn't the kind of a reception we had been hoping for. But up in the little whitewashed town everything began to smooth out. We were taken to a general store, almost like a New England general store in some place like Barnstead, New Hampshire, or Wallingford, Vermont. The owner of the store spoke a little French and less English, but he was on our side. He waved the men with rifles aside, and when he found that we were Americans he told us to be seated and he would serve us with coffee. In that part of the world people drink about twenty or thirty cups of thick Turkish coffee a day, just as we smoke cigarettes.

We sat down, and soon the whole town was swarming into the little shop. We were dizzy, all of us. The store floor seemed to be tossing around, just as the *Makedonka* had been doing for so long. But we didn't care. We didn't care about the stares of all those people and the shop rolling back and forth and the suspicion of a lot of our audience. We were on dry land. We were on Greek territory. We were safe. The *Makedonka* had made it. The good old *Makedonka*. Suddenly we started pounding one another on the back and saying, "Well, we made it, didn't we?"

Those poor Corfu people thought we were crazy, I suppose. We acted like hysterical children. I guess we were a little hysterical. But we were on land. Friendly land. The great adventure was over. Or we thought it was over. We didn't know that it had only begun. I looked around at all those Greek faces and wanted to do something to make them as happy as we were. They were all men and boys, and so I asked the shopkeeper for twenty or thirty packages of his best cigarettes, and I passed cigarettes to all those people with the suspicious faces.

It worked like a charm. They became friendly right away. I even lighted the cigarettes for a lot of them. And then we all smoked cigarettes ourselves, which was a treat, because on the

Makedonka we had been smoking nothing but bad pipe tobacco wrapped in pieces of newspaper or stuffed into a pipe. Greek cigarettes are about the best cigarettes in the world, and so after all those spectators had been taken care of we leaned back and inhaled deep drafts of that good Greek tobacco. We felt like a million dollars.

Then the shopkeeper brought on the coffee, and while we were drinking it he showed us what had happened here in Casopi the day before. Just yesterday. An Italian plane had come over Casopi and had fired machine guns at the village. See, here was where some of the bullets went right through the door and got buried in the counter. No one was killed, because they were all hiding. He seemed as proud of those bullets in the counter as you would be if your infant child suddenly sprouted some new teeth. Italian machine-gun bullets right in the counter! That was something to talk about! He'd be showing those bullets to his grandchildren!

And then he sneered at the Italians. He told us how all the people on Corfu were living on fish. Fish that had been killed by Italian bombs that fell into the sea. The fish were killed by the bombs and then washed up onto the shore. They weren't damaged in any way, just killed by the repercussion. Exploded fish, he called them. It was a joke. A big joke. He laughed with a deep belly laugh as he said it. It was a joke because the Italians had been trying to hit bridges and ships and barracks and things like that when they dropped those bombs, only they were such poor shots that the bombs always went into the sea and just killed a lot of fish that got washed up onto the shore and got eaten by the people of Corfu.

After he told the story to us in a mixture of French and English he had to repeat the whole thing to all the villagers in Greek. Everybody laughed. And then we laughed again. And I went around the place passing out more cigarettes. Now a lot of the men shook hands with us. We felt we finally had established ourselves as friends of the people of Corfu. But just then there was a roaring noise, and everyone ducked out the door, because that same Italian bomber had come over again. When the plane finally left, and the men returned to the general store, they were just as antagonistic as they had been in the first place. I didn't blame them. We probably had attracted the Italian plane. We might be responsible for a bombing, and this time the bombs might land where they were supposed to land, because the plane was flying too low to miss.

So the men with the guns took us to the office of the commander of Casopi. It was just a little shack on a hill overlooking the cove. Things began to straighten out when we got there. The man in charge was a Greek naval officer. He spoke beautiful English with just a trace of an accent. He had been stationed for years in England. He was sorry, he said, but we were technically under arrest because we didn't have the proper visas, and, of course, Atherton didn't even have a passport or identification papers of any kind, because he had scattered them in bits on the waters of the Adriatic. But even if we were technically under arrest that didn't mean anything. We should make ourselves at home while the naval officer called the authorities in the city of Corfu and got some instructions about us. In the meantime he told us how for hours he had watched us heading south toward Corfu through his glasses. He watched us being tossed around out there on the Adriatic and, he said, "I really didn't think you'd make it."

When he said that I was looking at Mike. Mike grinned, and his expression was one of intense pride. He seemed to be answering this fellow back and boasting about the crew of the good ship *Makedonka*. Mike was about the most loyal friend any of us had ever had.

The commander said they had figured out we were refugees fleeing from Albania. Probably Italians or Albanians. That was why they had been so suspicious. It had never occurred to them that we had come all the way down from Yugoslavia. And if they had only known we were Americans! America! How he wanted to visit America some day. *Après la guerre* he was going to

America himself. What a country America must be! How lucky we were, to be Americans!

Then the naval officer said that maybe we hadn't known it, but an Italian plane had been following us for hours, trying to keep out of sight in the clouds. We mustn't blame the people of Corfu for being angry with us. We had, after all, attracted that plane to Corfu. He said we had been just like a magnet, and please understand that Corfu is in a hell of a spot. With the Yugoslavs all folded up, it looked like curtains for Greece too, pretty soon.

While we talked with him he kept pouring out little glasses of ouzo for us. I had difficulty getting the stuff down, but I didn't want to offend him. Ouzo is the native Greek drink. It's like raki in Turkey, the color of water, with a taste like Italian anisette. A liquorish taste. Before you drink it you pour it into a glass of plain water and the whole thing turns milky.

Then the naval officer told us a lot of stories about the Italians that made it very clear what the Greeks thought of them. He said the Italian planes had tried to destroy the town of Pantokratoras and had dropped one thousand two hundred bombs, of which three had hit the ruins of an old monastery while the other one thousand one hundred and ninety-seven had fallen into the water.

Then he told us that if we had time (I guess he forgot we were under military arrest) we should visit the palace not far from here where old Kaiser Wilhelm used to spend his summers. It was interesting, he said, because the big room in which the Kaiser used to receive visitors was lined with statues. All of them were of old philosophers like Plato and Socrates, but there was one statue of an Englishman, Shakespeare, for whom the Kaiser apparently had a profound respect.

In between stories we asked the officer about communications. Wasn't there some way we could get a dispatch to Athens, and from there to America? He laughed good-naturedly, but he shook his head. No, not a chance. We could telephone to any place on the island, but there were no lines to the mainland. And no radio. And no cables. We were stymied again. But we weren't so bothered now, because we figured we'd be in Athens by to-morrow. What difference would twenty-four hours make any-way? Of course that was a dangerous state of mind for American newspapermen to get into. Twenty-four minutes still meant some-thing. But time was beginning to take on a timelessness. We were thinking in weeks instead of minutes. We agreed to forget com-munications until we somehow got to the mainland. And then we turned our attention back to the officer's stories of Italian bun-gling and Greek bravery.

It was all another pleasant interlude, that hour or two while we were under strict military arrest in the little town of Casopi, where the people hated us because we had attracted the Italian bomber.

The instructions finally came by telephone. The naval officer was to send us under heavy military guard to the city of Corfu by automobile. In the meantime we were to be stripped of all our firearms, our cameras, our identification papers, and anything else he decided should be taken from us. But, we asked, can we do something about the *Makedonka* before we go?

He said we could, so we went back to the shore. The whole village gathered around us. We took one of the gunny sacks and put the ham we hadn't touched into it along with a couple of loaves of Serbian peasant bread and a can or two of sardines that were left, and then we gave the sack to Mike and said, "Here, you may need this."

Mike grinned his thank-you. Then we gave everything else in the boat to the natives. It was just like a Christmas party, with the five of us playing Santa Claus, but some rather cutting re-marks were addressed to the member of the crew who had been given the job of rationing the food.

We damn near starved out there and yet look at all the bread and raisins and cookies we've got left!

What made you think it would take us ten days? No faith in the *Makedonka*, eh?

But it was all in fun, because we were too doggone happy that we had made it to be serious about anything.

Finally nothing was left but the empty boat with its sail and its oars and the motor, and our knapsacks and typewriters. Then we made out a legal document deeding the *Makedonka* to the naval officer if Mike or one of the rest of us didn't come back for it within a week.

Two cars were waiting to take us to the city of Corfu, which was halfway down the island, a winding drive of at least fifty miles through beautiful hilly country. Our chauffeurs were two tough Greek soldiers, and they insisted on stopping at every hamlet and every four corners to give the natives a chance to look at the curiosities, the Americans who had just come from Yugoslavia. Most of them treated us as you would treat striped baboons at a zoo or a bearded woman in a side show. They clustered around the cars, stared for a few minutes, then grinned, and away we went to the next settlement.

Corfu was dressed in her spring finery that warm Sunday in April. The air was heavy with the smell of lilacs and a lot of flowers we hadn't ever seen before. Fig trees were in bloom. The corn was seven feet high. The whole countryside was alive with colors and smells. Good colors and pleasant smells. For two hours we tried to pretend that it was all a nasty nightmare. All we had seen and heard and smelled back in Yugoslavia. Here was proof. Here life was going on as life probably had gone on without interruption for hundreds of years. It was Sunday on the pleasant little island of Corfu. Just another Sunday, like millions of Sundays in the past.

The people were doing the same things they always did on Sunday. They were sitting in front of their whitewashed cottages talking with neighbors, probably about the crops and the thickness of the sheep's wool this spring and the girl in the next village who had just had her first baby. I don't remember the men, but I do remember the women. They all wore freshly laundered white veils tied around their heads like turbans, then hanging in generous folds down their backs. Their eyes were nearly all dark and bright. The veils let a little of their rich black hair show. Just enough to serve as a frame for their olive-colored faces. There were a lot of sheep and jackasses and young lambs around the countryside, and children playing at the edge of the road and young couples walking arm in arm through groves of olive trees with gnarled trunks that gave you a feeling of great age.

That was the dreamy pleasant countryside of Corfu. But soon we left the countryside and clattered down a hill, and suddenly we were right in the city of Corfu. We knew now that we hadn't had any nightmares. Yugoslavia had been real, and now we were back in the land of realities again.

The city of Corfu was a place of desolation. They told us that normally forty thousand people lived here, but now I don't think there were many more than four thousand left. Those who hadn't been killed had fled into the hills. Why the four thousand stayed I don't know. Few of the four thousand ever appeared above ground in the daytime. The city fathers had opened up some of the ancient catacombs, which wound far down into the bowels of the earth under Corfu. Men and women and children had taken cots, mattresses, and food down into those dark, musty tunnels, and that was home for them now.

You couldn't blame them for not having much interest in what was left of their city. The shops and houses, which once had been so pretty to look at, because they were whitewashed in pastel greens and pinks and yellows, now were a mass of ruins. Not all of them, but so many of them that you stopped short and looked when you passed one that was undamaged.

Once, we were told, the people of Corfu, being proud people with a great sense of civic responsibility, hauled the debris out of the streets and cleaned things up as fast as the bombs sent another building collapsing into a heap of rubble. But they had given that up long ago. It was too big a job, and they just didn't care any more. That was the spirit of Corfu now. No one cared. No one cared about anything. They just took a dull, force-of-habit interest in keeping alive a little while longer.

You couldn't drive through many streets, because the wreckage of buildings was where the streets used to be, and where the buildings used to be there might be one wall standing or a chimney that remained like a sentinel in a graveyard after everything else had crumbled.

We stopped at the gendarmes' office, where they gave us back our revolvers but kept our cameras. They said we might need the revolvers. They didn't explain what they meant. Then the officers dug a bottle of cognac out of a desk, and we all had a drink. They said if we came back tomorrow we could get our passports back.

Then a soldier who spoke English because he had once lived in Chicago asked if we wouldn't like to see the city before it got dark. He must have had a deeply ingrained sense of morbidity, because all he did was to take us stumbling through the debris and show us where the greatest tragedies had taken place last Christmas Day. That was nearly four months ago, and there had been many raids since then, but none like that Christmas Day raid. More than a thousand people had been killed in the city of Corfu alone in that one raid. A thousand people out of forty thousand. One out of forty. And most of them had by some strange twist of fate been women and children. Our guide took us all the way across the city to show us a place where bombs had dropped on a children's Christmas party, killing he didn't know how many dozens of little boys and girls. But all that we saw was a pile of bricks and stone. He wasn't sure whether they ever did dig out the bodies.

He said that for six months now the people who refused to leave the city had spent three quarters of the time in a state of alarm. Every day for six months planes had been overhead three quarters of the time. That's why almost everyone was resigned to living underground. Only there weren't any sanitary facilities down there and the air was pretty bad and a lot of people had died below ground from disease.

The only cheerful note in his whole conversation was the remark that not a bomb had been dropped on Corfu for twenty-nine days. It would be a month tomorrow. But still the planes flew over every day, and they kept the people in a constant state of nervousness. To judge from the way they talked in Corfu I don't think the population at large had any idea that for fifteen days their country had also been fighting the Nazis.

By the time we finished our tour of the city it had grown dark. And then a strange thing happened. The narrow streets, which had been completely deserted all afternoon, suddenly began to fill up. We could see dark groups coming up out of the ground. Ghosts they seemed. Shadows of people from another world coming back to populate this city of lost souls. They swarmed out of the ground and into the streets until it was difficult to get back to the gendarmes' office, the crowds were so thick. They were like ghosts too, because none of them seemed to speak like human beings. They didn't laugh and they didn't talk out loud. All you could hear was just a dull, heavy mumble. No one seemed to be going anywhere in particular. They just roamed up and down the dirty streets, stepping around bomb craters and avoiding glass and rubble and the wreckage of their homes. It was after midnight before this promenade of hopeless people stopped. We saw them, before we went to bed, going back into their holes in the ground. Deserting their city again and going back into those musty catacombs, which held all there was left of life for them.

We had nothing but Greek cheese, some fried eggs, and some bad Greek wine for supper that night at the Hotel Angleterre, but it tasted like nectar and ambrosia. Then we took our clothes off for the first time in more than two weeks and had a bath. And then we went to bed. I don't think a bed ever felt better. Our bones were sore. Our hands were cut and blistered. Our faces were raw from wind and salt water and gasoline. Our muscles all ached. The food we had stuffed into our mouths wasn't being accepted very well by stomachs that weren't used to food. But we slept that night. The sleep of the weary.

We probably would have slept for days on end, without ever waking up, except for the air-raid sirens early the next morning. Big Italian seaplanes were roaring back and forth over the city. They kept it up all morning without dropping any bombs, but they had the people of Corfu terrified.

We tried to send out for some clean clothes, but the hotel people laughed. Only one or two shops were even making a pretense of doing business any more. And they wouldn't be open today because it was a holiday. Easter Monday. So we put on the filthy rags we had been living in for more than two weeks and went out into the street.

Mike was one of the happiest men in the world that morning. We had rented three rooms. The rest of us doubled up, but we gave Mike a room all for himself. It was probably the first time he had ever stayed in a hotel room. And the Angleterre, in normal times, was a high-class tourist establishment. Of course now it was badly banged up. Windows were broken. Plaster lay all around the place. But it was luxury to Mike. And we were treating Mike like one of us, which made him mighty proud. He strutted around the lobby and took great delight in asking one of the clerks, who spoke English, "Where are my shipmates?"

He was especially pleased about his new wardrobe. I think it was Atherton who dug into his knapsack and found an old pair of trousers and a white shirt and some incidentals for Mike. Everything was ten sizes too big, and Mike looked like a movie comic character in them, but it gave him one more thing to feel proud about. The little Serb fisherman in Bond Street clothes! Life really had begun at sixty for Milan Francisikovicz.

He strutted out into the street with us. We all pretended we weren't afraid of the planes over our heads. I really don't think we were. Fear had become dulled by now. We ignored the shrieking sirens and started out for a walk, but angry Greeks grabbed us by our arms and forced us down into their catacombs. It was probably just as well. The bombs began to fall all around us. The first bombing Corfu had had in exactly a month. An Easter Monday bombing.

"Well," Hill said, "the story's still following us all right."

"Yes," someone else said, "and communications are still keeping one jump ahead of us."

The air down in those dark tunnels was so vile, because of the lack of any ventilating scheme and because so many human beings were living down there in such a primitive way, that we stood at the entranceway even though several people told us how last month men had been killed because they hadn't gone deeper into the ground. But it was worth the risk, because otherwise we wouldn't have seen the boy bugler of Corfu. He was a barelegged, barefooted youngster of twelve or fourteen. He had on a tattered pair of trousers and a dark blue shirt, open at the neck. His face was the color of half-ripe olives. His legs and arms were almost black. While the rest of Corfu, with hardly an exception, hid below the surface of the earth, this child stood on the parapet of an old fortress just above us, silhouetted against the bright blue sky. He kept twisting his head, now this way, now that way, watching the planes. When he saw one of them approaching close he put a dented old brass bugle to his lips and sounded a clear call of warning. I saw one bomb fall directly on the fortress. I don't know whether the pilot had been aiming at the child or not. I do know that pieces of stone flew all around him. But the boy just ignored them and went on sounding his signals. I don't think there was much sense to the performance, because everybody in Corfu seemed to be down there with us, but maybe the signals meant something to someone.

The boy bugler of Corfu reminded me of the old story about the boy bugler of Cracow who stood on a tower blowing a warning that the enemy was coming, until a sniper put a bullet through his throat. His call, the story said, was broken off in the middle of a note, and so buglers all over the world still have one call which they break off like that in tribute to the boy bugler of Cracow. I looked up at the Corfu boy and uttered a little prayer under my breath for him, a prayer that he wouldn't get knocked off in the middle of a note.

Thinking of the Polish bugler made me think of Warsaw and those people in the Warsaw radio station who gave the world a modern version of the Cracow story. I remembered how we used to sit in the AP office in Budapest from which that Polish campaign was being covered. I remembered long nights after all the newspapermen had left Poland, when the only way we could tell whether Warsaw was still holding out was by listening to Warsaw Radio. I remembered how the mayor of Warsaw and some Polish newspaperman and a girl with an amazingly calm voice used to stand before that microphone twenty-four hours a day to tell the world that Warsaw still lived. I remembered the final night. The night we could hear the noise of shooting and bombing coming from Warsaw so distinctly over the air. And how suddenly the station went dead, and we knew then that the fight to hold Warsaw was all over. The three voices were silent forever. I wondered, as I stood in the entrance to the catacombs of Corfu, what they had done to those three people who shouted Polish defiance over the air right up to the very end.

I lost sight of the boy bugler of Corfu when a bomb landed within a few rods of the entrance to our tunnel. I tried to steady myself with one hand against the wall, but the next second I was flat on my back. I wasn't sure what had struck me. I jumped to my feet and looked behind me down the tunnel. No one had been killed or even wounded, and so what I saw was just funny. I guess it was the only funny thing any of us had seen for a long time. The repercussion from the bomb, the blast of air down the tunnel, had been so great that it had knocked a lot of us off our feet. Just the force of the air. And when we fell we knocked over the people behind us. Just like all the tenpins go down when a bowling ball hits the first one.

We could look down into the dark recesses of the tunnel and see women with children in their arms and we could hear babies crying. Someone told us that a number of births had taken place down here under the earth in the last few months. That made me wonder what kind of human beings they would grow up to be, these children born during an air raid in a dark, musty tunnel while bombs were dropping on their homes up above and anti-aircraft guns were making the air vibrate with thick noise and people were screaming in their fright and hell was moving to Corfu.

Then a man beside us who spoke a little English turned and said, "These Italians are Christians, you know."

He said it with more bitterness than I ever heard wrapped around words before. He said it with a hatred that seemed to have possession of every fiber of his body and every corner of his brain.

"These Italians are Christians, you know. It must be wonderful to be a Christian. I'm glad I have no religion. If I were a Christian maybe I could do like they do. You know about how they helped us celebrate Christmas, don't you? Well, they helped my whole family celebrate Christmas. And now—now I have no family. And today they come again. You know what day this is? This is Easter Monday. It is one of our most important religious holidays. And so the Italians who are Christians come to help us celebrate."

During a lull between raids we went to the gendarmes' office to see about getting back our passports and getting some kind of permission to leave Corfu. We felt we had wasted another twenty-four hours already. We were well aware that we still hadn't found the one thing we were supposed to be hunting: communications. And besides, although we were getting used to bombings, there wasn't much point in just parking ourselves in Corfu if the Italians were going to try to wipe it off the map, which a lot of the people of Corfu were convinced was the plan. But we couldn't get any attention from the gendarmes. They were so panicky that most of them refused to come out of the tunnels, even between raids. I guess there was some excuse for them, because someone told us that this was the fifth or sixth or seventh building the gendarmes had used for headquarters in the last few months. Each time they moved, the Italian pilots landed a load of bombs on the new headquarters. It might have only been coincidence, but the gendarmes were sure some Greek fifth columnist was signaling each new location to the Italian pilots.

Then we went with Atherton to the British consulate to get a new passport to replace the one he had lost. The building was surrounded by a tall iron fence, and at the gate a guard barred our way. Atherton said he was an Englishman and he wanted to see the consul.

"But," said the guard naïvely, "I have been warned against parachutists. I cannot let you in unless you can prove you are not parachutists."

It was the old, old story. Prove that you are not enemy agents. Prove that your typewriters are not radio sets. Prove that your knapsacks are not parachutes. But this time it was more difficult than ever, because our American passports were locked up by the gendarmes, who refused to come out of the ground long enough to give them back to us.

Somehow we finally got inside the building and into the office of a very terrified young British consul. Atherton told him his story. The rest of us explained that we could vouch for everything Atherton said. And if the consul wanted to check up on us, all our documents could be seen at the gendarmes' office.

First the consul said we mustn't bother him now, because he had much important work to do. He was getting ready to evacuate from Corfu. He expected that Corfu would be taken soon, and he must burn papers, pack his baggage, get ready to leave. Couldn't Atherton wait until he got to Athens or Cairo or some other place? But Atherton patiently pointed out that the Greek officials insisted he couldn't travel any farther until he got a passport. Then the consul wanted to know again exactly what had happened to Atherton's passport, and Atherton told his story once more. The consul kept saying, "Most irregular. Most irregular."

He went off and consulted an assistant. Then he came back and said "Most irregular" again and told Atherton there didn't seem to be any precedent for issuing a new passport under such conditions, and besides he didn't have any authority to issue passports even under regular conditions, and, besides that, he really must start packing now.

Calm, patient Atherton, so typically English in so many ways, finally blew up. He grabbed the consul by the shoulder and told

him in short simple words exactly what he thought of bureaucracy
in general and British bureaucracy in particular. He told him that
unusual situations demanded an unusual solution, and . . .
Well, the rest of us walked out of the room about this time to
avoid embarrassment for everyone. But finally the consul came
through. He came through with a single sheet of plain white
paper that said, as close as I can remember the exact words:
"Terence Atherton claims to be a British subject. I, the Consul
of Corfu, as yet have no reason to believe that he is not telling
the truth."

That was as far as he would go. But we all knew enough about
the Balkans to know that if it only had some red seals and rubber
stamps and some of the other hocus-pocus look about it, it might
possibly impress minor Greek officials who couldn't read English
anyway. So Atherton asked to have the document decorated. I
think he finally got the consul to put a rubber stamp to it.

The narrow streets of Corfu echoed all day with the noise that
bombs make. Our hotel was among the buildings that got their
faces lifted. But the real damage was along the water front. A
number of ships in the harbor were hit and sunk.

The biggest building in Corfu was the one on the quay con-
taining port authority offices. A modern structure of stone and
steel. The most modern building we had seen since we left Belgrade. We went there to see about getting a boat for the Greek
mainland. They told us to come back in an hour. When we
went back the whole quay was a mass of wreckage. The port
authority offices just didn't exist any more. A six-story hotel
near by had been gutted. Bomb craters almost as large as the
ones in Belgrade dotted the whole water front.

Even when the planes weren't overhead we heard deep
rumbling noises, but someone said, "Don't worry, that's just
workmen blasting open the entrances to more catacombs under
the city that were sealed up generations ago but have to be used
now for people to live in."

We went to the naval commander of the island and had a
talk about the transportation problem. He told us quite frankly

that Corfu's days were numbered. These Easter Monday air raids were probably a prelude to an invasion by the Italians. And if invasion came, there wouldn't be much of a fight, because there were few soldiers on Corfu. The invasion might come even tonight or tomorrow. He and his staff were getting ready to evacuate themselves. If we wanted to go to the mainland by boat, he would give us an order to the master of a caïque leaving during the night. The boat he had in mind, he said, was the *Spiradon Piraeus.* A two-hundred-ton, three-masted schooner. A Greek army food ship, which was going to take a load of bread to the Greek troops at Preveza, just across the Ionian Sea on the mainland. He thought it would sail as soon as it got dark. Hill and I said fine, and took the permit.

But White had a different idea. He suddenly asked the commander if he had a sea chart he could spare. The commander gave him one, and when we got outside, White announced that he had just had a hunch. He couldn't explain it, but he had a hunch that taking a Greek boat was too much of a gamble; that we wouldn't get off before the Italians arrived; and even if we did get off, we'd never get to the Greek mainland. He was going to play his hunch and go back to Casopi and push off toward the mainland in the good old *Makedonka.* Mike agreed to go with him. Hill and I said we had had about enough of the *Makedonka.* Besides, we reminded White, the engine had gone dead just as we pulled in to Casopi. We had given away all our provisions and gasoline. And what was the matter with the *Spiradon Piraeus?* He hadn't even seen it. But White had made up his mind. Then he turned to Atherton, and Atherton, after a few minutes of indecision, decided to play White's hunch too. So Russell and I said good-by to them and we started out to look for the *Spiradon Piraeus.*

CHAPTER ELEVEN

Interlude

————◆◆◆————

Iᴛ ᴡᴀs ɪɴᴋʏ ʙʟᴀᴄᴋ when Hill and I strapped our knapsacks onto our backs, picked up our typewriters, and stumbled through the darkened streets toward the quay where the naval commander said we would find the *Spiradon Piraeus*. Silent people wandered the narrow streets, as they had done the night before, only the crowds were much thinner tonight. We wondered whether it was because there had been so many casualties in the afternoon raids or because so many people had been frightened into remaining below ground even after it got dark.

Down on the water front there was evidence on all sides of confusion and disorganization. While it was still daylight and planes were still overhead the quay had been so deserted you would have thought the people of Corfu had no intention of ever moving a boat in or out of their harbor again. But when night came and they could work behind a screen of darkness, hundreds of men popped out of hiding and scurried around. Crowds of them were working blindly, trying to fill in the bomb craters so that trucks could get down to the docks.

Sailors were struggling to do something about a Greek destroyer that had been hit during the afternoon and now lay on her side with an ugly wound in her midribs. She looked in the dark like a grotesque animal some hunter had brought down in the woods. A large schooner had been struck by bombs in such a way that she was thrown partly out of the water and now lay with her three masts up on dry land, blocking the road so that vehicles had to detour into a field. There must have been a hundred boats tied up there in the harbor. They ranged all the way from little things like the *Makedonka* up to ships of almost a thousand tons. But regardless of their size, men were preparing to get them under way tonight. The hunch that this might be the last chance for anyone to get off Corfu appeared to be almost universal. These boat-owners seemed determined that if the Italians came tomorrow they wouldn't get their hands on any prizes of the sea.

We couldn't find anyone who had ever heard of the *Spiradon Piraeus*. But when we said "Preveza," men would start arguing among themselves as to where the boat was that was going to Preveza, and we would end up by investigating all their suggestions and still not finding the *Spiradon*. On the dot of nine o'clock, the scheduled hour of sailing, we saw a three-master of about two hundred tons slip away from the dock and glide out into the night. We asked a sailor who talked a little English if that was the *Spiradon*. He screwed up his eyes, stared out over the water, then said, "Yes, I am sure that is the *Spiradon*."

Hill instinctively yelled at the boat. I guess I did too. If we missed the *Spiradon* we might get stuck for life on this miserable little island, because Atherton and White and Mike had probably sailed away already. Our yelling riled a lot of the Greeks who were standing around the quay. Some of them came at us with doubled up fists. They pointed to the sky and shook their fists in our faces. The poor fools were trying to tell us we'd bring the planes here with our shouting. Then there were others who seemed convinced we were enemy agents. They were even more threatening.

It wasn't fun stumbling around the bomb-torn water front,

looking for a ship that probably had already sailed away, and being constantly threatened with mob action, and having the feeling that we were strangers in a hostile land from which the chance of escape was growing slimmer by the hour.

We found the *Spiradon Piraeus* quite by accident. She was anchored in the shadow of two other boats. We had passed by her several times without being able to make out her form in the dark. But we located her finally because a stevedore with a gunny sack on his back bumped into us in the dark. The sack dropped and split open. Loaves of hard, black peasant bread started rolling around at our feet. The stevedore cursed us and we started to curse him back, until Hill suddenly said, "Bread!"

I didn't get the point. "So what?" I asked him.

"Bread!" Hill said again. "Don't you remember what the naval commander said? The *Spiradon* is carrying bread. Bread for the soldiers at Preveza. If we follow this stevedore we'll probably find the *Spiradon*."

And that's how we found her. She was an ancient-looking boat, but in trim condition. Her decks were clear, her sails were neatly furled, and her five-man crew stood at the rail, watching shadowy figures lift sacks of bread out of a motorbus, which the army apparently had commandeered, and carry them up the gangplank, and then dump them down into the hold. We slipped into the bread line and got aboard. Apparently they had just started loading, because the hold was nearly empty, and there were two or three truckloads of bread on the dock. So Hill and I sloughed off our heavy knapsacks and relaxed.

It was an eerie night. Ghostlike. Unreal. Filled with implications of impending disaster. The noises men were making as they loaded dozens of boats and started them on their way were not normal noises. It was as if someone had thrown a gigantic blanket over the entire water front, muffling all sound.

Boats around us suddenly eased away from their docks without any warning and were swallowed up in the black of the sea. They sailed away without a trace of light, and the wonder was that they didn't collide with one another and sink.

Suddenly Hill grabbed my arm and pointed. Three lights, which looked miles away up in the hills, were blinking on and off. Then there were four. Then a dozen. We thought of stories about fifth columnists signaling to enemy planes. We sat there rigid, waiting for something to happen. But nothing did happen, because the dozen lights soon became a hundred. Then a thousand. Finally we realized we were watching fireflies just across the dock road. But that's the kind of a night it was. Even a completely sane, completely unimaginative person would have had a few hallucinations that night. Everything was so unreal, so eerie.

A little dark man who we decided must be the skipper of the *Spiradon* paced his deck like a beast of the jungle does when he's locked up in a cage. There was another man doing a lot of pacing too. His head was wrapped in white bandages. We decided he probably was a fellow passenger and we asked him if he spoke English. "No," he snapped back in perfect English, "I do not."

It was like asking a man if he had been stricken dumb and having him answer by saying, "Yes, I no longer am able to talk."

We never did quite figure out the man with the bandaged head. Hill thought he had probably been hurt in the afternoon raids and had lost his mind. That was just the way he acted.

Occasionally a stevedore dropped a sack of bread. When the black loaves rolled around, other stevedores tripped on them and dropped their sacks. Then there was a babble of cursing and the skipper would go down and tongue-lash the men until they stopped arguing and got to work again.

Hill and I dozed occasionally on each other's shoulders as we sat on the deck propped up against the gunwale. We were more relaxed than we had been since the morning Belgrade was bombed. We still hadn't reached communications or a stopping place, but it looked as if we would soon find them both. By morning we ought to be on the Greek mainland. And tonight we didn't have to worry about sails or engines or navigating. There was a five-man crew to do that. We could just doze and watch the fireflies and the silent ships and thank God we hadn't decided to follow White's hunch.

The hold was nearly full now, and the trucks on the dock were nearly empty. It was two A.M. We ought to make the mainland before it got very light. We would escape what might be a final bombing of Corfu or the beginning of an invasion. Thank God for small favors. Thank God for the *Spiradon*. We felt warm inside and our minds were at peace for once.

But suddenly we were stirred out of our calm by a violent argument. There was no hushed blanket character about the voices now. When Greek argues with Greek it's quite an argument. Now dozens of Greeks were arguing all at the same time. A naval officer was stopping the men from coming up the gangplank with the last few sacks of bread. He was forcing them to turn around and put the sacks back in the trucks. The skipper was in a rage. So were some of the crew and some of the stevedores. Now the officer barked another order, and the stevedores reluctantly began to haul the sacks of bread out of the hold and up onto the deck. That went on for half an hour; then the naval officer went away. As soon as he was out of sight the skipper gave some orders himself, and the stevedores quit work and lay down on the deck and went to sleep.

Hill and I asked the passenger with the bandaged head what it was all about. We could tell by the way he shrugged his shoulders that he understood us. But he wasn't doing any talking. Then we asked the captain in English and French, and Hill tried to form a question with the few Greek words he knew. But the skipper just stalked away, and so Hill and I strapped on our knapsacks, took our typewriters, and ran down the bomb-torn road looking for someone to talk to. We found the naval officer who had started the trouble. He spoke some English.

He said, "We have just had bad news. Very bad news. The enemy has reached Preveza already. The *Spiradon* will not be able to sail to Preveza. But she will sail for some other port all right. We don't know where to. We don't know if she will carry the bread or not. You see, we don't know where the Greek army is now. We are—we are very confused."

So we went back to the *Spiradon* and parked ourselves on the deck again. Now the passenger with the bandaged head got panicky. He collected his two suitcases and duffel bag and vanished over the side. We never saw him again, the poor fellow.

Hill and I weren't feeling very joyful right then. The first faint light of morning was beginning to chase away the dark. If we didn't get under way before sunrise it would be too late to start, because surely the captain of the *Spiradon* would never risk being spotted by planes out there on the open sea. That would be suicide. And if we waited another twenty-four hours Corfu might be in ruins and the *Spiradon* might get knocked over on her side like that Greek destroyer. Or the island might be occupied by the Italians. Or even if none of those things happened, White and Atherton would be getting a long start on us and might beat us to communications by a whole day. Wouldn't we look foolish back in New York! Risking our lives for two weeks and being beaten on the last lap. Then we got another bad thought. White and Atherton and Mike had planned to start out at dusk the night before. They probably hadn't heard about Preveza falling before they started. And Preveza, of course, was the place they would be heading for, because Preveza was the closest port on the mainland. Within a few hours all three of them might be in Axis hands, and there was no way for us to warn them.

Suddenly, with the stevedores still sleeping and the bread still half in the hold and half on deck, the ship's engines started up. They churned away for half an hour and then, while we were trying to figure out what was going to happen next, they were stopped just as suddenly and as unexplainably as they had been started.

We hadn't seen the skipper for more than an hour. Now he came back and started his deck-pacing again. He kept mumbling three words in Greek. Hill understood them. "My poor boat, my poor boat," he kept saying. Then he stopped abruptly, looked down into the hold, and barked some orders, and the stevedores began tossing the sacks of bread out onto the dock. Apparently the skipper had come to a final decision. He was going to sail away. Sail away without the bread. He had decided not to wait any longer for naval orders. If this be treason . . . That was what he was probably saying under his breath. To hell with the army and the bread and official indecision. The skipper was going to save his ship.

That guess wasn't far wrong. The next day we found out that that was exactly what had been going through the skipper's mind.

It was getting dangerously light when we sailed. I guess the only reason we didn't get a good bombing that morning was because the Italian planes had bigger jobs on their schedule than trying to hit a two-hundred-ton schooner. When we got out on the Ionian Sea we saw them circling over the city of Corfu just a little after dawn. Then we heard the noises of war and we saw smoke going up and we knew the naval commander and everyone else had probably been right about this being Corfu's last day of what they call freedom. I had a sinking feeling in my stomach, standing there on the deck of the *Spiradon,* watching Corfu disappear on the horizon. It seemed symbolic. Corfu was disappearing all right. It might be a year or a generation or a century before Corfu would come back. Poor little Corfu, where the people lived like animals down in the bowels of the earth because of what machines up in the sky had done to their homes and to their minds. Then I wondered about the barefooted boy on the parapet of the ancient fortress. He'd probably be blowing that dented brass bugle until the people of Corfu finally hoisted their white flag of surrender.

We stopped thinking about Corfu when we saw the skipper run to his cabin and come out with two big rifles under his left arm and a rusty old revolver in his right hand. He barked orders to the engineer and to the man at the tiller. The engines went dead. The man at the tiller swung the *Spiradon* around so that we were heading straight for the Greek coast where we knew the Italians had already planted their flag. Hill and I followed the skipper. He went into the bow and handed the revolver to one of his crew and the smaller of the two rifles to another fellow. Then he loaded his own rifle with a shell from his pocket.

It wasn't until then that we saw what was causing the excitement. The *Spiradon,* now that she had changed her course, was bearing down on an open boat about twenty feet long. The same thought must have hit Hill and me at the same time. The *Makedonka!* The skipper had his rifle to his shoulder and he was ordering the other two men to take aim. I was standing right beside him. My first instinct was to knock the rifle from his shoulder, but there was still time. He still didn't have his finger anywhere near the trigger. I strained my eyes trying to make sure if it really was the *Makedonka.* I started breathing normally again when I noticed that the sail on the little boat was dark yellow. The *Makedonka's* sail was pure white.

Hill relaxed, too. Thank God! I said quietly in his ear, so as not to disturb the skipper, who still had a bead on the boat. We almost rammed it before the skipper put down his gun and ordered the *Spiradon* back on her course with full steam ahead. There were six boys in the boat who were obviously Greek. Anyway they shouted some Greek words at the skipper, and that was when he put down his gun. Hill and I went back to our corner of the deck and figured out that the skipper must have thought the boat was the advance guard of an Italian invasion party, because it seemed to be heading from the Greek mainland toward Corfu. If that guess had been right he probably would have shot them. Or been killed himself in trying to perform one last patriotic service for his native Corfu.

After it got light the crew's chef, a bent old man of seventy or eighty, began preparing breakfast. He had a crude brick fireplace built right on the deck. It looked like the open fireplaces you see in public parks. He put a pot of water on to boil and then he took the head of a lamb and cooked it. When he called them, the four other men in the crew came around for their share. The head of one lamb, even if you eat the eyes and all, as they did, isn't much food, but those hard-working sailors insisted that Hill and I have a nibble too. We tried to repay their kindness by sharing with them a loaf of peasant bread and a bottle of wine we'd picked up in Corfu.

As soon as we were on friendly terms with the crew we learned that the skipper did speak a little English and so did the engineer. It was the skipper who later told us how he was trying to run for some safe port to save his ship, and it was the engineer who said we were heading for Patras, down on the south shore of the Gulf of Corinth, which means the north coast of the Peloponnesos. We would travel by night and hide in out-of-the-way coves by day. We ought to make it in two more nights.

We hid that first day in a cove of the Greek mainland near the town of Murtos. Murtos was thoroughly Moslem. The men wore fezzes and the women veils, and the churches were mosques. It reminded us of Sarajevo. Only Murtos would never be bombed, because it was already occupied territory. The Germans had gotten this far during the night. We heard that from three Greek gendarmes, two Greek soldiers, a Greek sailor, and eight native boys who came down to the water's edge to meet the *Spiradon*. But they said we were safe, because the Germans had passed right through Murtos, and anyway, if we climbed to the top of the mountain overlooking the cove we could keep an eye on the *Spiradon* and at the same time watch all the roads leading to the sea.

That's what we did. The skipper left one man on watch on the schooner, and all the rest of us climbed the mountain. When we got up there, he had one man watching the roads all day while everyone else slept. Everyone else, that is, but Hill and I. We had our typewriters with us and we started pounding out stories about Corfu and stories about Yugoslavia. We were sure that when we got to Patras we would be able to send them by telephone to Athens, where other American newspapermen could get them censored for us and relay them on to New York.

There were plenty of distractions while we worked. One member of the crew snored like a bass horn. The eight Greek boys crowded around watching us pound our typewriters, their eyes wide, their mouths open. A Greek sailor who had once made a trip to America and was quite proud of the six or eight English words he had picked up looked on in silence for half an hour and then, when it finally dawned on him that we were newspapermen, he blurted out, "Ah, New York *Times.*"

Hill, who had the typical *Herald Tribune* reporter's disrespect for the rival *Times,* corrected him immediately. "No, not New York *Times.* New York *Herald Tribune.*"

The sailor grinned. "Ah yes, New York *Times.*"

Hill shouted, "No! New York *Herald Tribune.*"

It went on for minutes, the sailor shouting *Times* and Hill shouting *Herald Tribune.* They sounded like two rival newsboys peddling their papers. Finally Hill groaned and gave up. Then the sailor called over some of the other Greeks and pointed to Hill and his typewriter and said a lot of Greek words which ended up with, New York *Times.*

I'm glad Hill was never able to send the story he wrote that afternoon. I'm afraid it wasn't up to his usual standard. He was too angry to think while he pounded the typewriter keys.

Another distraction was an Italian reconnaissance plane that spotted the *Spiradon* about noon. It circled twice right over us and then went streaking off toward Italy. The skipper was worried. He didn't sleep after that. He paced the hilltop for an hour. Then he went down with one of the crew and pulled the schooner a little closer into the cove. When he came back he paced up and down for another hour. It was the two big Italian bombers coming out of the clouds that finally ended his nervous perambulation. We were sure the reconnaissance plane had given them our location and ordered them to bomb us. Maybe we over-estimated our importance. Anyway the bombers never found us, and when the sun began to set we put to sea again.

Hill and I curled up in a corner of the deck and went to sleep. The *Spiradon* was rolling gently from side to side. We fell asleep almost immediately. The thing that finally woke us up was the salt spray on our faces. We had had a full night's sleep at last.

It was nearly dawn. The *Spiradon* was cutting through the water at a reckless speed. We wondered why, and then we noticed that while we had been sleeping, the crew had hoisted two huge sails. Both the wind and the engines were pushing us on toward Patras. Helping us to get away from Germans and Italians. Helping us to get to a safe port and communications. That was what we thought.

We anchored that morning in a cove in the Island of Leukas. An old newspaper lay on the floor of the sea, thirty or forty feet below the surface. The water was so clear we could make out the Greek characters in the headlines. A mountain rose straight up from the shore. The skipper winked at us and told us to follow him. We climbed the mountain for more than an hour. We dodged behind trees or boulders every time we heard a noise, because we had been told that the British, Greek, German, and Italian front was right opposite us on the mainland and that Leukas might already be in Axis hands.

The island looked uninhabited until we got to the summit. Up there we came onto a little village and on the outskirts of the village a crumbling old monastery. The Monastery of St. Nicholas. A monk with a white beard and white hair tied with a ribbon and then hanging in two braids down the back of his black cassock came out to welcome us. He seemed to belong to another world, and so did we after we stepped through the doors of his monastery and sat around him on benches in a semicircle and listened to his soft, low voice as he talked with the sailors. Of course we couldn't understand the words. But it was like listening to muted organ music. It was a bit of peace on the very fringes of war.

He talked to the sailors, they told us later, about religion and philosophy. The war that was so close was never mentioned. We knew at the time they weren't talking war, because when men talk war they get excited and lose their tempers and get red in the face and you can see hate and fear in their eyes, even if you can't understand what their lips are saying. But the old monk and the sea-hardened sailors had peace and calm in their eyes.

While they talked, Hill and I wandered off into a little chapel with silvered ikons and ornate pictures of saints. It was quiet in that miniature cathedral on the top of a mountain. Not a hint of sirens or whistling bombs or screaming victims.

We just stood there drinking it all in, all this quiet. One of us went over and put a handful of Greek drachmas into a wooden box on the wall with a slit in the top. And then we lighted some candles, as we had seen people do in other Greek Orthodox churches. We didn't know much about Greek religious procedure, but we wanted to make some outward sign of how much we appreciated this first real peace we had found since that Palm Sunday morning when planes roared out of the sunrise over Belgrade and crucified peace.

When we went back, the old monk had dug out a tattered guest book. He would like our signatures. We looked at the other names. They were headed by the signature "Elizabeth, Empress of Austria and Queen of Hungary." The ink was faded. It had been a long time ago that Empress Elizabeth had stopped on Leukas. And now her descendants were killing the Greeks just across the water on the mainland.

Then the padre took us outside and pointed over to another island and he made us understand that it was the Island of Ithaca, where Ulysses was born. Ulysses who had never dreamed of war like this. After that we went back inside again and were served with luncheon. We were served by a young woman whom someone should have painted. She was a plain, simple, peasant type, but there was something almost Madonna-like about her simplicity. Her delicately carved face, framed by braids of black hair, made you guess that maybe she was twenty-five. Her body looked as if it had been doing hard labor for at least forty years. But it was her hands that most people would have noticed. Her hands looked sixty years old. They were just like Mike's hands. Brown and gnarled. They looked like the hands of a peasant man who had used them so long and so hard that the joints were enlarged and the fingers were shapeless and stocky. I think they were the ugliest pair of hands I have ever seen on a human being. They didn't really look human. They were grotesque and horrible.

But I forgot the woman when she started setting food down in front of us. First she brought on a dish of pancakes made from herbs that had been stewed first. She must have gathered the herbs herself in the forest. I don't know what they were and I can't describe the flavor, except that it was exotic. They had the taste of deep, musty woods. Then there was goat's cheese, and finally small plates of honey, raisins, and almonds all mixed together, with a rich red wine to wash it down.

When we had to leave I tried to slip some money into the old monk's hand without anyone seeing. He wasn't angry and he wasn't offended, but he was insistent that not one drachma would he take for his hospitality. He made it clear that this was a holy house, consecrated to the service of God. We had been his guests and the guests of Saint Nicholas. Saint Nicholas wished us a happy voyage. If we ever came by the island of Leukas again we must be sure to stop and climb the mountain to the crumbling monastery. We understood few of his actual words, but we could tell that that was what he was trying to express to us. He told us all those things with gestures and with simple Greek words, which we seemed to comprehend.

We went straight from the world of Saint Nicholas back into the world of Hitler and Mussolini. Back into a world where men were hating and killing for all they were worth.

Stepping out of the otherworldliness of the St. Nicholas Monastery and then seeing Italian planes circling low over Leukas and over Ulysses' birthplace on Ithaca was a shock to the emotions. That other world had seemed real. This world of bombing planes seemed like something out of a bad dream that we thought had ended. But the planes were real all right, and they might drop bombs this time, and so we dodged from tree to tree and made for the *Spiradon*. The planes were gone when we got ready to sail away.

That night, Shorty, the *Spiradon's* engineer, said we could sleep in his bunk. He had to stay awake to keep the engines going. So we got another good night's rest, which was lucky, because it was going to be our last for a long time.

We made Patras harbor as dawn broke. The skipper threw a hawser to a man on the quay, and they were just tying up the ship when sirens began screaming. We scrambled over the side and hid in the most perfect air-raid shelter we had seen anywhere in the Balkans. It was nothing but blocks of concrete piled on top of one another, with a few narrow slits between them where men could hide. But those blocks were fifteen feet high and about ten feet thick. Since we knew we might survive even a direct hit with that protection, we stretched out between the blocks listening calmly to the thunder of the planes and the noises the bombs created out of silence when they hit their targets. The noises were just as unpleasant as the noises bombs had created in Belgrade and Sarajevo and everywhere else. Those noises were beginning to get monotonous.

"Well," Hill said, "I guess we've still got horseshoes around our necks. We made the Peloponnesos, and the story is still following us. What a break!"

CHAPTER TWELVE

Under Fire

--◄◆◉◆►--

No one agreed about how many people the German bombers killed in Patras, but they surely did a job. A Greek hospital ship with tremendous red crosses painted all over its sides got a direct hit. It was listing badly and before long would go to the bottom. Someone said it was the last hospital ship the Greeks had. The rest were already at the bottom, some of them still weighted down with the bodies of their wounded passengers who hadn't had a chance when the planes came over. The hospital ship in Patras harbor had been full of wounded too. Some said the flimsy wooden boat had been turned into a morgue for at least two hundred soldiers. Others put the casualties lower than that. But the worst job the planes did was on hundreds of refugees.

The people of Patras had had a hunch, like the people of Corfu. Only the Patras hunch came too late. The hunch was that life wasn't going to be pleasant much longer in Patras and they had better get moving. And so they had flocked down to the water front. It had been a well-organized exodus. They were all going away in flat-bottomed barges towed by a large ship. They brought their most precious and their most essential possessions down to the water front with them. They loaded them onto the barges until there was hardly room for the human freight. They were about ready to shove off when the planes came.

Of course it was a stupid mistake. They never should have tried to get away in daylight. Some of them managed to hide between the blocks of concrete on the quay, but most of them just huddled down on the barges, burying their heads in the blankets and mattresses and tin kettles and baby cribs and all the other stuff they wanted so much to save. They tried to play ostrich, but bullets from a machine gun in an airplane can hit people just as well and kill them just as dead even if their heads are buried. That was what happened. The planes dropped some bombs and then they used their machine guns. No one ever counted the bodies exactly. The estimates varied greatly. Anyway at least seventy were killed.

After the planes went away and the dead and the wounded were removed the rest of the people of Patras lost all interest in going places on barges. They fled from the water front. They never wanted to see that water front again. And that was why it was that when we shook hands with the skipper and his crew they weren't paying much attention to us. There was a lot of stuff to look over on those barges. Stuff no one was interested in any more, because most of it belonged to people who were dead now. I saw Shorty's eyes brighten as he stood in the middle of one of the barges holding up a silk dress you could have bought in Klein's, New York, for about ninety-eight cents. He was holding it up at arm's length and admiring it and probably trying to decide whether it would go around his wife's figure. Other members of the crew of the *Spiradon* had their eyes on frying pans and blankets and flashlights. We thought it was a rather sordid scene, because a lot of that stuff was covered with the blood of the people who had owned it, and it didn't seem right for anyone to be touching it. At least not until the blood was dry.

We went straight from the water front to the office of the *État Major*. Up there we ran onto a Greek lieutenant who had once been in Detroit. He said he thought we would be wise to get out of Patras immediately. The Germans were just across the Gulf of Corinth and they might come over with a landing party any hour now. It was about a hundred and fifty miles along the gulf to Athens, but there wasn't any motor traffic moving along the highway. Too dangerous. Too many planes overhead all the time. However, there was a train leaving at four o'clock in the afternoon. He helped us buy tickets so that we would be sure to have places. It might be, he said, the last train that would ever leave Patras.

We were walking back into town when the sirens went off again. We decided to ignore them, but it was the old story again. The natives started shouting at us and pointing up into the air where the planes were. When we just smiled and tried to keep going, angry gendarmes came running after us.

"This thing is getting damned monotonous," Hill grumbled.

"Yes," I said with some sincere bitterness, "it's like a phonograph when the needle gets stuck in a groove and keeps playing the same bars of music over and over again until you think you'll go crazy unless someone shuts the machine off."

But you can't argue with a gendarme if he's got a rifle in his hand, and we were forced up the street to an air-raid shelter. Over the door it said in English as well as Greek, "Built with funds contributed from America." I grinned when I read that sign. The greatest nation in the world had helped the Greeks. Never let it be said that we hadn't. I had seen the proof with my own eyes. We had gone to their help when they were attacked by all the forces of evil. When vast mechanized armies rolled down from the north, America had stood behind little Greece. We had—contributed funds to build an air-raid shelter. And I suppose America would have been hurt if she could have seen the Greeks pouring into that shelter without paying a bit of attention to the sign or giving a thought to the great generosity of the United States.

There were more people trying to get in than the place would hold. Gendarmes barked and cursed. The planes came closer. The gendarmes looked nervously over their shoulders and then put their knees in people's backs and pushed. But there was a wall at the far end of this shelter built in the side of a hill, and the people between the door and the back wall were already packed in there so tightly that it was difficult for any of them to breathe. But the gendarmes kept on pushing, and a woman whose head was inside the shelter but whose broad backside stuck out began to scream her fear of being hit in the rear. It wasn't a pleasant scene, because human beings were acting like terrified animals. The lower the planes came and the more bombs they dropped around the city, the more these people were metamorphized into animals, bent only on self-preservation.

Hill and I finally turned away in disgust and sat down a few yards from the entrance to the shelter. When that raid was over we wandered down into the messed-up city and found a café where we couldn't get any food but where we could set up typewriters on a dirty marble-topped table and pretend that we were right on a dead line and that a telegraph operator with a wire open to New York was sitting beside us waiting to flash our news to America. It was all make-believe, of course, because the lieutenant at army headquarters had just laughed when we asked about communications. The only communication center left in Greece, as far as he knew, was at Athens. And there was no way to telephone to Athens. We'd have to wait until we got there. But since we were going to take a train at four o'clock for Athens we pounded our typewriters and told about the people who had died like rats on the quay of Patras and the wounded soldiers who were given their *coup de grâce* as they lay on the hospital ship.

We talked several times about Mike and White and Atherton. We were worried, because we had asked a lot of people around town already about them and no one had seen them. Anything might have happened, but our guess was that they had fallen into the hands of the Axis when they hit Preveza.

Then Atherton walked into the café. He had blood all over his shirt. Dark, clotted blood. Almost black. His face had tragedy written all over it. He was limping badly. He tried to smile when he saw us. We knew he was glad to see us. And we were damned glad to see him. But he couldn't smile. He just said two words, and then we all sat down and didn't say anything else for quite a while. The two words turned something to stone down inside of me. I guess Hill felt the same way too.

All Atherton said was, "Mike's dead." Then we knew where the blood had come from. We didn't ask any questions. We didn't know yet how Mike had died. But we knew he had died with his head on Atherton's chest. We knew that because we knew Atherton and we knew he felt about Mike just like we did. Mike was sixty years old and he was a tough little fisherman with big gnarled hands like boxing gloves that mashed your hand when he grabbed it. And Mike wasn't the kind of person you'd invite into your home for a cocktail party. But Mike was worth most of the people I had ever met at cocktail parties all thrown in together. We had lived with Mike for days out there on the Adriatic and we knew that Mike was a real man, with an honest, open heart. But a heart that wasn't beating any more now.

"Bombed?" Hill finally asked.

"Yes," Atherton replied. "Killed outright. A Stuka dropped something that got him in the head. Mike never knew what hit him."

We finally got some weak tea by arguing with the café owner. Then the story gradually came out. White and Atherton and Mike had started out from Casopi about the same time we started from Corfu. They had found out about Preveza, and so they went right by it. The trouble began when all the gasoline they had leaked out of the fuel can. They hailed a Greek mine sweeper, which took them aboard and towed the *Makedonka* on behind. But the mine sweeper went so fast that the towline broke, and the *Makedonka* capsized, with everything in it. Then the

Greek ship, as it got near Patras, was dive-bombed by those same planes we had been hiding from under the concrete blocks. That was when Mike got it. And at the same time a piece of shrapnel had buried itself in Atherton's right knee, so that it was difficult for him to walk now. White had come through the whole thing without a scratch, and now he was looking around town for communications.

A little before four o'clock we all went down to get on the train that was going to take us to Athens, but the railroad men said it had been canceled. They didn't think there would be any more trains to Athens. Things were getting bad. The Germans were sweeping down from the north. Nobody seemed to be able to stop them. They would probably be here in Patras soon. Thousands of people wanted to get out of Patras. Who were we anyway? Were we any better than the people of Patras? This was their town, their railroad. Even if a train did come along, we couldn't get on it anyway. If a train did run, the people of Patras would be given first chance, but there were thousands of them, and there probably wouldn't be any train anyway.

Of course those railroad men were right. But still, you've got to think of yourself when the sky is always full of planes, and people are being killed all around you. You've got to go Nietzsche and look out for your own skin. We spent all the rest of the afternoon and all evening watching the highway to Athens for some sign of transportation and chasing to different army head-quarters trying to get some help.

Late in the night we were ushered into the "Great Presence." I guess he was a general. He had enough gold braid on his uniform for all the officers at West Point. You never would have known a war was going on and that right now Greek soldiers were fleeing like frightened rabbits from the German motorized army all over the country and leaving the poor Anzacs to hold what was left of battle lines. We could tell from the fragments of conversation while he conferred with his aides and kept us waiting that they were being just as petty and bureaucratic as ever about a thousand little details that didn't matter a bit now. Greece was falling, but how many carbon copies did the general want his orderly to make of this letter?

Finally he turned to us. So we wanted transportation, did we? Of course we should have it! An army truck was leaving for Athens soon. We had his permission to go on it. No, we didn't need any papers or passes. Just tell the officers out in the ante-room that the general said we were to go on the truck to Athens. We went out and told the officers. They looked puzzled. They talked to other officers. Then they told us the truck had left two hours ago. They were sorry, but that was the last truck going to Athens. There wouldn't be any more. Not tonight or tomorrow either. Maybe later in the week, if—if nothing happened. We asked to see the general again. They told us they were sorry, but the general had gone off to dinner and he wouldn't be back tonight.

Dinner? We decided that we'd like some dinner too, but the food supply of Patras apparently was reserved for generals and people like that. We couldn't find any anywhere. Then Atherton remembered that once when he was down in Greece before the war he had stopped in Patras and had met an engineer who lived at the Cecil Hotel, and so we went to the Cecil. The place had been badly wrecked by bombs, but we crawled through the debris and got up to the engineer's quarters.

In some ways going into the engineer's rooms at the Cecil was just like finding the Monastery of Saint Nicholas on top of the island of Leukas. As soon as we got inside and shut the door we were in another world. Outside, most of Patras was in ruins. There was hardly a building in town with its four walls still standing. But here in a little room in a bomb-damaged hotel a man who spoke four or five other languages as fluently as he did his own was sitting in front of a fireplace listening to soft orchestra music on a radio and reading, of all things, one of Lamb's essays. He had water boiling on a little alcohol stove and he asked us, with that tone you associate with English parlors, how we would like our tea, with milk or lemon?

I wanted to say, "You don't have a sirloin steak hidden away anywhere, do you?" But I didn't, because the engineer was Atherton's friend, not mine. So we sat and drank tea, and when he brought out some English cookies I guess all of us acted as if we had never seen cookies before and thought the thing to do was to make a sandwich of half a dozen and jam them all in our mouths at one time. But the Greek engineer pretended not to notice. Soon he and Atherton were talking about Lamb and mid-Victorian poetry and then about Nietzsche. And that's how we got around finally to that irrelevant subject of the war, which was being fought almost outside this man's windows.

He said the people of Patras hoped to be occupied by the Germans because they didn't have any feelings about the Germans. They hated the Italians and they'd fight until hell froze over if they were just fighting the Italians. But not many Greeks wanted to fight the Germans. It wasn't that they were any more afraid of the Germans. Not that. It was simply that they had no quarrel with the Germans. Germany was a long way off geographically. Also the Greeks had a great admiration for German thoroughness and German discipline and the German way of life.

"You don't mean the Nazi way of life, do you?" Atherton asked, disgustedly.

The engineer said he did. He talked for an hour about how wise Hitler had been in setting up an economic scheme that wasn't based on gold, and then he expounded a lot of other pro-Nazi arguments.

Atherton answered him, point by point. But he failed to convert the engineer.

I began to understand why Greece was falling so quickly. The country must be lacking in unity of thought and unity of purpose just as much as France and a lot of other countries had been.

While Atherton and the engineer went on talking I looked over the hundreds of books that jammed the little hotel room. The engineer was very catholic in his tastes. He had read everything from Sinclair Lewis to the Koran, but he seemed to specialize

in the field dominated by Nietzsche. Perhaps that was the clue
to why he thought as he did.

After many hours had been idled away we got down to basic
things. We told the engineer we had to find some way to get out
of Patras, and quickly. He picked up a telephone and called a
friend. It seemed strange to have a telephone operating. It was
the first telephone we had seen in use in nearly three weeks. We
asked, while he was waiting for his number, "Can we get Athens
on your phone?" He shook his head. He asked his friend, who
was a railroad executive, about trains, and he found out that at
five o'clock in the morning a long train would be loaded at the
Patras station and would set out at once with Greek soldiers for
Corinth, about a hundred and twenty miles down the gulf and
only a short distance from Athens. It was supposed to be a
military secret, but if we went down to the station before the
train came in there wasn't any reason why we couldn't smuggle
ourselves aboard.

We were at the depot at four-thirty. The place was jammed
with soldiers and civilians. If the arrival of this train was a strict
military secret, the Greek army surely let a lot of people in on its
secrets. About five o'clock the train pulled in. Ten coaches, old,
dirty, some with broken windows. But it was a train and it had a
locomotive that ran, and it was headed toward Athens and
communications and maybe safety for a while. We fought just
as viciously and as much like hungry animals as all the rest of
the people. It was dark, and no one could tell that we were foreigners. The only way not to be mistaken for foreigners there
in the dark was to fight for a foothold on that train just the way
the Greeks were doing themselves.

We made out rather well, in spite of Atherton's game leg. We
found two seats facing each other with only one place taken.
White and Hill and I took those three places. Atherton got a
seat across the aisle. We sat there in the dark grinning over our
good luck and listening to the noise of battle going on out on
the platform. The cursing and fighting was being done with a

vehemence that might have terrified enemy troops if it had been directed against them. Finally the train got started. There were about seven hundred men aboard, which you'd agree was a lot for ten cars if you knew the size of those Greek coaches.

The sun came up in a burst of red splendor as we were being shunted around the railroad yards. Finally we really got under way. Hill and I spread a map on our legs and studied the route. The tracks followed the very edge of the Gulf of Corinth all the way. We couldn't see the other shore of the gulf at Patras, but we knew that the Germans were in possession over there, just out of sight. The map showed that the farther we went the more the gulf narrowed down, until it ended at Corinth in nothing but a canal. A trainman came through, and we asked him when we would get to Corinth. He said, "With luck, in about fifteen hours." That meant we were going to average exactly eight miles an hour.

The train was full, and we weren't scheduled to make any stops, but every time we hit a town, which was every few miles, we stopped anyway. The engineer couldn't help it. Soldiers, when they saw the train coming, swarmed onto the tracks, waving their arms. Some of them hadn't thrown away their guns yet, so they waved them too. When the engineer put on his brakes rather than mow down a whole Greek regiment, the panicky soldiers clamored to get aboard. Now they were fighting just like the soldiers at Patras. Finally the train started up. Men were hanging onto the steps and some were even sitting on the roofs of the cars. The train looked like a ship covered with barnacles. That same thing happened at each town. Then we began to realize why it was going to take fifteen hours to go a hundred and twenty miles. Fifteen hours would get us into Corinth just after dusk. We would be going along the edge of the gulf all day long. Each hour we would be getting nearer to German territory, because of the way the gulf narrowed down. We thought of all those things as we stared out the window.

That trip in peacetime must be the most delightful, the most scenic in the whole world. The cliffs are high. They drop straight down from the tracks to the sea. A drop of several hundred feet. And at the bottom there's the smooth blue water of the gulf. The map showed that we would never be out of sight of that smooth blue water.

"It's going to be a lovely trip," Hill said.

I knew what he meant, and so did the others. Any minute now German planes might come over from the other shore and pay us a call. After all, our train was a natural for a plane. The men on the roof and the men hanging onto the platforms were living advertisements that this was a troop train. And there was nothing to stop a plane from flying right alongside the train and giving us all guns.

Those were the things we were all thinking, and then I thought, what a hell of a seat I chose! Right next to the window on the gulf side of the car!

"It looks like today's the day," White said.

The rest of us pretended we didn't understand.

"I mean today's the day we'll probably really get it," White went on grimly.

"Well, as long as we can't do anything about it, let's play poker," Hill suggested.

We put a typewriter on our knees, and the three of us tried not to think of what we might soon see out the window. We didn't have any chips or any money, but Hill got out the black notebook in which for more than a year he had been entering material for newspaper stories, magazine articles, and the book that every newspaperman is going to write some day. We didn't play long, but we were playing for high stakes, and Russell had some astronomical figures chalked up in his book. Astronomical if you know what newspapermen's salaries are. Later we tried to remember who owed whom how much, but those poker winnings were destined never to be paid.

I remember I had just lost a pot and was looking out the window while Hill was making another entry in his notebook. I was facing toward the rear of the train. We were in the next to the

last car. The first thing I saw was the wing of the plane. The men
in that last car could have reached out and touched it, it was
so close. But no one did, because just then the plane's machine
gun started to bark out its nasty message.

I never saw men move so quickly. And so instinctively. No one
had ever told us what to do if we were riding in a train and an
airplane started machine-gunning us. But we knew without any
lessons.

White and Hill were next to the aisle, and they fell onto the
floor first. Then a lot of fellows from the other side of the car fell
on top of them. I was last man. The plane was just about
opposite our window when we all got settled there in the aisle. I
kept thinking, what a target I am with my head buried but with
my tail sticking right up in the air!

The rattle of the machine gun lasted for about seven seconds.
That was long enough for the pilot to go the whole length of the
train and give every one of the cars a good dose of lead. Then the
plane roared off to make a big circle and come back again.

About that time the train stopped with a jerk. Windows on the
far side were thrown open. Hundreds of Greek soldiers dived
through them. I saw Atherton go out head first.

White was quite a way under me, but I could hear him hollering, "I've been shot. I've been shot."

By the time the plane had lined up for its next visit there
wasn't anyone left in the car but the three of us. Hill and I tried
to carry White out before we got a second blasting. But he was
heavy. His right thigh was useless. There were three bicycles in
the vestibule of the car. We were having our troubles. We were
both standing up, with White's arms around our shoulders, when
the car got its second dose. Somehow the sprinkle of bullets missed
us that time.

While the plane was circling around again we got White under
the train. It was impossible to follow the Greek soldiers up into
the woods, because the hill leading away from the tracks was so
steep and White was so heavy.

By the time the Messerschmitt came back for its third visitation the three of us were hugging the gravel and ties under the car.

White was cursing a blue streak. "Why the God-damned hell doesn't someone fire at him? The son-of-a-bitching bastard! The God-damned Nazi whore!"

But White's other opinions were drowned out by a roar that almost split our heads open. The pilot had dropped a heavy bomb on the right of way a couple of hundred yards behind the train.

Gravel and pieces of ties and rails were flying through the air. There wouldn't be any more trains following us now. There was nothing but a big excavation where the roadbed had been.

I guess we all held our breath for the next second or two. If the pilot dropped a bomb like that on the train, it wouldn't save us to be hiding underneath. I clawed the gravel and gritted my teeth. White was just groaning now. Hill hadn't said a word since the show began.

Now the plane was alongside the train. Now the machine gun began to bark again. Now we could hear the bullets tearing through the windows and the wooden sides of the car. One bullet ripped through a tie just behind us. Another sailed over our heads so close we could feel the heat from it. But the plane was past us now. It was working on the cars up ahead. Now we could breathe again. We could swallow. We could wet our dry lips. We could lift our faces up from the cinders and gravel.

When the plane went off that last time we knew we were safe, because we remembered that a machine-gun belt only has twenty seconds of fire in it, and we surely must have had twenty seconds of punishment by this time.

But just then the engineer got panicky and started off with a roar of steam. Hill and I rolled White out between the wheels just in time.

How many men were killed and how many were wounded inside the cars we never knew, because we never saw that train again.

But the right of way was sprinkled with men who had jumped

or been shot off the tops of the cars and with others who had dragged themselves out of the cars and then had collapsed.

Anyway, after the train left we had a problem of what to do with White. He was in great pain. We finally ripped a shutter off a house near the tracks and used that for a stretcher. Then we carried him up the steep hillside to a highway. There wasn't any traffic moving, just as the military people had said. But Hill and I walked in opposite directions down the road and finally one of us found a broken-down R.A.F. truck. The driver said yes, he'd take us all in to Corinth if we could help him get the truck going. It took about an hour.

Hundreds of Greek soldiers from the train were still up in the woods, some of them in the tops of trees and others hiding under rocks. A lot of them were screaming like mad. We never could figure out why.

A short distance down the road we picked up half a dozen Greeks who had been wounded. Some had shattered legs or arms, and some had machine-gun bullets through their heads or shoulders and were in bad shape, but the worst victim of all was a man nearly fifty years old who kept screaming for his mother. He just lay on top of the truck screaming the word "Mother." When a British ambulance went by we stopped it and asked the driver to look at this man, because his screams were driving us almost crazy. We helped undress the fellow, but the ambulance driver couldn't find a mark on him anywhere. Still, nothing would make him stop screaming. We figured out that he had probably fallen from the top of one of the cars and had had a brain concussion.

On the way into Corinth my right leg felt as if it were asleep and I kept pounding it. Finally I had Hill pull it a few times to loosen the cramped muscles. Since it didn't seem to do any good, I just tried to forget it. Somehow I never thought about being shot. I guess I was too damned tired to think. And besides, things kept happening to keep a man from thinking very much. Like the return visit of that damned Nazi plane. We were about half an hour along the road when someone yelled, "Christ! Here he comes!"

There were no trees along the road, but there was a thicket off in a field. The R.A.F. driver jumped out and started across the field. He yelled at us to follow him. All the Greeks on the truck who could move by themselves went off into the thicket with the driver. But there were two Greek soldiers wounded so badly they couldn't get out of the truck. And then there was White. He was still lying on the shutter. The shutter was on top of a lot of cans of gas. The truck had no top. There was nothing at all between White and the sky. We looked at the plane. It was coming lower and lower. We tried to lift the shutter.

White yelled, "I can't stand the pain, being moved like that. Leave me here."

We didn't like the idea of running off and leaving White lying there on top of the open truck. It didn't seem right. So we buried our heads in some blankets that the other wounded men had left behind and waited. It's crazy how you always want to hide your head. Especially crazy for a newspaperman, who ought to keep his eyes open and see all he can. The plane made a hell of a noise as it came down. Finally it seemed that the landing wheels must be almost touching our backs. As I lay there waiting for something to happen I thought, I wonder whether he'll just drop a bomb or whether he'll play with that God-damned machine gun again. But he didn't do either.

After he disappeared in the clouds the R.A.F. driver and the Greeks came back and we started off again. The driver told me to stand on the running board because he had something he wanted to say. He had to shout so that I could hear him above the noise the truck was making. He said, "Listen, my dear fellow, bravery's a fine thing, but only when there's some sense to it. You and your friends were just sticking your necks out for no good reason. If it happens again you may not be so lucky. Next time you hide with the rest of us. You can't save the wounded men from getting hit just by staying with them. You might as well save yourselves if you can't save them."

Then he told all of us to keep a sharp lookout because he thought the plane would be following us all the way to Corinth.

We should hammer on the roof of the cab to warn him if we saw it again. It was only about ten minutes before we did see it. It was coming right down at us again. We all ran into a field. All except White and the poor Greeks who couldn't move either. I saw White pull his coat over his head as we left.

There weren't any trees in the field this time, and we just crouched behind a stone wall. The driver said it was a good safe hide-out. But I didn't feel at all right inside. I could see the truck through a hole in the wall. White and the other wounded men looked as if they were dead already. I was sorry I had left them in spite of all the driver had said. The driver was right, but I felt mean and selfish. I felt that I'd always be ashamed of running away like that, even though I couldn't have done anybody any good by staying on top of the truck. The R.A.F. driver was right beside me. He pulled out his service pistol and got it ready for use. We were only a few feet from the truck. If the plane skimmed over it again the way it had done last time, a good marksman could plant a bullet where it might hurt. I remembered the automatic that King Peter's bodyguard had given us. I yanked it out of my pocket. I know I couldn't have hit the broad side of a barn then, because I was shaking all over, but it gave me some strength to tighten my fingers around the little gun.

The plane didn't come down so low this time. The pilot seemed to be losing interest in the truck. In a few more minutes we were on our way again.

That R.A.F. driver was really a fine person. He tried so hard not to jostle White around when the road got rough, because every time we did hit a bump Leigh screamed in pain. I guess the driver winced as much as the rest of us did when he heard those screams. We kept giving White drinks of cognac to dull the pain. Halfway to Corinth another truck was waiting for our truck. They switched the gasoline cans, and we transferred all our wounded men. The first truck driver said he had to turn around now and go back to Patras. We shook hands and wished him luck. I had a strange feeling that he was in for trouble. That's why I pumped his hand so hard and said, "Happy sailing! You've probably saved a couple of lives today. We're damned grateful. Hope you can save your own on the way back."

He just grinned and said, "What the hell?" and then he was off. Somehow I felt he was going to get it before he ever reached Patras.

CHAPTER THIRTEEN

Bombs and Hospitals

———————◄•◆•►———————

THIS CHAPTER is going to be difficult to write. It will be difficult for many people to read too.

If I can put down the things I saw and heard and smelled that afternoon in Corinth, Greece, just as they happened, it will give you a fair picture of what war really is when it comes to a town like Corinth. But I doubt if many people in America want to know what war really is when it comes to a town like Corinth, because they may realize that Corinth in many ways is not much different than Darien, Connecticut, or Middletown, Indiana, or a lot of other American towns. And that may lead to other thoughts.

Anyway, Corinth was a sleepy little place on the afternoon of April twenty-sixth. People were doing just the same things in Corinth they were doing in Darien and Middletown. They were having lunch and some of them were reading novels and some of them were tending shop. All of them were trying to pretend that nothing was likely to happen to disturb what they were doing right then.

The hospital in Corinth was modern in a lot of ways, except that there weren't any doctors. Just a lot of Greek nurses, most of them so young and sensitive looking that it didn't seem right that their lives should be all wrapped up in war and blood and death. They had on lettuce-crisp uniforms. When we carried Leigh White into the operating room they cut his trousers off and washed the wound in his thigh and gave him an anti-tetanus injection when we insisted. They said there wasn't anything else they could do until a doctor arrived in town. They didn't know when that would be.

While White lay on the operating table a little old lady with white hair—I think she was an English missionary—came over and said, in a professional bedside manner, "Does the poor boy speak English?" When we told her he did, she said to him, "My dear boy, wouldn't you like me to stand beside you and talk English for half an hour?"

White groaned. She thought it was the pain. We knew it was because the very idea of a woman, however fine her motives, standing there chattering small talk to him for half an hour in a professional bedside manner was too much even to contemplate. All he wanted was a chance to rest and maybe sleep and forget his troubles. So we took the old lady down the hall and asked her about the other patients, and she said, "Come and see my Australians." We went into the big ward room and the Australians acted as if they were pretty glad to see someone who didn't want to get sentimental and maudlin about them. Most of them were in bad shape, and some of them were going to die before sunset, but they were a cheerful lot. We smoked a cigarette with them and talked about the things they wanted to talk about, and then we went off into the town.

We wanted rest more than anything else, and so we rented a room in the Hotel Belvidere, which was on the main street, facing the water front. It was in the Belvidere that I discovered that White wasn't the only one who had been shot up by the Messerschmitt. I couldn't get my trousers off because they seemed glued to my right leg. Then I noticed that the cloth was stiff with caked blood and that there were two neat holes right through the cloth. So that was why my right leg had felt asleep and stiff!

We had been in bed just forty-three minutes when the visitors arrived. It sounded as if there were at least ten or fifteen of them. When they started dropping their bombs the Belvidere shook like I once saw a big pine tree shake in a New England hurricane. Glass from the broken windows flew all over the place. I ran out into the hall. So did a girl in the opposite room. We bumped into each other. She started jabbering in Greek about the raid. She seemed to be afraid the roof was going to collapse on us because we were on the top floor.

She was one of the prettiest girls I'd seen in all the Balkans. Even the expression of terror on her face didn't detract from her beauty. We had been standing there almost a full minute dodging falling plaster and pieces of glass when I suddenly saw a new expression cross her face. There was a little lull in the bombing. Now she suddenly realized that she had been talking to a completely nude man. She gave a little scream and dashed back into her room. I had forgotten myself all about the proprieties. I really hadn't realized I was naked. And anyway it wasn't anything to get hysterical about. But I was shivering with cold, so I went back and put on some clothes, and we all checked out of the Belvidere without even paying our bill for the forty-three minutes of rest, because the whole hotel staff had fled.

I was worried about White and the hospital, because hospitals are so often targets in air raids, and we wandered down there. Now we could see what the planes were aiming at. A train had apparently just pulled into the depot. Every car had a red cross painted on the roof. The Stukas were screaming down and dropping incendiary bombs smack on the crosses. There must have been about thirty cars. Even though we were more than half a mile away we could hear the screaming of the wounded men who were being killed and cremated inside those twenty or thirty cars. We could also hear little explosions when the air wasn't full of bigger noises like the noise wings make in a power dive. We decided the little explosions must be the shells in the rifles of the wounded men exploding when the heat of the fire set them off.

At the hospital the nurses were white-faced and tense. They knew they were about to experience the worst few hours of their lives. Hours that would be indelibly stamped on their minds for all time. They stood in the door of the hospital and waited for the parade to begin. While we stood there with them watching the black smoke that wood and clothes and human bodies send up when they burn, the old lady who seemed to be a missionary came running down the hall sobbing at the top of her voice. He just died. He just died in my arms. The poor Australian boy is dead.

But no one paid any attention, because just then the stretcher-bearers began to arrive.

I don't know how many wounded soldiers there were in that hospital train, but there must have been hundreds. There wasn't any ambulance in town, and so they had to carry the men on stretchers. A continuous line of stretchers with bodies coming up the right side of the main street and a continuous line of stretchers with nothing on them but blood stains going back the other side for more victims.

What was on the stretchers coming up from the train wasn't pretty to see and isn't pretty to write about now. Up in Bucharest during the Iron Guard revolution I had seen some good examples of what happens when mass passions are let loose. I had seen the body of a soldier who had been captured by the Iron Guard and drenched with gasoline and then set afire. People called that performance a proof of how bestial men of low mental caliber can be. They showed movies in Rumania of that human torch. Women fainted. Men had to leave the theater. Now this was just as bad, only on the grand scale. Not one human torch but hundreds. This time it was done by long distance. I suppose that makes it all right. If you burn a man to death by something you do up in the sky over his head, then that's nice clean warfare. Quite according to the rules. Anyway, it's easier on the man who's doing the job. He doesn't see what we saw as we stood in front of the hospital looking at what was on the stretchers.

It was foolish for them to bring most of those charred bodies to the hospital, because they had no life left in them. It only made the nurses vomit, and that made them less able than ever to do anything for the bodies that still had a spark of life left in them. I suppose wrapping bandages around stumps of legs and pieces of arms and split-open heads keeps the dirt out and does some good. But it all seemed so futile. Here were hundreds of amputation jobs, but there was no one to do any amputating. Here were hundreds of wounds that needed to be sterilized, treated, probed, but there were no doctors to do any of those things. Here were men who should have been given narcotics, because there is some limit to the suffering a human being can bear. But that handful of nurses just went on tying clean white cloths around filthy, torn human flesh.

I know it doesn't sound pretty. Well, it wasn't pretty. It made me damned sick inside my stomach. It made Hill say he guessed he'd walk around and try to find some way to get White out of town, because there wouldn't be a chance in the world of getting any more attention for a man who had merely been shot up a little with machine-gun bullets. But I wanted to stay. I thought I might be of some help. I did carry a few stretchers into the hospital and a few dead bodies out of the hospital. I did what I could to help keep up the morale and courage of those girls in their uniforms which weren't lettuce crisp and white any longer. But I guess maybe my real motive in staying there was to see if I could take it. Anyway, whatever it was, that afternoon in Corinth, Greece, I really found out something firsthand about war and the results of war and the price of war.

As fast as the stretchers arrived, the victims were rolled off onto the floor of the reception room, and then the stretcher-bearers were sent back for more. The room was soon two deep with bodies. For an hour, about all the nurses and interns could do was to try to keep the victims sorted out. They took a quick look at a man, and if he was dead or they decided he didn't have a chance, they made a motion with their thumbs, and someone hauled the victim out into the courtyard. Before long the courtyard began to fill up with the dead and the dying, all in one big heap. That courtyard scene was a little too much for anyone to stomach, and I tried to turn my back on it, but a Greek who somehow realized what my nationality was came running up to me. With gestures and a word or two of English he begged me to go with him into the courtyard because, he said, there was an American out there.

By the time we got to where he said he had left the American, other bodies had been hauled out and he couldn't find the corpse he wanted me to look at, and so I had to join in the hunt. I looked at each one of them. Ninety per cent of them might have been Chinese or Russian or Hottentot as far as I could tell from the condition of the bodies. And I couldn't find anyone who looked like an American among the other ten per cent.

I wish that the Greek hospital attendant hadn't taken me out there. I wish I hadn't heard the moaning and looked into the eyes of some of those men who weren't dead but who had been placed there among the dead because someone thought they didn't have a chance and weren't worth bothering with. After two years in the Balkans I was accustomed to people who held life cheaply. But this was too much. The eyes of those dying men were so damned accusing. They seemed to be saying words that had been said once in Gethsemane. My God, why hast thou forsaken me? They seemed to be accusing me and everyone else around us and the whole rotten world for doing this to them. For letting this happen to them.

I once looked into the eyes of an animal that had been cornered and shot by a hunter. I was glad then that I wasn't the hunter. The eyes made such terrible accusations. The eyes of these men in the Corinth hospital yard were just like the eyes of that animal. Only I wasn't the one they should have been looking at with all that hate and fear and terror. They should have been looking into the faces of those men who were still in the sky over our heads pulling levers and playing a game called war. I thought, I wish I could get one of those pilots down out of the clouds and make him spend the rest of eternity just looking into the eyes of these victims of his. Yes, and listening to the moans, which cut deep into the soul of anyone who stood there helpless, the way I did. Death rattles? The courtyard echoed with death rattles. Death rattles are not pleasant things to hear.

In some ways the smell was worse than the noise. All Corinth was permeated with the smell of burning human flesh. Human flesh burns with a sickening sweet smell. It's a smell you never forget. I tried to breathe through my mouth so I wouldn't have to get that stench up my nose. It was just like the smell at the Dunning Insane Asylum fire. That was in Chicago, back in the twenties. It was my first big newspaper story. A lot of lunatics had been trapped in a dining room and cremated. This smell in Corinth was just like that smell at Dunning. But you could take a taxi and get away from the smell back in Dunning. Here in Corinth we couldn't get away from it. The smell seeped into every corner of the city. Even after we left Corinth the smell seemed to follow us.

Maybe I would have stayed on in Corinth if there had been anything helpful to do, but we were all just in the way. There wasn't room left in the hospital for the people who were trying to work there. And I didn't even know how to make a simple bandage. Therefore, I joined Hill and Atherton in the hunt for some way of getting White on to another hospital where we could get attention for him. We wanted to go to Athens, of course. Finally we found a young R.A.F. officer who wanted to go there, too. He went out to try to beg a truck from someone.

It was almost twilight now. The Stukas had gone home. The pilots by now were probably sitting around their mess hall congratulating one another on a job well done. Twenty or thirty carloads of men set on fire. Hundreds of Greek soldiers who wouldn't ever fire another rifle at the enemy again. Neat work. You pull a lever and that's all there is to it. Science takes care of the rest. The progress of civilization has made all these wonders possible. Civilization, isn't it grand? You pull a lever and you cremate twenty or thirty carloads of your fellow human beings. And I used to get furious, when I was a poultry farmer in New

Hampshire, because hens were so uncivilized that sometimes they went cannibalistic and pecked one another to death! Now, as I stood on the edge of the Gulf of Corinth, looking out over the clean blue water, boiling with contempt for my fellow human beings, I thought how much more cannibalistic we are than those hens I used to curse.

The sun, as it went over the horizon in the west, was brilliant red. The flames, which were still going up from the burning hospital train in the east, seemed like a reflection. The air was still. The evening was warm. I was far enough away from the hospital so that I couldn't hear the groaning and moaning. My back was to the hospital so that I couldn't see anything. I could see only clean blue water, and beyond the water green hills. As long as I looked in that direction the world seemed at peace for the moment. It had been a hell of a day. This morning the machine-gunning of our troop train. This afternoon the bombing of the hospital train. But it was all over for another few hours, because the Greeks in Corinth had told me that the enemy pilots always knocked off work at sunset so that they could get back to their bases by dusk.

I was staring blankly across the water when I saw the formation sail in. There were about ten big planes in the squadron. There wasn't a sound from any of their motors. They were just coasting along. As silent as a hawk when he glides down on an air wave. I was perplexed by the ten planes, because I didn't know the British or the Greeks had that many. I hadn't seen a British plane anywhere in the Balkans up to now. And I had understood that the Greek planes had nearly all been shot down. I thought, I wonder why these big fellows weren't here this afternoon to fight off those damned Stukas?

It never occurred to me that this was an enemy squadron. Enemy planes wouldn't fly that low or come in such a mass, because right across the gulf there were a whole line of machine-gun nests and anti-aircraft batteries. I had seen them in action all afternoon. The gulf was only about a mile wide at this point. The planes were just skimming the surface of the water. They were within half a mile of the batteries. They couldn't be enemy planes, because they had already passed two or three of those gun nests and nothing had happened.

Then the show began! Some alert gunner woke up. He began firing point blank at the squadron. Then every gun within miles started going off. But it was too late. Now the squadron was over the bridge. The bridge that connected the Peloponnesos with the Greek mainland. Now they were unloading. I thought I saw pieces of the bridge fly into the air and nearly hit the planes. I did see the bombers go on over the Corinth Canal and let the rest of their cargo drop where it would do the most harm. I also saw them drop a few odd bombs on the burning hospital cars. Then they climbed fast into the clouds and went back home.

The R.A.F. officer said this last raid had cooked our goose. We couldn't get to Athens now because the only bridge over to the mainland was destroyed. We decided to head for Argos. Argos is about the largest town in the Peloponnesos. It's a long way south from Corinth. We all figured that things would be quiet down there. He knew that Argos had a hospital, and he thought maybe it had a doctor. Maybe we could get some attention there, as long as the war hadn't progressed that far south. We got a nurse in the Corinth hospital to let us take a cot with a spring on it and we used that as a stretcher for Leigh White. We started off while it was still light and we had the road to ourselves. We had to go slowly because of the bumps and White's pain.

As soon as it got dark we found we were in a caravan of hundreds of British lorries. Huge lorries. Lorries packed with Anzac troops. Where they suddenly came from I don't know. When we got on a hill we could look back and see the road black with the parade of British lorries. It suddenly dawned on us what was happening. The British were evacuating Greece! These were some of the three hundred thousand soldiers who had been sent up from the Middle East to help the Greeks and the Yugoslavs. This was the army Pappas had told us about when he was up in Belgrade. But now they were in flight. They were heading south to get ships and to sail away. The Balkan War must be nearly over. Greece must be collapsing fast. The parade to the sea had begun.

We crawled along now at a snail's pace. Officers on motorcycles scooted in and out of the column barking savage reprimands whenever a driver used his lights. The troops who were getting ready to leave were weary, frazzled out. They bore all the signs of having been through hell. Their faces were grimy. Their uniforms were often in tatters. Some had rifles, others had lost them. Some had steel helmets, others had left them behind. Some had full packs, others were traveling with nothing. But their morale wasn't gone yet. Occasionally we heard singing coming from inside one of the covered trucks. When the column stopped for a minute or two because some truck had gone off into a ditch or had turned over when it ᵣissed a curve, the men shouted greetings to one another. Their voices were weary voices, but not beaten voices. They were tired and they were part of a defeated army, but they personally hadn't been defeated.

Once when we stopped I walked up to the next truck and got a light from an Australian and passed around some cigarettes I had wangled out of a café owner in Corinth. That's how we got talking. One of the Australians said something about the two divisions that had been fighting in this Balkan War. I asked some questions about the rest of the divisions.

"Rest? What do you mean, rest?" he asked.

And that was the first time i found out that there had been not three hundred thousand British troops in Greece; only two divisions. One division of Australians, one division of New Zealanders, and about ten thousand miscellaneous English and Canadian soldiers attached to units like the R.A.F., the ambulance corps, and headquarters companies. Forty thousand in all, the men told me. Forty, not three hundred. Forty thousand all together. I didn't believe them at first. I asked the men in other trucks. I asked dozens of soldiers. I checked up on the figures later in Argos, and still later in Crete, and after that in Cairo. The figure wasn't ever exactly the same. Some said forty-one thousand, some said thirty-nine thousand, but they all agreed that there were just two full divisions. And when I told them about our figures of one hundred, then two hundred, and then three hundred thousand, they just laughed.

I was stunned. Probably just as stunned as the Yugoslavs were when they learned the grim truth. I know, because later I talked to some Yugoslav General Staff officers in Cairo. They told me how stunned they had been. They told me they had believed the officially-denied-but-unofficially-confirmed stories that were sent up to Belgrade about the British strength in planes and men.

Forty thousand. No wonder we hadn't seen any British help arrive for the Yugoslavs. No wonder Yugoslavia was able to hold out only ten days. And no wonder what was left of the British Expeditionary Force was fleeing now toward the sea. Even three hundred thousand men with a real air force would have had a tough job holding back that sea of men and machines that I had seen sweeping down like a wild cascade from Germany through Hungary, Rumania, and Bulgaria into Yugoslavia and Greece. Forty or fifty thousand against millions of German soldiers who had no other job on their hands at the moment than to take the Balkans at all costs.

The last part of that drive was tough. The R.A.F. officer was having a lot of trouble keeping the truck on the road.

"I didn't want to tell you," he said, "but the only reason they let me take this piece of junk was because it had been condemned. The two front wheels point in opposite directions and the front axle is broken. I hope we make it. But if we don't, I don't want you to think it's because I can't drive."

After what we'd been through already that day a little thing like an automobile accident wouldn't have bothered any of us very much, but the road was almost as full of curves as those roads back in Bosnia and Serbia, and part of the way we were going through steep hills, so that the officer had a real job on his hands.

As we got near Argos our way was lighted by bright red flames reflected in the sky. We tried for an hour to figure out what it was. Then, once when we got stopped in a traffic jam, somebody beside the road told us. It was a burning ship in Argos Bay. The British *Ulster Prince*. It had run aground and then been dive-bombed by the Germans. It served as a beacon for us, and it also illuminated some rather unpleasant sights along the road-side. Abandoned British lorries. Many of them full of machine-gun bullets. Some of them wrecked by bombs. Some of them stained with blood. The remnants of a previous caravan. I was glad, when I saw those wrecks, that we had made our trip under the cloak of darkness. And I understood why the officers on the motorcycles had been so insistent about our not using lights. Apparently the Germans knew all about this flight of the British army to the sea, the evacuation from Greece.

"It looks as if the story's still following us," Hill said.

"Yes, aren't we the lucky newspapermen," someone else said with rather obvious sarcasm.

We got into Argos at midnight. We stopped. The other trucks went right on. They kept coming through all night long. The narrow streets of Argos thundered with the dull noise that British lorries make. Occasionally we heard the muffled voices of men when their machines got tangled up in a traffic jam or broke down or rammed into one another. But it was an efficiently run evacuation; we could see that. This wasn't anything like the flight of the Greeks. None of that helter-skelter, every-man-for-himself business. No breakdown of discipline and organization. The British were whipped again, but they were still functioning as an army.

We carried White into the little hospital and they dressed his wound again and put some iodine on my leg and Atherton's knee. Then they said the first thing in the morning the one doctor in Argos would be around and he'd get to work on White. Just to be sure no one else got taken care of first, we left White on the operating table, covered with a blanket and sleeping with the help of some medicine.

Then the rest of us curled up on the floor of the ward and

went to sleep. The hospital must have been full of fleas, because it was their bites that woke me up. I looked at my watch. I had been asleep just ten minutes. Then I heard the sound that kept me from going to sleep again that night and that still makes real sleep impossible. It was nothing but the whimpering of a child. The low, muffled whimpering of a child with its face buried in a pillow. But that little voice will always be the symbol of war to me. I guess it got inside of me so deeply because I was so exhausted that night. I think all the misery of war was wrapped up in that child's whimpering. When a nurse came by flashing a torch around the room I got up on one elbow and saw where the voice came from. She was about five years old. A pretty child, with jet black hair. But there wasn't anything pretty about her right arm. It hung in black, tattered shreds. Just as if the hand had been chewed off by some animal. I had seen far worse sights a few hours before in Corinth. Some day I may forget those charred bodies in Corinth. But I shall never forget the arm of that little girl who lay in the same hospital with me in Argos. And I'm afraid that her whimpering will always pound through my brain. Afraid? No, I'm glad, because I know that as long as I hear that whimpering I shall be aware of what war really is. And that seems important to me.

I called the nurse over. "What," I asked, "does she say?"

"She sobs for her mother," the nurse answered me, rather coldly. She had to be cold. I knew that. I knew that if she wasn't cold and hard she'd have to run from all this refuse of war.

"Can't you send for the mother?" I asked naïvely.

"No, the whole family was snuffed out in the raid. All except this one."

So I tried to bury my head in my arms. I even put my fingers in my ears so I wouldn't hear. But those cowardly tricks didn't work. I still heard. Some time along about morning I dozed off for a few minutes. But I was glad to wake up again, because during those few minutes pieces of human bodies swirled around in my mind's eye, like pieces of glass swirl around when you twist a kaleidoscope.

We got up at four-thirty, and Atherton found that there was a British ambulance unit not far out in the country. We sent a New Zealand soldier on a motorcycle to ask one of the doctors to come in and look at White. The dispatch rider brought back a promise that the doctor would appear at nine o'clock. But before nine o'clock ever came, the Nazi planes came. They didn't do a great deal of damage in that first raid, and so as soon as it was over we carried White across the town to the home of a man who owned an X-ray machine. He didn't have the right kind of film and his apparatus was almost an antique, and it took him a couple of hours to make a lot of small pictures and patch them together.

The rest of us waited in the courtyard of the house. It was pleasant there, between raids. The family sat around under lemon and olive trees sipping sweet Turkish coffee while a neighbor who had once been in America told them how proud they should be to be offering sweet Turkish coffee and Greek hospitality to men who came from the great United States. While he talked I lay on freshly cut grass and sniffed the warm earthy aroma. I thought of Bosnia and its fields of blood red poppies and yellow buttercups. I thought of the heavy scent of lilacs in Corfu. I thought of all the pleasant things I had seen and smelled in these last twenty days, and I tried not to think of the other things I had seen and smelled.

Finally we left White at the X-ray station and said we'd be back in a few minutes. We went to the hospital to talk to the local doctor about the operation and to see if the British doctor had come. We were just going into the hospital when the big raid began. They may have been aiming at the hospital itself or they may have been after the railroad yards just behind the hospital. Everywhere in that part of the world the people who planned the location of hospitals seemed to manage it so that these buildings, which should have been as far away as possible from military targets, were always right next door to a barracks or a railroad station or a munitions depot. Anyway the bombs were falling all around the neighborhood. One of the nurses asked us to help them carry the patients out on their cots. Most of them were Anzac soldiers. We put them down the street a way, under some trees.

Then we got a little jittery ourselves and jumped into a slit trench just behind the hospital. All the nurses were in there, and a lot of Greek soldiers. The trench was about ten feet deep and just about as wide as a man. The planes were all Stukas, and they were landing those bombs right where they wanted to land them. This was worse than the Srpski Kralj bombing, because we could actually see the planes as they drove at us. I remember the first one that came down. Its wings were screeching, but that wasn't enough. It had a siren too, just in case the screeching didn't impress us. I don't know how many thousand feet high it was when it started, but it was just a dot in the sky. Then the noise began and the dot got bigger and bigger. I lay curled up on the bottom of the trench watching. Atherton was beside me.

"It's got our number," Atherton said.

I couldn't say anything. I was too busy watching and listening. The plane was driving its noise right into my brain. Just the way a hammer drives a nail into a block of wood. I could feel the noise splitting my head into two pieces. Down, down, down. Right at us. Then I heard another noise, and I knew it was the bomb coming. Someone had told me the bomb itself travels faster than the noise. That's a lie. You hear the noise first. I heard it. And I knew the bomb was coming right after it. Right at the slit trench. Right at Atherton and me. I stuck my head down and tried to force it into the dirt on the bottom of the trench. Then I heard the bomb land. It landed ten feet away from the trench. Right on top of a garage full of trucks. I looked up in time to see pieces of the trucks flying over our heads. The air was full of pieces of tires and wheels and roofing.

Atherton and I were both taking a deep breath when we heard the second plane diving down. He was headed right for us too. Only he was coming faster than the other one. I ducked again. I heard the bomb land. It seemed even closer. Then something hit me on the back of the neck and head. A million blows right on the back of the skull. I thought, why did they have to do that? My head's already split in two pieces.

Then everything went blank for a second. After that my head began to break into little pieces and I realized that people were running back and forth over me. I could feel the steel of hobnailed boots on my skull, but I couldn't see and I couldn't yell, because my face and head were buried in dirt and stones. I could hardly breathe until Atherton dug me out. The soldiers were still running up and down in the trench like madmen, yelling and cursing and shaking their fists up at the sky. I spit dirt out of my mouth and wiped it out of my eyes.

Then I saw what had happened. The second bomb had hit a big R.A.F. truck loaded with oxygen tanks for the hospital. It also had blown back into the trench on top of us a lot of the stones and dirt they had left in a pile when they dug the trench. Just then we saw fire. The oxygen tanks were burning, and so was the truck. There would probably be a hell of an explosion when the fire got to the gas tank, and so we climbed out of the trench.

The planes were still up there, but we walked around a little anyway. The hospital was a mess. All the windows were broken and all the doors were blown off. Some of the wounded men out under the trees had been wounded again. The nurses, who had been so brave, had finally lost their grip. We saw them running toward the hills on the edge of the city. Other bombs had sent houses and shops all over Argos tumbling down into the streets. Several young hospital interns were taking newly wounded people into a basement air-raid shelter, which was going to be the dressing station now. I wondered why Argos had built its hospital near a railroad yard in the first place. And why someone hadn't thought of using the air-raid shelter for a dressing station before this? Why aren't all hospitals in war zones put underground?

There wasn't a trace of the city's only doctor. Why in the hell wasn't he working over these mangled bodies?

And why had the weather been perfect during the Yugoslav
war, and then stormy when we were fighting our way down the
Adriatic and wanted good weather, and now so perfect again?
The German pilots for three days had had just the kind of a
sky all pilots pray for.

We suddenly remembered White and we started running for
the X-ray man's house. On the way we saw the whole family
racing up the street toward us. We tried to stop them to ask
where White was, but they were panicky. They had blankets
under their arms, and one of them had an antique clock. They
ran right past us without stopping. When we got to their home
we realized what had upset them. Bombs had landed all around
the place. The olive tree and the lemon tree were flat on the
ground. Everything in the house, even the antique X-ray
machinery, was smashed. The green grass I had enjoyed smelling
was covered with rubble now. There was no trace of White, but
a man across the street made us understand that he had seen
White being taken to the private clinic of the doctor who was
supposed to be attached to the hospital that was now in ruins.

We finally found the clinic all right, but I wish we never had,
because out in front on the sidewalk lay what had once been a
man. We heard him before we saw him. But this time the sight
was worse than the sound. His screams turned your blood cold,
but wait until I tell you what he looked like. Both his hands had
been blown off at the wrists. One leg was in shreds. A piece of
shrapnel had ripped open his stomach, and a yard or two of his
intestines were hanging out. He also had blood gushing from
his head and foaming from his mouth. Yet he screamed. He
screamed like a maniac. Not just a noise, but words. Words
that he kept repeating over and over and over again.

"We're dead, Atherton," I said, grabbing onto his arm to
steady myself. "We're dead and we're in hell. This isn't Greece,
this is hell!"

I wasn't trying to say something clever. I meant it. I really
thought as I looked down at that poor piece of a man that we
must be in hell. Maybe it was the blow on the back of my own

head that made me a little crazy myself. Anyway, when we got inside the clinic and the screaming wasn't so loud, I got a grip on myself. White was in there, and the doctor's wife said her husband was going to operate on White as soon as it got dark and the raids stopped.

"But can't your husband also do something about that man on the sidewalk?" I asked her.

"We can't stop to work on people like that," she said. "That man will be dead in a few minutes. There are dozens, maybe hundreds whose lives we may be able to save."

We went out, and then I noticed a human hand on a plate on the grass. It looked like a surrealist painting. A dirty, bloody hand on a clean white plate. It must have been one of the hands the screaming man had lost. But why on a plate? The doctor or someone with a pair of scissors probably had stopped long enough to snip it off, but why put it on a plate? Why leave the plate on the grass?

Just then a British ambulance came down the street. I had an idea. I ran out and stopped it.

"What in the hell do you want?" the driver yelled. "We're busy!"

I said, "Just give me three grains of morphine tablets for a friend of mine."

"Three grains would kill a man," the driver said.

"I know they would. That's the idea."

"But that's against regulations!"

"So what? Look over at that fellow on the sidewalk. Is it still against regulations?"

The driver looked over at the fellow on the sidewalk. He hesitated a second. Then he shook his head again.

"I can give you only three quarters of a grain. But that's enough to stop his pain."

While the ambulance was driving off, Atherton and I got a glass of water and forced the tablet down what was left of the man's mouth. I was sure he swallowed it. Then Atherton said we hadn't seen Hill for a long time and that we had better

look for him. We found him in the basement air-raid shelter.
Then I remembered that Leigh White had been worried about
leaving his passport and all his papers in the hospital and I went
back to look for them. Someone had moved two or three of the
wounded Anzac soldiers back into what was left of the hospital,
but there was no one taking care of them. One of them saw
me and hollered to get some help and get them out again,
because the hospital was on fire. It really wasn't, but flames
from the burning R.A.F. truck were spewing up and it looked
as if the hospital might go any minute. I ran down to the main
street and got some British officers to help me carry the cots.

After that I went back to the shelter to rest and then remembered I still hadn't found White's passport, and so I returned
to the hospital and was just walking through the corridor of
that shell of a building when a bomb landed right outside the
front door. The repercussion, the rush of air through the corridor, picked me right off my feet, like a gale picks up a leaf,
and the next thing I knew I had been thrown against a car
parked out in the hospital yard.

My nerve was completely gone now. I was all through. I got
down to the air-raid shelter and told Atherton to keep an eye on
me because I felt strange. The thing that finally sent me off
were the noises down in that cellar. They had brought the
screaming man there, but no one was paying any attention to
him. The morphine apparently hadn't had any effect on him.
I asked an intern who knew English what those words were he
kept screaming. I recognized them as the same words he had
been saying all day.

"He's trying," the intern explained, "to get his hands into
his pocket to get some Greek money. That's why he thrashes
his arms around. But of course he doesn't have any hands. He's
hollering to someone to take his money and go to a chemist
shop and get him some aspirin to stop the funny feeling in his
head."

I began to have a funny feeling in my own head.

Then I saw a child lying beside me with only a stump of a

leg. She was bleeding badly. No one had done anything for her
either. She was about four. She seemed to be all alone. Then
there were several babies who had been badly injured. Their
mothers probably were roaming the streets looking for them
right now. A man who had been hit on the head by a block of
stone moaned and foamed at the mouth. Another man had had
his lungs crushed, and every time he breathed it was like the
noise when you drag your fingernail across a blackboard.

The last thing I remember doing was trying to get to the door
for air. But there was another raid going on, and someone pulled
me back.

Atherton told me afterwards that I raved like a madman for
an hour, completely out of my head. During that hour Atherton
and Hill took turns watching me while the other went out between raids and made more arrangements about White. They
saw the doctor several times. He renewed his wife's pledge that
he would operate as soon as it got dark. They explained to the
doctor that the rest of us were going to move on unless he
thought we could be of some assistance to White. He told them
we should go. Then they asked him if there was any possibility
of taking White with us if we stayed another day or two, and
he said he doubted it. The bullets were in too painful a position.
They wouldn't be able to move White for a long time.

It was late in the afternoon when we decided to try to get
an hour's rest and then push on toward the sea. On the edge of
Argos a mountain rose to a great height. There wasn't a single
building on that mountain except a monastery near the top.
Atherton and Hill decided that if we had the energy to climb
the mountain we would be safe from bombings and we could
sleep up there for a while and be a little fresher for whatever lay
ahead of us.

I wasn't sorry to get out of that improvised hospital in a cellar
in the heart of what was left of Argos. It's foolish to call it even
an improvised hospital. It really was nothing but a morgue,
except that most of the victims hadn't had sense enough to die
yet.

When I said that out loud, Atherton said, "Cheer up, they'll probably all be dead soon."

It wasn't a hospital at all, because the doctor never came down there, and there weren't any nurses around town any more. And no medicine. And no bandages. Nothing. Nothing but four walls, a thick ceiling, and a concrete floor. It was really just a place where people could die with company.

There were three or four young Anzacs down there. Some of those same boys we'd been moving around all day. Just before we left the cellar, a British ambulance driver came in and said, "The last evacuation ship leaves tonight, boys. We're going to take along all of you who're in any fit shape to be moved."

An old New Zealand cowpuncher lying on his back, quiet as a mouse but with agony written all over his face, spoke up in a feeble voice, "How about me, Doc?"

The ambulance driver looked over his wounds. His body was torn all to pieces by shrapnel. His insides were in bad shape.

"Sorry, Jack," the ambulance driver said softly, "but I'm afraid you can't be moved. You'll have to stay behind."

Before anyone else could say anything, a handsome young Australian spoke up. He'd been standing beside Jack's bed. He hadn't ever left the cowpuncher's side. We had first seen him the night before in the hospital. Then during the raids he had been one of those who helped us move the cots in and out. But he never got far out of sight of his New Zealand friend. We'd commented on the two of them earlier in the day. There must have been twenty years' difference in their ages, but there was some great bond between them.

"You mean the two of us will have to stay behind," the Australian said. He didn't say it with any braggadocio. He said it quietly. He was really saying it to the man on the cot, who apparently couldn't move a muscle without torturous pains sweeping through his whole body. The man on the cot smiled and held out his hand. The younger fellow grabbed it and shook it gently. The ambulance driver moved on, arranging for the evacuation of the others.

When we got our typewriters and knapsacks together we said good-by to the Anzacs. The Australian walked to the door with us.

"I'll probably be getting captured tomorrow," he said, in his deep but unemotional voice. "But I can't desert my pal, Jack, at this stage of the game. The doc tells me he hasn't but a day or two to live. Maybe he'll die tonight. He's got lead all through him. If I left him now he'd pass out cold right away. So I've got to stick by him. But, say, fellows, how about taking a letter to my family for me? It may be a damned long time before they hear from me again. I don't think the Germans let their prisoners write letters to the folks back home. So just drop this in a mailbox somewhere, will you?"

We took the letter and we left the hospital in the cellar that held so little of life and so much of horror. We felt like cowards. We felt rotten inside. But after all, we weren't soldiers. We were just leeches. Reporters trying to suck headlines out of all this death and suffering. That's what I was thinking about as we started to plod up the mountain. The Nazi planes were still banging away at Argos. At poor little Argos down in the valley Argos, which was suffering today the tortures of the damned.

CHAPTER FOURTEEN

Evacuation from Greece

———◆———

WE COULDN'T EVEN REMEMBER when it was we had last eaten, but it seemed like months ago, so that when we passed a Greek bakery on the way to the mountain, the warm smell of bread in an oven made us forget that we'd better hurry. The three of us stood in front of the bakery just breathing in lungs full of the hot air. Food was as scarce here in Argos as everywhere else. The owner of the bakery came out and asked if we were Americans or English, and when we said we were both, he grinned. Then he glanced around to be sure no one was looking and slipped us a large loaf. When we finally got to the mountaintop we split it into three chunks and started in on it. It was white bread. The first white bread any of us had seen in months. Even before the Balkan War began there wasn't any white bread. Some of those countries in southeastern Europe hadn't had white bread for a year or two.

It's a common sight in countries like Rumania and Hungary to see a peasant going down the street with a loaf of bread under one arm. Occasionally he pulls off a chunk and stuffs it into his mouth. Then he pulls an onion from a pocket and takes a nibble. For two years I had watched peasants living like that, on bread and onions. I used to feel sorry for them. Now I didn't any more. No sirloin steak or cake or caviar ever tasted as good as that loaf of white bread did. It was a good object lesson in comparative values.

We lay on the top of the mountain chewing bread and looking down into smoking, dying Argos. There were still German planes having their fun with Argos. But it was all remote enough so that we could feel now like spectators in a gallery watching a drama of life and death that meant no more to us than a drama on a Broadway stage. That's the way it's supposed to be with a newspaperman. He's always supposed to be the disinterested observer. Remote from the story. Personally unconcerned. Above and beyond the story. That's the only way a newspaperman can work on the comedies and tragedies that make up the front page and not crack up emotionally. He mustn't ever give a damn about the hero or the villain in his piece. He mustn't like the hero or hate the villain. He must deaden his own emotions. Otherwise he'll suffer all the time. He'll suffer with the victims of every single tragedy he covers.

On the mountaintop the noises that airplanes create out of silence and the noises buildings and people make when things fall out of the sky on them were dulled by distance. I thought, this is as close as anyone ought to get to war. Why can't all the people in the world sit on hilltops while planes do their stuff on empty cities? If we have to have war, why can't we be as intelligent as they were back in those old days when each army chose its best swordsman and the two rival champions met in a clearing and battled to the death, with victory in the whole war going to the army whose champion won? The issues today could be decided just as well by letting the planes bomb empty cities, while the people sat on hillsides and watched. Then there never would be men with their guts sticking out of their bellies and children with arms and legs blown off.

Those are the things I was thinking as I looked down into the valley where Argos lay. Hill and Atherton had gone to sleep, and I might have gone to sleep too if I hadn't felt ants crawling on my arms. I started to move to some antless spot, but the activity of those thousands of crawling black insects suddenly fascinated me. They were building a new home. I could pick out those who were directing the job and the ones who were doing transport duty and then the actual construction gangs. They were working in perfect harmony. In clocklike rhythm. With Ford assembly line efficiency. They reminded me of the German army I had seen in Rumania and Bulgaria. Hitler's generals must have studied ants, I thought. But the difference was that German efficiency had death and destruction as its sole object. The labor and efficiency of these ants was directed toward construction. Toward making the life of their community more pleasant, more comfortable. Toward building houses and roads. I looked closely to see if any of them were killing one another over such questions as who should have this or that piece of territory. Maybe there were battles going on, but I couldn't see any. Ants. We step on them. But maybe, I thought, after we intelligent humans wipe one another completely off the face of the earth with our guns and our planes and our other products of intelligence and civilization, the ants will still be here, building and constructing.

This may sound like schoolboy moralizing to you, but I'm telling you just what went through my head, that's all. And my head was pretty sick after that day down in the valley.

Anyway, it was a good thing those ants kept me awake, because otherwise I might not have seen and heard the planes just over the other side of the mountain. They were sailing high over a peaceful country valley. I shook Hill and Atherton. They were annoyed at being awakened.

"Planes!" I yelled.

"So what?" Hill said sleepily. "They won't bomb three men on top of a mountain."

But something about that squadron of a dozen or twenty planes fascinated me. They look different from other war planes. I realize now that it was because they were the first fleet of transport planes I had ever seen in action. They were flying in perfect formation. There wasn't even a machine gun to annoy them, because the batteries in Argos on the other side of our mountain couldn't see them. Then I suddenly grabbed Hill's arm and pointed. We stared with wide eyes as the parachutists started to drop. We knew then that it was time to get moving. There wouldn't be any more sleep for any of us now. Parachutists! The Nazis were dropping parachutists in the south of Greece. Greece surely must be about through now.

We got down that mountain in a hurry. In Argos we could see that the British evacuation was nearly over. But stragglers were still coming in. Argos had been the chief crossroads of that evacuation. Columns of trucks had been pouring down into Argos for days from all parts of Greece. The trucks were full of war-weary Australian and New Zealand boys who had been fighting an amazing rear-guard action against the Germans. When the trucks got to Argos they branched out. Some went down the west coast of Argos Bay. Some went down the east coast. For nearly twenty-four hours we had watched them. A truck would come roaring into town. The driver would shout out a number, like S234, to a British officer standing at the cross-roads. The officer would say, "Bear right all the way," or he would say, "Take the next left and keep going."

We picked up one good story before we left Argos that afternoon. I mean good in a newspaper sense. A hundred and fifty British lorries had been heading into Argos. They had to cross a flat strip of land just north of the city. We had crossed that same spot the night before, and it had made me think of my native Illinois. Flat. No trees. The road straight as a ruler. But the poor bastards in those one hundred and fifty trucks I'm talking about had to travel by day, because the Germans were so close on their heels that they couldn't wait to take advantage of the dark. The Stukas were waiting for them when they hit the strip of Illinois territory. When the Stukas came diving down, the Anzacs took to the ditches. But for half an hour the German planes worked on the big British lorries. When they got through with their bombing and machine-gunning there wasn't a single truck in the convoy in workable enough condition to carry the wounded to a hospital and the dead to a morgue.

And now there were parachutists in the neighborhood!

Hill was the freshest of the three of us and he said he'd run back to say good-by to White and see if he was all right. Atherton went off to try to rent, buy, or steal three bicycles. While I stood waiting for them I saw a tough-looking Australian soldier eying me. Finally he called to a Greek gendarme, and they came over and arrested me. I was arrested, they said, as a fifth columnist. A foreign agent. I showed them my passport, but it didn't impress them. Finally I got angry. Damned angry!

"Listen," I said to the tough Australian, "I've been hauling your wounded Anzac soldiers in and out of that bombed hospital all day. I risked my life a couple of times to save some of your Australian buddies. Now for Christ sake stop this nonsense and call off your bloodhound. I'm no foreign agent. Even if I do wear a beard."

He understood that kind of language and he ended up by apologizing.

"No offense meant, Yank, but we've got to be careful. The country's full of them, you know. Where are you going?"

I told him we wanted to get out of Greece. If Atherton didn't locate some bicycles we'd have to walk. We were going to walk to some little fishing village and try to rent, buy, or steal a small boat. Then we'd hop-skip-and-jump from Greek island to Greek island and try to make Turkey. Probably Smyrna.

"It's a long walk," he said. "If you don't find bicycles, I'll give you a tip. A couple of miles south on this road we've been abandoning a lot of our lorries. They're all either alongside the road or in a thicket of trees. Help yourself. No one will care."

When Hill came back and Atherton arrived with the bad news that the bicycles he had had his eye on were locked in a shop with steel shutters which he couldn't break open, we started off on foot.

We began seeing abandoned lorries a few miles out of town.

But they either didn't have ignition keys, or the tires had been shot full of holes, or the gas tanks were empty, or something else was wrong. We wasted a lot of time trying to get some of them to run.

When it got dark, the road filled up with hundreds of lorries all jammed with haggard soldiers. During a traffic tangle a pleasant young Australian truck driver offered to pick us up. We threw our knapsacks and typewriters into the back and then hopped in ourselves. We bounced around in that truck for an hour or more. The soldiers were all young. Just boys. That was probably why they were so cheerful. They had had a month of hell. Now they were going to leave it all behind. Tonight they would sail away from this country they had tried so vainly to defend. Thousands of their friends lay dead in the mountain passes of Greece, but they were still alive to fight another day. So they sang. They sang all their Australian favorites. The one they liked the best was "Waltzing Matilda." Then they sang about what they were going to do after they got out of the army. Between songs they talked about Australia and their girls and their plans for the future. Then they sang a lot of American songs. We were embarrassed when they sang "Marching Through Georgia," because they knew more of the words than we did.

We told the driver we wanted to get off at Myloi. We picked Myloi because it looked on the map as if it might be a sleepy little fishing village where, this late at night, we could steal a boat in the dark. We also chose Myloi because we had found out where the British evacuation ships were sailing from, and this wasn't one of the ports. We didn't want to get mixed up in that British evacuation, because we knew how little air support the British had and we had a hunch the evacuation ships were catching hell from the Stukas; that the Argos Bay exodus might be as bad as Dunkirk. Why get mixed up in anything like that? Our interest in saving our own necks was finally getting stronger than our interest in the story. These poor Anzacs didn't have any choice. We did have. We could get ourselves a little boat like the *Makedonka* and stage our own private evacuation. We even had a course charted on a map. All we needed was a boat, a sail, and some oars.

Suddenly the truck stopped on a deserted section of the road.

"We passed Myloi a couple of miles back," the driver shouted. "Sorry. I just realized it."

We hopped out and started plodding back those couple of miles. Then Russell Hill got the foolish idea of changing his socks. He had been saving one clean pair for what he called an emergency. Now, no matter how we argued, he was going to change his socks. Atherton and I said we'd walk on slowly ahead. We did. We walked for twenty minutes. Since Hill didn't catch up with us, we turned around and went back. We walked all the way to where we had left him. But there wasn't any trace of him. We turned around toward Myloi again.

For the next hour or so Atherton and I were stopped repeatedly by British and Greek soldiers with revolvers and bayoneted rifles. They popped out of shadows and ordered us to throw our hands up. All of them were tough. They didn't hide what it was all about. They were trying to round up parachutists dropped by the Germans during the afternoon. The few who hadn't already been executed. We looked suspicious to those patrols. We had black typewriter cases, which they were sure contained portable radios. And they looked with great suspicion at the knapsacks on our backs. Several young soldiers pointed to them and said significantly, "Parachutes, eh?"

I blew up once. "You idiot," I yelled at one young soldier, "did you ever see a parachutist who'd bailed out of a plane walking around with his parachute still neatly folded up on his back?"

My American passport wasn't much good either.

One British lieutenant said, "If I were a German parachutist I'd do just what you're doing. I'd get hold of an American passport and I'd say I was a New York newspaperman."

I don't know how many parachutists landed that afternoon. Rumor put the number as high as seven hundred. But I think most of them were rounded up and shot. Every time we heard a volley of rifle bullets off in the woods, Atherton and I would turn to each other and say, "Another parachutist biting the dust!"

We went down the road calling Hill's name every few minutes. That kept getting us in trouble with the patrols, but it was a good thing we had the idea, because finally we got a response to one of our calls. It was Hill's voice all right, but just as he started to yell something to us from the woods another voice said, "We'll shoot you on the spot if you don't shut up."

We scrambled over to where the voices came from, and after a lot of explaining Atherton got them to release Hill. I think Russell was more frightened then than when we were machine-gunned. I didn't blame him, but all we said to him was, "I hope you got your socks changed!"

We had missed each other because Hill had picked up a ride in a truck. The driver had refused to stop when they sailed by us on the dark road.

The three of us continued on toward Myloi. On the outskirts of the village we found a parked limousine. Behind the wheel sat a boy soldier so young I don't think he had even started to shave yet. He was studying a map. He told us he was connected with British G.H.Q. and was trying to get to the harbor at Myloi. We asked him to take us along and he told us to pile in. He didn't even ask our nationality, which was a relief.

We said, "Why Myloi?"

He said, rather subtlely, "Things are happening at Myloi harbor tonight."

When we got near the town we realized what he meant. British lorries were lined up as far as you could see. The dock in the little harbor was jammed with men. They were going off in small boats to Greek caïques and fishing schooners lying in the shadows out some distance from shore. It was another eerie scene. No lights. No loud talk. Great confusion. Much dashing around. A lot of commands barked in low voices.

"Tell your men to stand by their lorries," one officer yelled to another. The order was passed along.

"Tell your men to drain the oil from their crank cases."

That order was passed along.

Fifteen minutes later: "Tell your men to start their engines and run them at top speed."

"Tell your men to shoot the tires full of holes."

We heard the simultaneous cracking of hundreds of revolvers and rifles.

"Tell your men to drain the gas tanks."

Here was another set of sounds and smells we'd never forget. The noise of those racing automobile engines sounded like the noise a squadron of Stukas makes when it's getting ready to dive to the attack. The smell of those overheated cylinder blocks was like the smell of hell and brimstone. We looked down the road and saw dots of bright red gradually emerge out of the darkness. One red glow every ten or twenty feet. Blood red. We started to count them. But our eyes got fuzzy and we stopped. We had some strange thoughts as we watched a fortune in rolling stock being destroyed. Thousands of men and women in Britain had been risking their lives, working through air raids, to build this equipment. Sailors had risked their lives to get the trucks to Greece. Now they were being destroyed because they couldn't be taken along. The Germans would salvage them, of course, but they'd have to equip each truck with new tires, find gasoline, rebore cylinder blocks, and fit the engines with new pistons.

After the job was done, the truck drivers got into small boats and went off to the ships waiting in the dark. One by one the boats weighed anchor and slipped out into the night.

We also saw mounds of cigarettes, hundreds of thousands of cigarettes, and tons of foodstuff being destroyed. A lot of Greeks might starve in the next few months, but the British didn't dare let all these military supplies remain behind. The Germans were coming. The British argued that if the food and cigarettes fell into Nazi hands it wouldn't do the Greeks much good. Then we remembered that every few rods along the highways of Greece we had seen five-gallon cans of gasoline in piles, often twenty or thirty feet high. The gasoline would be destroyed, too. The highways of Greece tonight or tomorrow morning would be lined with fire. Vast wealth was being destroyed because another phase of the war had ended in failure.

Once during the evening there was quite a commotion on the dock. Everyone snapped to attention as a group of men came quickly from a big military car. At the head of them was a British army officer they all called "The General." I still don't know who he was, but he must have been very important. There were two young R.A.F. officers with him in clean, new uniforms. One on each side of him. They got into a motor launch, which took them out to a big Sunderland flying boat anchored in the harbor. A few minutes later the flying boat's engines were started, and then the ship sailed away into the black sky.

We got the story just by listening to the men on the dock talking. They laughed when they talked about it. Those R.A.F. boys were really girls. Two British nurses. Sisters, as the British call their nurses. They had been on the staff of a British hospital in Athens. All the rest of the British in Athens had been evacuated, but somehow everyone forgot about the dozen or two sisters in the hospital. By the time the nurses realized that they were being left behind to be captured, everyone in authority had fled. Even the army evacuation officers. But there were two R.A.F. boys in the hospital. Pilots who'd been smashed up. The two nurses we'd just seen taken off in the Sunderland had asked their matron for a leave of absence for a few days. Then they went to the R.A.F. patients and borrowed their uniforms. In that disguise they worked their way down here to the south of Greece and hunted up The General. They put the whole thing up to him. They insisted that they'd make life miserable for him if he didn't see that all the girls back in the Athens hospital were evacuated. The General gave them his solemn vow that he'd make some arrangements immediately. Whether he did and how he did, I don't know. The men on the dock didn't know either. But The General did promise the female R.A.F. officers that the matter would be taken care of. And then he took the two of them off in the Sunderland.

Hill said, "That's one of the stories that'll still be worth sending back to our papers when we finally find communications."

"If we ever find communications," Atherton put in.

Finally we were left alone on the pier with about twenty men. They were all tall and young. They all wore dark blue coats. British naval officers. So far we hadn't made our presence known. We were just eavesdropping newspapermen, snooping around and seeing at close range how an army flees from a country where it's been defeated.

Bit by bit we pieced together the last chapter of this Myloi drama. These naval officers had been in charge of the entire evacuation. Now their job was over. The last of the soldiers had shoved off. The last who could be saved anyway. There were many being left behind, but the Germans would probably be in Argos and Myloi by dawn. The great evacuation was over.

Argos, which had taken such a beating all day, was being bombed again tonight. We could hear the planes. We could see the fires. We could imagine horror being piled upon horror back there in that little town. That town which tomorrow would be a place of ghosts. A place of silent people. We thought of Leigh White and we said a prayer that the bombs would miss the clinic where the doctor should be operating by now.

The naval officers had sent for a British destroyer to come and take them away. We learned that by listening to their conversation. They had evacuated thousands of men. Now they were waiting to be evacuated themselves. They had sent word that they would wait for the destroyer until midnight. If it didn't come by midnight they would assume it had been impossible to meet their request. If the destroyer didn't come by midnight they would have to face the same prospect a lot of other Britishers in Greece were going to have to face. The prospect of capture.

We looked at our watches. Everyone on that dock kept looking at his watch. Eleven-thirty.

Now it's eleven forty-five.

Now it's eleven-fifty. The men in the navy blue uniforms stand in silent little groups. They all peer out over the water.

They strain their eyes trying to spot something that might be a destroyer out there just beyond the line of visibility.

Eleven fifty-five.

"Well," says one officer, "I guess we're done for. Eleven fifty-five. No destroyer. I did want to see my family again. But—what the hell!"

"Cheer up," another fellow says, "we've still got five minutes. I've seen both hell and heaven open up in five minutes."

Eleven fifty-seven. We all suddenly see the same thing. Hill and Atherton and I are in the spirit of the game now. We all see it at the same time. Just a pinpoint of light out there on the black water. Then the light goes out.

"Who's got a torch?"

"Blink at him! Quick!"

A young officer pulls a flashlight out of his pocket and starts clicking it on and off. Dot, dash, dot, dash, dot, dot, dash . . .

When he finishes his message we all wait with our mouths hanging open and our eyes glued on the spot where we had first seen the pinpoint of light.

"What did you ask him?"

"I asked him what ship he was."

"You bloody fool, he won't answer that!"

"Well, it's his turn to do something anyway."

But nothing happens. No answer comes. Nothing shatters the blackness out there on the Aegean.

"Well, I guess it wasn't our destroyer after all!"

Then suddenly the pinpoint of light again. Only this time it's a little larger, a little nearer. It blinks on, then off. On, then off. It spells out a message, slowly, cautiously. Obviously the men on the bridge are afraid these men on the dock may be the enemy trying to trick them.

Now there's a furious blinking back and forth. The signalers are shooting their messages across the water with the excitement of two men both trying to talk at once. The staid British naval officers are as excited as school boys.

"Give him PSB," one of the ranking gold braiders says in

what would have been a shout if he hadn't been trying to whisper. "Give him PSB right away!"

Quickly the man with the torch flashes the signal. Dot, dash, dash, dot. Dot, dot, dot. Dash, dot, dot, dot. He flashes it over and over again. PSB. PSB. PSB.

"What in hell," we ask one of the officers, "does PSB mean?"

He looks at us the way some New Dealer would have looked at you a few years ago if you'd asked him what AAA or NRA meant.

"Please send boat," the officer answers curtly.

The men on the ship must have gotten it, finally, because pretty soon a motorboat comes chugging through the water. When we make out the forms of the men we can see that each one has a gun of some kind in his hand ready to use in case an error has been made. They're a grim-looking bunch of British sailors, but they relax and put away their firearms when the officers on the dock identify themselves.

The motorboat bumps against the side of the dock. Someone makes a rope fast. And then we hear the good news.

The greatest destroyer in the British navy has arrived. The *Havock!* The destroyer that has already taken part in every major naval engagement of the war without the loss of a single life!

The naval officers begin to load their duffel bags and guns and other baggage into the launch. We approach them timidly. "Can we go, too?"

There's some debate. Several of the naval officers look us over with suspicion. They examine our passports and our other documents. There's no precedent for it. You aren't British. You aren't soldiers. Or sailors either. There isn't much room. You may be cheating some weary Anzacs out of a place.

But finally they nod their heads. They agree to waive regulations. We can go!

Now we're in the captain's lounge on the *Havock.* We're under way at last. The engines are churning. We're going full speed ahead. We can tell by the way the whole boat throbs and vibrates. We're on our way to Crete. We still have plenty of danger ahead of us, but we're steaming away from Yugoslavia and Greece. We're leaving the enemy behind. All we have to fear now are night bombers, submarines, E-boats, and mines. But they're nothing compared with what we've been facing and what we've been through. Or they're a change anyway.

We slap one another on the back. It's a recklessly happy gathering. The captain's steward offers us Scotch and soda. It warms us up inside. What we really need is food, but this is better than food, because we're too tired and too unaccustomed to food to put anything solid inside our stomachs yet. We must have some sleep before we can think of eating.

"What a break!" we tell the naval officers, and they answer:

"Yes, it was lucky the *Havock* came just when she did. In another five minutes we would have given up. But now we're through with worry and danger—for a while, anyway."

And then we notice two young army officers who raise their glasses in all the toasts but for some strange reason seem to be entirely out of the picture. Entirely out of the spirit of the gathering.

Now it's four o'clock in the morning. The two young officers look at their watches. They nod to each other. They put down their glasses and pick up their revolver belts. They grin as they get ready for—for what?

Then they go around the circle shaking hands. The naval officers seem to know what it's all about. They wish the two young officers luck.

"Where are you going?" Hill asks them.

They only smile and say: "We're getting off here. We've got one more little job to do."

"Getting off? Where? In the middle of the ocean? And one more job? What do you mean?"

But they are already halfway up the iron ladder that leads to the top deck. We watch their feet disappear through the hatch. That's the last we ever see of them.

One of the naval officers echoes our thoughts by saying: "I guess none of us will ever see them again!"

And then he lifts his glass and suggests a toast to "those two chaps." We drink without fully understanding.

Just then the throbbing dies away. For a minute or two the engines remain idle. Then they start up and we are on our way to Crete again. On our way without the two young army officers.

They had gotten off at the tip of Greece. They had gone back, we were finally told, to do a little job of sabotage. A suicide assignment, for there would be no other ship to take them off to safety.

CHAPTER FIFTEEN

Crete

———————◄•●•►———————

CRETE was an island of confusion, disorganization, and fear, even before the Germans started dropping their parachutists down there. We spent days on Crete. We hunted communications. We hunted the Greek government. We talked to hundreds of army officers who had a weird premonition that the worst chapter of the war was going to be written right here on Crete in a week or two. Men in the permanent garrison who had been stationed on Crete for months shook their heads and frowned.

This is obviously the next hot spot, one of them told us. We've been fiddling around here on Crete and we're still fiddling around. We aren't prepared for anything. We haven't any fortifications and we haven't any planes. The island is full of spies. And if Jerry ever comes after us, we boys here are going to catch hell.

Everyone we talked to told us about the spies. Everyone knew the spies were there. Some said there were nearly as many fifth columnists, and even German officers disguised as Balkan refugees, as there were British soldiers in the permanent garrison.

Every day for weeks small Greek caïques had been putting into the many coves and harbors scattered around the island. Each boat had a few passengers. Maybe five. Maybe twenty-five. Some of them were legitimate refugees from places like Rumania, Yugoslavia, and Bulgaria. And from Greece itself. A lot of them were Jews. But most of them were German agents. An Australian lieutenant told how he himself had caught a German army officer who had come to Crete on one of these boats. The German captain was trying to pass himself off as a Rumanian Jew. He had all the papers to prove it.

I asked what they did with spies when they caught them, and the Australian winked and said, "We know what to do with them when we get our hands on them, but after all, this is a Greek island and our hands are tied. If the Greek government gives visas to people we think are German spies, there isn't much we can do about it. Except that there have been a lot of accidents here in Crete. The Anzacs are a tough lot, you know. They don't put up with official hocus-pocus if they can help it. So, unfortunately"—and here his voice became slightly sarcastic—"unfortunately there have been quite a few men killed by stray bullets on Crete. Hunting accidents and things like that. The Australians like to hunt jack rabbits, and sometimes they hit a man by mistake. Purely accidental, you understand. But it would surprise you to know how many of their victims happen to be— just happen to be suspected foreign spies."

At Canea, which was so soon to be literally drenched with blood, I was arrested because someone thought I was one of those spies. I was alone. Hill and Atherton had gone off to get a shave. I didn't have to worry about that because I was boasting a beard, and so I was arrested by a Greek who was conducting a one-man spy hunt. No one at headquarters spoke anything but Greek. I couldn't even make them understand I wanted to telephone to the British consulate. They were giving me a trial without even giving me a chance to be heard.

I got angry, but the angrier I got the more sure they were that I was an enemy agent who ought to be liquidated. Finally I was

saved by a Greek pimp. If this loathsome creature the night before hadn't charged a New Zealand soldier seven hundred drachmas more than the regular price for procuring a woman for him,
I'm afraid I wouldn't have gotten out of that mess alive. But at
the psychological moment the Greek pimp was brought in by a
member of the British Military Police, who listened to my story
and got me out of the trouble by persuading the Greeks to let me
go. I never did find out what happened to the pimp.

There were no hotel rooms in Canea and very little food and
no communications or diplomats or Greek government, and so we
went back to Suda Bay. Now that all the British soldiers who
were going to be taken out of Greece had been dumped here on
Crete, something had to be done with them. If the Germans had
dropped a few bombs on Suda Bay and Canea that last Sunday
in April they would have killed thousands of Anzacs, because
seldom has anyone ever seen such military congestion in such a
small area. But for some reason the Nazi planes didn't come.
On Sunday night the destroyer *Hotspur* pulled into Suda Bay
and G.H.Q. decided to use her to take several thousand soldiers
down to Herakleion, the other big Crete town. We wanted to go
to Herakleion to look for all the things we hadn't found in Canea,
and so we sneaked up the gangplank of the *Hotspur* and stowed
away until she steamed out of the harbor. Then we presented
ourselves to the captain. He gave us whisky, cigarettes, a little
food, and a corner of his cabin floor where we could sleep for
an hour or two.

It was three o'clock in the morning when we got to Herakleion. The city was blacked out. We dodged behind trees every
time we saw a gendarme or a soldier, because we didn't want to
be arrested as spies. We wanted to find a hotel. We finally did
find one. The Hellas. It was lucky that Hill knew a word or two
of Greek. The sign in front merely said, "Xenodocheion," but
Hill knew that that word meant hospitality for strangers, which is
the Greek way of saying hotel.

Atherton said, "I like that. Hotel in English is surely a mean-
ingless word. Hospitality for strangers says something."

But actually we didn't find much hospitality for strangers. The door of the Hellas was unlocked, but no one was on duty upstairs. We looked over the hotel register. It indicated that every room was occupied. We even tried the trick of looking for a key in a door, but no one had been that careless in Herakleion. Then we curled up in a corner of a hallway and went to sleep. Looking for the key in a door had reminded me of Sonia. As I dozed off I had some uncomfortable thoughts. I was safe on Crete. But how about Sonia? What had the Italians done to her when they found her in Cattaro? Should I have stayed behind with her? If I had, could I have done any good? They were troublesome thoughts. Thoughts that made sleep pretty difficult.

We hadn't been lying in the hallway long before a porter or hotel manager, I don't know what he was, routed us out. It was dawn anyway, and so we started looking over the town. We found a telegraph office, but the Englishman in charge of the place said it would take them weeks to catch up with their official dispatches. They had only one key. A lot of equipment they had been expecting for days hadn't arrived yet. All was confusion, he said, with a hopeless gesture of his hands. But one thing was certain. Press messages were out of the question for a long, long time to come.

Then we hunted up the British vice-consul and found that his chief interest in life had always been and still was the ancient ruins of Minos, which were only a few miles out of Herakleion, at Knossos. He'd written a book years ago about the ruins. He wanted to talk about both the ruins and the book. I tried to point out that as the Australian officer had said, hell might break loose on Crete any minute. But Atherton got interested in the ruins. The vice-consul presented Atherton with a copy of the book, at cost plus postage. He even autographed it. Then Atherton autographed something for the vice-consul. Hill and I were getting impatient, and when the vice-consul finally persuaded Atherton that he shouldn't miss this opportunity of going out and spending an afternoon looking over these relics of the oldest ruins in the world, we had our first row with the Balkan Correspondent of the London *Daily Mail.*

We said we'd seen the ruins of enough cities already. Modern cities. We weren't interested in ancient ruins right now. Atherton grumbled a bit about how all Americans lack any real appreciation of art, history, and archeology and other things that really count. But he backed down, and we left the vice-consul. A little later we ran into someone who said the boy king of Yugoslavia was staying on the estate of an English millionaire near Knossos. Now Atherton had a double reason for wanting to take the afternoon off. He thought we could get an exclusive interview with Peter as well as see the ruins. But Hill and I argued that down by pointing out that we had too much news already. What we needed was some way of sending it.

We were in the bar of the dirty little Minos Hotel at Herakleion when we met a British chaplain having a glass of wine to brace himself for a trip to Canea. The British Minister to Greece was here in Herakleion now, but he was going to Canea by motorcar. The chaplain was taking all the Minister's personal luggage, which would just about fill a sizable British lorry. The Minister was looking for the Greek government, just as we were. He had a tip that the Greek government was at Canea. We bought the chaplain another glass of wine, and he agreed to take us along.

We hadn't gone far in his lorry before we were threatened with the necessity of walking the rest of the way. It was all because of a rather heated argument that broke out between the chaplain and Atherton over religion. Atherton, who I think was a member in good standing of the Church of England, said he had seen some of this two-year war and he was convinced that Christianity was virtually dead. We finally got the two of them off that subject, but I kept mulling the question over in my mind as we went through that quiet countryside, which was so soon going to be one of the most blood-drenched battlefields of the whole war. Where was God in this war? In the last war they had talked about God being in the trenches of France. This time I hadn't heard anyone mention God except another British chaplain who had sat glumly on a curbstone in Argos when we were there and kept saying, "This is bloody. This surely is bloody."

I asked him what attitude he thought God took to this sort of thing. For a second or two he seemed perplexed by the question. Then he said, "God is always on the side of right and justice."

That day back in Argos we didn't pursue the discussion any farther, because just then bombs started to fall and the chaplain scurried for cover, just as I did. I don't think he heard me say, "A hell of a lot of people are being killed on God's side, whichever it is."

Atherton's short discussion of contemporary religion also reminded me of the interview Frank Gervasi, of *Collier's,* had had with General Smuts in South Africa. Smuts during the conversation expressed a firm conviction that the British would win. Gervasi, zealous for concrete facts, asked Smuts why he was so sure. Smuts hesitated; then he said, "Because, my boy, God's on our side."

Gervasi broke up the interview right there by saying, "Excuse me, General, I don't mean to be sacrilegious, but how many planes does God have?"

But to go back to Crete, the merry-go-round on Crete was beginning to wear us down. Suda Bay, Canea, Herakleion, and now Suda Bay and Canea again. All in search of communications, which probably didn't exist, and the Greek government, which by now had probably fled to Egypt. We decided that we wouldn't continue the hunt any longer. We wouldn't go on to Canea again. We'd drop off at Suda Bay and see if we couldn't catch a boat for Alexandria. In Alexandria there would surely be some way to get dispatches to New York. But the seat had suddenly broken out of Atherton's trousers, and he still was worrying about not having a British passport, and so he decided to continue on with the chaplain and try to get a new pair of pants and a passport. He agreed to meet Hill and me at the Suda Bay military and naval headquarters at eight o'clock that night.

While Hill and I were roaming around the jetty waiting for

Atherton to return we noticed that a great many large British ships, both merchantmen and warships, were apparently getting ready to sail that night. The evacuation of Crete obviously was going to get under way soon, the evacuation of the troops that had been dumped here from Greece. We talked to naval officers about our going on one of the ships, and they said we would have to get a military pass from G.H.Q. down in Canea. Then—maybe, just possibly—a place could be found for us on some ship. It was doubtful, but there was a slight possibility, if we only had a military pass.

Hill went off to Canea to get passes for all three of us while I stayed to guard our typewriters and knapsacks and to try to make a little more progress with the transportation problem. Hill also agreed to be back at exactly eight o'clock that evening.

As darkness closed in on Suda Bay things started happening. The whole harbor was naturally blacked out. But off on the water workmen were using an acetylene torch on a wrecked British destroyer that had been badly banged up by Stuka bombs. They did everything they could to hide the nasty blue light from that torch, but the whole harbor seemed to be illuminated. The British needed the destroyer. They were working twenty-four hours a day on her. If they had only known! If they had only known that just about the time they finished the job more Stukas were going to drop from the clouds and give that warship her *coup de grâce*.

Streams of British lorries poured down onto the quay. They were loaded solid with black masses of humanity. The lorries would stop. British army and naval officers would dash up and bark out evacuation orders. The tired, sleepy men would tumble out of the trucks and try to get into some kind of military formation. Then they would shuffle off toward the ships tied up to the docks or to lighters that would take them to boats anchored far out in the bay.

Some of the men were Anzac soldiers. Some were Italian prisoners. Some were Greek volunteers who were enlisting for duty off in Africa. I kept wondering why, if Crete is going to be

the next battleground, they are taking off experienced Greek
soldiers. Wouldn't they be needed right here soon to defend their
own soil? I couldn't help remembering what that Australian
officer had said. How he had told me that all the men stationed
permanently here on Crete were positive that things were going
to happen soon, and how unprepared he said they were.

A young English officer who had come onto the quay with the
Greek volunteers walked over to where I was sitting and asked
for a light. We sat smoking our cigarettes together. I told him I
was an American. He said, "Well, you're lucky you weren't in
my boots today. I had to go out and persuade a lot of Greeks to
join up with us. To volunteer to go to Africa. We're trying to
salvage all the man power we can out of this mess. And what a
job it's been! The Greeks never were keen about fighting the
Germans. And I can tell you that it took a job of salesmanship to
get any of them to go on fighting, especially off their own soil.
But I got a few truckloads anyway. At least we'll be able to say
we have Greek volunteers. It will make a good story back home.
Yes, and in your country too. The Greeks fight on. Even after
Crete falls they'll be fighting on. Because after they get to Africa
they won't have any other choice."

Eight o'clock came and no sign of either Atherton or Hill.
Then nine o'clock. Then ten. About that time I got a tip that
just before daylight all these British ships were going to shove off.
Most of them were anchored out in the harbor. One big one, the
Delane, a British merchantship with her hull dented by bombs,
was tied to a dock. She was definitely going to be in the convoy.
That was our hope. We must get on the *Delane*. She was already
loaded with thousands of men. She was just waiting now for the
signal to weigh anchor. I paced up and down. Restless. Nervous.
This might be our last chance to get to communications and
safety. Crete might begin catching hell in the morning. And we
might never get off.

Then Atherton appeared. He had a new pair of trousers and
now he could walk with his head in the air again and without
holding a newspaper over his rear. He didn't have to worry

about indecent exposure any more. But he had not succeeded in getting a passport. The British officials here had been just as suspicious and bound by red tape as that consul on Corfu had been. Atherton and I took turns watching our luggage while the other one called every possible telephone number in Canea for Hill. But no one in Canea had seen him.

A faint light was beginning to streak the sky over Crete. They were beginning to cast off the ropes that held the *Delane* to her dock. We wrote a note to Hill and left it with the commander of the port. Then we tried to walk the half mile to the *Delane* with our luggage and Hill's, but we couldn't make it. Hill had put almost everything he owned into that big knapsack of his. We rummaged through it and took out all his papers and everything else that seemed to be of value. Then we left the knapsack at the exact spot where we had told Hill to meet us without fail at eight o'clock. We put a sign on the knapsack telling him we had waited all night and now were shoving off. And then we took his papers and his typewriter along with our stuff and sneaked up the gangplank of the *Delane* when no one was looking.

We spent two days and two nights on the *Delane* on our way to Egypt. Two days and two nights of attack by Nazi bombers and by Italian E-boats. We learned more in those two days and two nights of what the Balkan war had meant to the British than we ever could have learned any other way. We lived those two days and two nights with the human wreckage of that disastrous campaign. Between air-raid warnings and E-boat attacks they talked. They wanted to talk. They wanted to tell how they felt about everything.

There were about seven hundred Italian prisoners on board, mostly officers. Every one of them had a minimum of two suitcases. When we saw how they clung onto those suitcases, no matter how great the danger of death, we realized how they had come to be captured. They seemed to be the happiest men of the lot. They were being well fed and well taken care of in every way. Some of the rest of us had to sleep, if we could sleep through the air-raid alarms, curled up on piles of rope or behind cases of bully beef to keep off the wind. But the Italian prisoners all had rather respectable quarters. And they didn't have anything to do but sit around and tell one another how lucky they were to have fallen into British hands. Some of them wore jaunty green Alpine hats full of the gaudy feathers of wild birds. They were the really lucky ones, because almost every Anzac soldier wanted one of those hats as a souvenir. The Anzacs knew that the girls back home some day would give anything for one of those hats. And then what a story could be built up around a souvenir like that!

"We were fighting hand to hand. It was a desperate battle. I—well, I finally won. I left him lying where he had fallen, but I took his little green hat to prove the story to you."

And so the Anzacs bartered and tried to outbid one another for the Alpine headpieces. The Italian officers played shrewd. They kept the price up. Many of them got in return for those hats a supply of food such as they probably hadn't seen since the war began.

Then there were about a hundred R.A.F. men. Pilots and mechanics and ground crew. They were "Men Without Planes." One of them told us something we knew already. As the Greek rear-guard action drew to a close, the R.A.F. wasn't able to give the Anzacs a bit of air support. Not only was there a dearth of planes, but all the Greek fields had either been captured by the Germans or were under such heavy and constant Nazi attack that landings and take-offs were simply out of the question.

He also told us how, just a few days ago, the slaughter of the retreating Anzacs got so great that the British command decided to take a long chance. They ordered ten Hurricanes up from the desert front. To make the long trip to Greece, extra fuel tanks had to be installed. That boosted the weight so much that the machine guns had to be taken out. But they knew there was a supply of extra machine guns up in Greece, which could be installed when the Hurricanes landed, and so the ten British planes took off. All of them got to Greece. But as they landed, one by one, on an airport in the Peloponnesos, the Stukas were waiting for them up in the clouds. The Stukas dove down. The

Hurricanes were bombed, machine-gunned, and set afire as fast as they touched the ground. Not one of the ten ever was able to do the job assigned to the squadron, the protection of the retreating Anzacs.

We also talked to the Anzacs themselves. They were bitter about the lack of air support. The favorite repartee on board the *Delane* centered around the wreckage of a Hurricane lashed to the boat deck. It had been shot down in Greece, had been salvaged, and now was being taken to Africa for repairs.

"Hey, Jack, here's a Hurricane," some Anzac would shout to a friend. "It's the first Hurricane I've seen in weeks. How about you?"

They were bitter about it because they said that although they were greatly outnumbered and might never have been able to beat the Germans in this Balkan theater of war, they were sure they could have made a good showing and held back the Nazi columns for months if they had only had something up in the air to help them. They blamed the British High Command. They talked about official bungling. They said that upsetting Berlin's timetable by a week or two wasn't worth the sacrifice that had been demanded of them.

But there were other things they were angry about, too. A whole group of them let off steam about the dilly-dallying of British officers who insisted on keeping their boots polished and their trousers pressed while a campaign was being lost and men were dying right and left. They were loudest in their denunciation of the "Old School Tie" spirit. It was dying in England itself, they had heard, but not out here. Not in the Middle East. They claimed that the British diplomats and the high-ranking British army officers were mostly upper-class snobs who had won their posts because they belonged to the right families and had gone to the right schools.

"I wish we had had some of those fellows up in the mountains of Greece with us," one cynical young Australian told us. "I wish they could have seen what it means when they issue an order for a sacrifice campaign like this one we've just been through. It may seem cheap enough to them to lose just a few tens of thousands of men to delay the enemy, but—well, it's been hell for us."

Then they would curse Hitler. I never heard them express any feelings about the German people, or even the German soldiers. It was always Hitler. That bastard Hitler. It was Hitler who was keeping them thousands of miles from home, forcing them into death traps, sending dive bombers at their heads.

We talked to one cheerful young Australian who was captured by the Germans and escaped. He was wounded in getting away, and when he finally reported back to his own outfit he was told to get his bullet-torn arm treated at a certain hospital some miles off. He made for the place on foot. He walked into the dressing station and asked the nurse for a little treatment.

"I noticed a funny expression on her face," he said, "and she seemed to be trying to get rid of me. But I was too dumb to understand, until suddenly a door opened and a German officer popped into the room. Then I discovered that the Nazis had advanced so much faster than our outfit realized that they had already captured the hospital."

They dressed his wounds and then they locked him up, but he fooled the Germans again. He escaped a second time and now —here he was on his way to safety.

Another thing those Anzacs wanted to talk about was what the Greeks had done to them. They were bitter about that too. They said the bravery of the Greeks was a lot of smart propaganda but that now it prevented anyone telling the real story of those last days of the Balkan war. No one would believe now that whole companies, battalions, regiments of Greeks had fled from their positions at the front when the German drive really began. They had left vast holes in the line. Holes which the Anzacs had had to try to fill up. But the Anzacs had barely enough men to hold their own sectors. That was the reason the Nazi sweep down through Greece had been so rapid. The Anzacs were furious about it because they felt their own reputation as warriors had been besmirched. We told them how we had plenty of evidence to back up their story. We told them we had seen Greek soldiers all over the Peloponnesos and later in Crete running in circles. Fleeing in disorganized masses. Jamming highways. Stopping railroad trains. Running they knew not where. But running just the same.

And yet history, one of the Australians said, will probably put them down as brave soldiers, just because they sat up there in the hills of Albania making faces at the Italians, who didn't want to fight any more than the Greeks did.

While they talked I remembered one midnight early in the year in Belgrade when the Greek Minister called me up and said twenty or thirty hospital cars of wounded Greeks were going through town. The men had been prisoners of the Italians. Now they were being traded across Yugoslavia for some prisoners the Greeks had captured. The Minister and I went down and spent an hour going through the train. Many of the Greek soldiers had lost legs or feet, but all because of frost bite. Not one of those hundreds of wounded prisoners had a shell wound, a bomb wound, or a bullet wound.

Another story they told us while we lay beside them on the deck of the *Delane* was about two thousand Palestinian Jewish soldiers who, as the evacuation was about over, were left on the tip of the Peloponnesos with just enough rations for two days and a small amount of ammunition. They were told that one final attempt would be made to take them off from a certain point on the beach. They were to hide meanwhile in the hills and wait. A British destroyer was sent for them, all right, but by the time it got there the Germans had completed their occupation. They were in control of the entire seacoast. The Palestinian soldiers saw the destroyer and made a dash for the beach. They used up a lot of their precious ammunition cleaning up the German patrols, but it was all futile, because the destroyer had difficulty getting in close enough to reach the men. Then Nazi dive bombers came out of the clouds and forced the warship to pull out to sea.

We also heard stories about treachery in high places in Greece.

One British officer told us how King George called a meeting
of his Greek cabinet just before the final collapse. It was held
behind locked doors.

"Gentlemen," the King told his Ministers, "we Greeks have
three enemies, not two. The Germans, the Italians, and also some
of our own people. Our Greek fifth column."

The Ministers all nodded their heads sagely in agreement.

"You don't know what I mean," the King went on, pound-
ing the table with his fist. "I'm not talking about the little fellows.
They're not the real danger. I'm talking about the fifth columnists in high places. And—some of them, the most dangerous of
them, are right in this room now."

The British officer said that the very next day one of the men
in that room, the Prime Minister of Greece, committed suicide.

There was also the Greek who poured gasoline into a ditch
encircling an important military airport that the British were
using as a base and then set a match to it. The Nazi planes
didn't have much trouble figuring out where to drop their bombs.

And the Greek who used a flashlight to signal a Stuka pilot
the location of a shipload of explosives in Peiraeus harbor.

No wonder the Anzacs were bitter. These were Greeks. Their
allies. Yet they were selling out their own country and also the
British.

The Anzacs lay around the decks those two days and two nights
reading books they had stored away in their knapsacks. It was
interesting to circle around and see what entertained them. Here
and there a boy had a Bible. Others, who had lived through
more adventure in the last few weeks than most novelists had
ever seen, were reading Sabatini adventure stories. But a lot of
them had their noses in serious books. One spent all his time
with *Propaganda for War,* by an American college professor.
It was a book that a British censor had once confiscated from
my luggage. Another was passing *Undertones of War* around
among his friends. A lot of them were thinking and talking about
the war and what it meant and what we're really fighting for
and what kind of a world we ought to try to create after it's all

over. That amazed us. Soldiers on the front line aren't supposed
to do much thinking. But we realized now that on both sides
common ordinary soldiers were trying to think the thing out.
And some of them were having their troubles reconciling this
and that.

One Australian asked if I would like to hear a few pages from
his diary. He had written this entry up in the mountains of
Greece one day while they were hiding for hours from Nazi
planes that were circling over them. A lot of his friends had been
killed all around him that day. But there was nothing any of
them could do but hide, because the Nazis had full control of
the air. So while he lay in a ditch waiting to see if his number
was up, he scribbled out his reactions. It was airplanes he hated
the most. After the war, airplanes should be abolished. Men who
invented planes should be put into prison. People should go
back to walking or riding automobiles, but airplanes shouldn't
be allowed. They were an invention of the devil. He hated
planes.

Just as he was reading the diary entry we heard the squeak
of a rusty pulley. We looked up. Someone on the bridge was
pulling up a piece of colored bunting so it would wave in the
breeze and be seen all over the ship. It was a bright yellow flag.
Preliminary air-raid warning, one of the sailors told us. If it
changes to a red flag that means enemy planes are directly overhead.

While he explained the signals, thousands of soldiers and sailors
all over the ship were looking for their steel helmets and fastening
lifebelts around their waists. The *Delane's* gunners sprang into
the concrete boxes that enclosed their anti-aircraft guns. A lot
of Anzacs grabbed machine guns and Breen guns, which they had
salvaged from Greece, and got them ready for action.

Then we heard the squeak of that pulley again. The yellow
flag was coming down. I looked at the man who had been reading his diary to me. He was six feet tall and as husky as most
of those Anzacs. But his hands were twitching nervously. He
kept his eyes fixed on the bridge. He wasn't the only one. The

whole shipload of war-weary men seemed to be holding their breath. Waiting. Waiting to see if the yellow flag had been pulled down because the danger was over and the planes had disappeared or because the red flag was going to be hoisted.

We heard the planes just as the red flag went up. The gunners' telephone rang. One man in the concrete pillbox answered it. The other started training his sights on the planes. Three thousand soldiers and sailors and two newspapermen looked around for the most protected spot in which to hide. My Australian friend with the diary was trembling like a leaf now. So were hundreds of other brave Anzacs who had lived through weeks of dive-bombing. Atherton and I knew exactly how they felt, because we felt the same way, with much less cause. The noise of Stukas does something to your mind. It makes even the bravest soldiers tremble after they've had a few samples of what dive bombers can do if they don't have any opposition. The bodies of all these Australians and New Zealanders were whole and sound. But their nerves were shattered.

The only living thing on board the *Delane* that didn't react the way the rest of us did was a little fox terrier, the mascot of the *Daedalus,* one of the British ships sunk by the Nazis. He stayed right in his corner and slept through all the red flags and all the danger. He'd had his big war adventure and he'd swum his way out of it. If any other came, he'd probably swim again. Meanwhile he wasn't bothered.

There were eight hundred shipwrecked sailors on board. Enough to run a small navy. Some were from British warships and merchantmen. Others were from Dutch, Greek, Chinese, and Norwegian boats that had been dive-bombed. When the air raids came, these men were just as jittery as the soldiers. They had seen enemy planes send their floating homes to the bottom, blow their shipmates into bits, and force the survivors to jump into the sea and swim against death, sometimes for twenty-four hours, before help came.

After that first raid was over we talked to some of these seamen. They had been through hell too. Some of them had been in Peiraeus harbor the night that that Greek fifth columnist gave a signal with a flashlight that brought on what was probably the most disastrous single bombing attack of the war. The full story had never gotten out. Greek and British censors had smothered it. Yet what happened that night in Peiraeus harbor had much to do with the collapse of Greece. It was the night of April sixth. Germany had just declared war, in its customary unofficial manner, against Greece. The first night of the Greek-German war. Many a Greek told us that the psychological effect of that bombing was really beyond estimation. Much of the damage, the extent of the destruction, was just luck for the Nazis. But a lot of Greeks argued that if the Germans could do that much destruction in the first night of war, Greece was through.

And so Greek spirit was broken that night of April sixth because a Greek fifth columnist flashed a torch up into the sky and let a Nazi bomber pilot know the location of a shipload of explosives. The bomber came down. The ship was hit. The explosion set other ships on fire. Some careless harbor master had allowed a string of railroad cars full of dynamite to stand overnight on the dock. They exploded. In a few minutes the whole harbor was ablaze. One ship after another was set on fire. The flames were a beacon for more Nazi bombers.

We lay on the deck of the *Delane* talking to a lot of sailors whose ships were lost that night. Their stories agreed on most essentials, but they didn't agree as to just how many boats were lost that night. A dozen or two anyway. Big ships. Ships loaded with war material for the British and the Greeks. Ships that would have helped in the evacuation a couple of weeks later. Ships that the British couldn't afford to lose.

They also disagreed about just how far the boiler of the munitions ship was thrown by the explosion. Some said half a mile. Some said as much as five miles. But anyway a huge steel boiler was catapulted through the air and landed a great distance away. It landed, quite by coincidence, in the center of a factory that manufactured, of all things, boilers.

Then they told how a piece of steel weighing many tons, which had been part of that exploded ship, landed in the masts of another British boat. Men had to go up with acetylene torches the next day and cut it down.

The sailors who had been in Peiraeus harbor that night still had terror written on their faces. They shuddered visibly as they talked of flaming Peiraeus. Of a harbor packed with ships all on fire.

Then some eyewitnesses told us another story. There were several ports from which the British evacuation of Greece had taken place. All were scattered around Argos Bay. As the ships loaded with Anzacs steamed down toward Crete they converged at a certain point and then followed the identical course. The Stukas spotted the point where they converged and remained above it, high in the clouds. Whenever a ship crossed that spot, it was dive-bombed. One of the first victims was a British merchant ship with three thousand Anzacs on board.

Before she sank she sent out an S O S. The call was answered by two British destroyers, the *Diamond* and the *Wryneck*. Between them they had almost two thousand men below their decks. They were jammed to the gunwales with men, most of them Anzacs. War-tired men. But the British navy always answers a call for help. The British navy has a tradition. So the *Diamond* and the *Wryneck* went back. They went back to that same spot where the Stukas were hovering in the clouds. And when they got there, the Stukas dived out of the clouds.

Then it was the turn of the *Diamond* and the *Wryneck* to send out calls. They were sinking now. Now there were nearly five thousand men in the water. But there weren't any more British ships within speeding range. Maybe that was lucky for the British navy. But it wasn't lucky for the five thousand. Five thousand men in the water with lifebelts that were guaranteed to keep a person afloat for twenty-four hours at the most. Five thousand men thrashing around in the water, and no ship within speeding range.

But down just off the coast of Crete was the *Griffin*. The *Griffin* was a great little destroyer. She had covered herself with laurels many times before this. A ship that had lived up to all the fine traditions of the British navy. The *Griffin* heard those calls for help from the *Diamond* and the *Wryneck*. But the *Griffin* was in a tough spot. She had taken the *Glen Airn* in tow. The *Glen Airn* was a story in herself. She was a British merchant ship. She went up to Greece to do some evacuating. On her way across that marked spot in Argos Bay the Stukas had come down at her. They had hit her. But since the only damage was the loss of her anchors, the skipper decided to take a chance. He went on into the evacuation port. He foundered around without being able to anchor. He took several thousand Anzacs aboard. Then he went on to Crete. It was a job to disembark those troops without being able to anchor. But he did it. Then he turned back. Again that same spot. Again the Stukas. This time the *Glen Airn* wasn't so lucky. She was machine-gunned as well as bombed. Her engine rooms were flooded.

The *Griffin* took aboard almost all her crew. Only a skeleton force was left on board the *Glen Airn*. Then the *Glen Airn* was taken in tow. On the way down to Crete the towline broke. It was a wild night. It took hours to get the two ships hooked together again. They were nearly to Crete when the calls from Argos Bay were picked up. The *Diamond* and the *Wryneck* were sinking. There was more important work than towing to be done now. Thousands of men were in the water. The *Griffin* turned the battered *Glen Airn* over to a Greek caïque. The little Greek boat would have to tow the crippled British monster. And then the *Griffin* put on full steam for Argos Bay. But when the *Griffin* finally got to the disaster spot, more than twenty-four hours had gone by, and she could find only fifty-four men in the water. Fifty-four out of nearly five thousand. Four thousand nine hundred and some odd lives lost in that one double tragedy.

That was the story they told us. The men who lay on the deck of the *Delane* telling us about it were some of those fifty-four survivors. They had been there. Their stories agreed. We believed them. Nearly five thousand men missing from just three ships.

But we had the shipwrecked crews of more than twenty other ships on the *Delane*. And the *Delane* was only one of six ships sailing down to Crete in this convoy, not counting the destroyers and cruisers protecting us. Our decks were cluttered with the skippers of boats that had been sunk. They were a pathetic-looking lot. Most of them were unusually silent, even for ship captains. They paced back and forth looking out over the water with grim expressions. I guess having your ship sunk from under you is damned heartbreaking, especially if you're an old sea dog.

One of them, more communicative than the rest, got statistically minded and interviewed all the other men of the sea on the *Delane*. He compiled a casualty list, which he showed us. That's how we knew that on the *Delane* were the survivors of twenty British and allied boats. Twenty ships, and their total weight came to more than two hundred thousand tons. But that wasn't all. There must have been many others sent to the bottom, because we knew there were more shipwrecked crews on the other evacuation boats. We began to realize that this withdrawal from Greece had surely been a real tragedy of the sea.

The only amusing story we picked up from our fellow travelers was the one about the *Quiloa*. She ran aground in Argos harbor. The British evacuated her. Men, guns, and material. Stripped her completely. When they finished the job there wasn't anything left on board worth saving. Not even a mess kit. Not a roll of toilet paper. Then they loaded her with depth charges timed to go off in four days. They figured that would be after the evacuation was all over. But the very next day, while the *Quiloa* was still loaded with those time bombs, the Stukas spotted the wrecked ship. They worked on the *Quiloa* all day. Finally their bombs took effect and they sank her. She went to the bottom on Thursday. Had the Stukas held their fire and saved their bombs, the *Quiloa* would have blown up on Monday anyway. Then there was the story of the *Hellas*. She was the old Vanderbilt yacht, the *Valiant,* which had been turned over to the Greeks for evacuation purposes. She had a thousand men aboard, British, Maltese, Palestinians, and a lot of other mixed nationalities. They told us that five hundred out of those thousand men were lost when the *Hellas* went down.

They also told us about the *City of Karochi*. She was sunk in Peiraeus harbor. Her crew of eighty, made up of mostly lascars, swam to shore. Then they walked fifty miles. They lived on the land, eating grass most of the time. Finally they bought or stole a fishing boat and got to Crete. We met the skipper on Crete. He was trying to ride a bicycle. The whole experience seemed to have done something to his mind. All he wanted to do when he finally got to Crete with his lascar crew was to ride a bicycle. And he didn't know the first rudiments of bicycle-riding. Now he was on the *Delane* with us. He seemed out of his head most of the time. At least a dozen of the *Delane's* crew told us the story of what happened to their sister ship, the *Devis*. She had been coming out of Argos Bay with a full load of troops when she was attacked from the air. The first bomb landed amidships and started a fire. It looked like the end of the *Devis*. But just as the flames were beginning to sweep through the ship, six more bombs came down. All of them landed in the sea but close enough to send a torrent of water washing over the *Devis*. The water put out the fire. The *Devis* was saved from destruction by the same plane that nearly destroyed her.

The crew of a small merchantman told us how they had been subjected to a long machine-gunning by a Nazi plane that flew back and forth, just skimming the decks. The ship was completely pock-marked when the attack was over, and she soon sank. But not a man was even wounded, because as soon as the attack started, the skipper and his whole crew let the boat founder around by herself and went below decks. Down there they hid directly under the heavy steel plating on which the deck guns rested. That was their only chance of safety. And it worked. They were here on the *Delane* to tell the story.

During one of our air raids on the *Delane,* two buxom young women came running out of a cabin, fastening lifebelts around their waists and jamming steel helmets on their heads. They wore crisp linen dresses. Their faces were properly painted and powdered. Their hair was neatly combed. About three thousand of us blinked. We rubbed our eyes. We wondered if the Stukas had driven us completely out of our minds. But after the raid was over we talked to the girls and got their story. They were Dutch. One had been a nurse and one a stewardess on the Dutch liner *Penland,* a sixteen-thousand tonner that was sunk three hours out of Peiraeus. They'd been among the lucky ones. They'd been picked out of the water. Now they were helping the ship's doctor dress wounds and hand out medicine.

Of all the men on board the fellow who interested us the most was a young Australian soldier not more than twenty years old. He stood, day and night, leaning over the rail of the *Delane,* looking out across the water. He seldom spoke. Most of the time he had his elbows on the rail and his chin in the cup of his hands. Just looking. I sensed some great tragedy. There was probably a good story here if I could get him to talk. I finally did. The great tragedy was that he was on his honeymoon but without his bride.

"She's—out there," he said glumly, waving his hand toward the horizon.

I looked intently. All I could see were the bare outlines of several other ships in the convoy. But gradually the story spilled out. The Australian had fallen in love with a Greek girl on the island of Crete. It had been a whirlwind, three-day courtship. They were married just a few minutes before the evacuation ships set sail. Then they pleaded with British officers to allow the bride to go along to Egypt. It was a mean problem for officers already busy trying to save the lives of thousands of men. There didn't seem to be anything in the regulations about a case like this. No precedent at all. Finally they agreed she could go. But the bride and bridegroom must not be allowed on the same ship. That was the compromise. So here they were. They were on their honeymoon, he on the *Delane,* she on a ship miles away, just visible on the horizon.

"A swell honeymoon!" the Australian grumbled, still staring off into the darkness.

The decks of the *Delane* were crowded, not only with men and their salvaged equipment but with big wooden crates of food. Crates of canned bully beef and thirst-provoking biscuits, as the English would say. Plain hardtack, we called them. But those crates, juggled around a bit, made a good office for the Associated Press and the London *Daily Mail*. Atherton and I set our typewriters up on top of a pile of them, and then we posted a sign saying, "Anglo-American Press Headquarters, Don't Disturb." Pretty soon we had sailors, soldiers, and airmen flocking around us to tell us their stories. That's just what we hoped would happen. Norwegians, Britishers, Dutchmen, Greeks, lascars, Chinese, and men of a lot of other nationalities helped us to get a clear picture of what had happened.

Before long we felt we had a rather complete story of that Greek campaign and the evacuation. We were certain, now, that there had been just one division of Australians and one division of New Zealanders in Greece. Veterans of fierce fighting in Libya. Two divisions that had been pulled out of the western desert to fight a delaying action in the Balkans, and while they fought in the Balkans, Axis troops regained all the territory down in Libya that these Anzacs had taken away from them earlier in the year.

A very minimum of equipment was sent up to Greece with the two divisions. And not enough planes to do any good. Not enough even to hold the airports. In addition to the two divisions there had been a few thousand Canadians and Englishmen attached to miscellaneous units. But not enough Englishmen to keep the colonial troops from doing a lot of what they call grousing. They complained frequently that purely colonial divisions had fought the campaigns in Ethiopia, in Libya, and now in the Balkans. In a few days they expected they would be back again on the western desert trying to regain the lost Libyan territory.

What they wanted to know was why there weren't some English troops in action in this part of the world. This was England's war, too, they said. And it wasn't a matter of transport, either, because when they started from home they were first taken around the tip of South Africa and then up the Atlantic to the British Isles, where they were paraded through the streets of English cities as a back-stiffening gesture. Then they were hauled all the way back around the Cape and were landed in the Middle East. England surely could have spared a few of her millions of trained soldiers to take part in these Middle East campaigns. That was their argument. It did no good to tell them that England needed all her military force in case of invasion. They snapped back that some of the Colonials could have been left in England and some of the Englishmen sent to the Middle East.

It would have been better psychology, better propaganda, one Anzac officer told us. It would have prevented a lot of this grousing.

Out of approximately forty thousand British troops in Greece, about twenty thousand had come out of it to fight another day. The other twenty thousand had either been killed in that devastating rear-guard action the Anzacs fought so bravely down through Greece or had been so badly wounded they had to be left behind, or had been taken prisoner, or had been lost at sea when dozens of ships went to the bottom. Twenty thousand! Fifty per cent of the original force! At Dunkirk the loss had been about ten per cent, and yet that evacuation was considered terrible. This was so much worse than Dunkirk that there just wasn't any comparison. Five times worse, by actual count.

Our Press Headquarters sign was a better idea than we had imagined. We had been stowaways on the *Delane*. Until the ship was well at sea, where they couldn't very well dump us overboard, we literally hid from the ship's officers. Then gradually we got up nerve enough to circulate a little. All the men were divided into units, and each unit was fed separately. For the first twenty-four hours we had to beg a biscuit here and a little water there. But now that we had identified ourselves with the sign, we began to eat a little better. The Australian press officer let us line up with his men. Now we got a can of bully beef a day and a regular ration of tea.

The sign also brought, during the evening, an invitation from the chief engineer to go down to his cabin and listen to the evening BBC broadcast. We were lucky. We turned the radio on just as Lord Haw-Haw was boasting from Berlin that the Germans were in complete control of the Mediterranean and that not one single Britisher would get alive from Greece and Crete to Egypt. That brought loud guffaws from everyone in the cabin. Another convoy had preceded us. Thousands of Anzacs were already on Egyptian soil. We were bringing up the rear with thousands more. Of course we weren't there yet, but this idle boast in the sickening voice of Lord Haw-Haw got under our skins.

Ships had been sunk already. Probably more would be sunk. But the British navy was doing a magnificent job, despite all the losses it had taken. They were getting twenty thousand men to safety, and that was twenty thousand more than Lord Haw-Haw apparently ever expected to survive. The British navy would have gotten a whole lot more men down to Egypt if it hadn't been that same old story about lack of air support. All the casualties, all the ship sinkings had been due to Nazi air force action.

We drank some sweet Greek wine with the chief engineer, listened to some more hair-raising evacuation stories, and then went down to the chief medical officer's cabin. For hours I had been doing a continuous St. Vitus's dance, because the skin all over my body itched like mad. The ship's doctor opened my shirt, looked over the red spots that covered my skin, and laughed.

"How long since you've had a bath?"

I told him, "Nearly a month."

He laughed again. "You're just filthy. There's nothing wrong with you except that you're filthy. You'll be all right when you finally get your clothes off and get clean again."

So I kept on scratching, and my body kept looking more and

more as if I had a bad case of measles, hives, impetigo, and flea bites all combined.

At all hours of the day and night there was a line of men in front of sick bay waiting to see the doctor. A large percentage of them were Italian officers. A lot of those tough Anzacs had rather serious wounds which they just ignored, but the Italians came flocking to the medical officer with ailments a man wouldn't even go to a doctor about back home in normal times. The medical officer was the only one on board I heard get tough with the prisoners. He always treated the ailment or dressed the wound, but each Italian officer got a stiff lecture about being a man. Most of them didn't understand English, so the words didn't mean anything, but I was sure, by watching their reactions, that they all got the point. But that didn't stop them from coming for more treatments and more pills and powders.

Between cases the medical officer told us that his big problem was diarrhea. Hundreds of the Anzacs had serious cases of diarrhea.

"It isn't anything they can help," the doctor explained. "It isn't any reflection on their bravery. It's just a result of the nerve-shattering experience they've been through. They're physically and emotionally exhausted. It's like a woman failing to menstruate for months after a shock of some kind. But, damn it, I'm running out of medicine for that particular ailment!"

Just then the door burst open and an excited young officer's orderly came rushing in. He was out of breath. We could tell from his expression, his intensity, his nervousness that something serious had happened. He clicked his heels and snapped us the customary salute. And then he blurted out the story, rather breathlessly:

"Sir, I—I have—an officer with—constipation!!"

I don't know why it struck us so funny, but anyway we all burst out laughing. The officer's orderly turned crimson. But the doctor finally gave him some pills for his poor officer.

After we left the sick bay we went up on deck, moved around the cases that formed press headquarters so that they would cut

off some of the cold wind, and tried to go to sleep. We didn't
have any blankets, and our legs were soon like cakes of ice. It
was nearly the first day of May, but a bitter wind was sweeping
the Mediterranean. I guess we'd just about gone off to sleep
when the sirens blew. It was the first time we had had a night
alarm. Three thousand men were on their feet in an instant.
The *Delane* was like an anthill when you suddenly put your
foot in it and stir up instantaneous activity. Gunners ran to their
posts. Everyone who had a lifebelt started putting it on. Atherton
and I couldn't remember whether it was his day or mine to wear
the one belt we had managed to filch for the two of us, and so
we ended up by neither of us putting it on.

Now that rusty pulley was squeaking again. But instead of a
piece of yellow cotton bunting, a red lantern was being pulled up.
We looked out over the rail. It was too dark to see even the outline
of ships, but scattered all over the water were red pinpoints of
light. And then the fireworks began. That was our first reaction.
Fireworks. Beautiful fireworks. They burst into existence a few
hundred feet above the water's surface. Bright yellow-white
lights that illuminated everything for a quarter of a mile around,
just as if it were high noon. They dropped slowly. Sometimes
they seemed to be standing still in midair. But finally, one by
one, they hit the water and went out. You could hear the sizzling
noise when they went out, if they were close enough. For a minute
or two Atherton and I stood on the deck of the *Delane,* fascinated by this impressive display of pyrotechnics. It was like a
Morris Gest stage effect. But then guns started going off, and we
suddenly realized that this wasn't a fairyland scene but a scene
out of war.

Now there were more shell stars than ever falling. The whole
sea seemed to be dotted with them. Now we could see the gray
outlines of ships. Dozens of ships. The sea around us was covered
with ships. Was this some kind of an optical illusion? There were
only six transports and six warships in our convoy when we
started out. When darkness had closed in on us there were still
just eleven beside the *Delane*. But we didn't have much of a

chance to try to figure it out. Now the flares were landing close
to the *Delane*.

We asked one another why we couldn't hear the noise of the
planes that were dropping these parachute flood lights. And why,
with the whole sea lighted up for them and all their targets
standing out so clearly, weren't they dropping any bombs? Guns
on almost every ship in our huge convoy were blasting away. But
at what?

It was all a grand mystery. We stood shivering on the wind-
swept deck. Three thousand of us. And out across the water, on
those other ships, there were thousands of other men shivering.
Any second now a lot of us might be out there on the surface of
that black water. I thought of the swimming medal I had at
home. I got it by mistake, for winning a canoe race. It had
always been a standing joke in the family. I, who couldn't swim
a stroke, with a swimming medal. I told Atherton about it as
we stood there shivering and watching the flares and listening
to the orgasm of noise from the guns.

"Well," Atherton said, "with your bum leg and my bum knee,
it wouldn't do much good if we were swimmers."

Then a sailor sauntered along, and we asked him a question
or two. He laughed when we mentioned planes.

"This isn't an airplane attack, you crazy fools, it's Italian
suicide boats. You know, those little one-man and two-man
torpedo boats. The pilot rides the boat and steers it right at his
target, then he jumps off before it hits. Those flares are our flares.
We're shooting them up into the sky, and they burst at a certain
height, then float down to the surface. We're trying to spot the
damned Italians. I guess we've got their bearings or else we
wouldn't be blasting away at them. But they're a reckless lot.
We still have a good chance of getting hit by a torpedo."

A whistle on the *Delane* was blowing almost continuously.

"This is the commodore ship of the convoy," the sailor told us.
"The movements of all the other ships are being directed right
from our bridge. That whistle of ours is signaling the other ships
to come into closer formation."

We saw that that was just what was happening. One ship after another was heading for us. We were like a mother hen when her chicks start clustering around her.

For what seemed like hours those parachute flares lighted up the water. The guns barked away. The ships went through a most elaborate series of maneuvers, all apparently directed by the *Delane's* whistle. Sometimes we all went around in big circles. Other times we went full steam astern. The flares now were dropping within a few hundred feet of the *Delane*. Closer and closer. That meant the enemy must be right in our vicinity. Then the lighted area gradually moved away. Finally, after the distant sea had been surveyed under the calcium glare, the guns stopped their noise. The *Delane* whistled for a normal course again. The Italian attack was over. We never did find out whether any of the enemy boats were sunk by all that shooting. Some of the *Delane's* crew said definitely yes. Others said they thought the enemy had been frightened off.

At last the pulley on the bridge squeaked again. The red lantern came down. We went back and tried to go to sleep. Finally we did. But Atherton and I woke up about the same time. We were freezing cold and we both agreed that there are some things worse than sleeplessness. We both had been having nightmares. Living over again Belgrade, Sarajevo, Corinth, Argos. We were suffering from complete emotional exhaustion. We walked the decks and finally found a place where we could stand in a hatchway close to the smokestack and keep warm. We leaned against each other and dozed out the night that way on our feet.

It was a clear morning. We counted back. The fifteenth clear day. The weatherman surely seemed to be with the Axis. The only bad weather during our whole experience was that first night on the Adriatic, when we wanted a clear sky so badly. But since then we had had more than two weeks of perfect flying weather. Perfect weather for bomber pilots.

When it got light we saw that our twelve ships had been joined by another huge convoy during the night. Now we had a

British airplane carrier, two or three battleships, and a lot of smaller warships protecting us.

The British airplane carrier kept six or eight of its fighters circling over us all the time. From then on we never even had a yellow flag. Not even a preliminary air-raid warning.

That confirmed an observation that a lot of other people had made. The Nazi pilots aren't a bit afraid of the largest array of guns on land or on ships that anyone can get together. But just the minute they run into British fighter planes they lose their reckless courage.

Atherton and I were about the first men on the *Delane* astir that morning, because sleeping standing on your feet isn't too much fun. As the ship came to life and the men saw that impressive lot of British warships around us, we could feel the morale and the spirit of the whole three thousand men perk up. A man who was blind and deaf could have sensed it. It wasn't anything anyone said. It was just an instantaneous feeling of confidence on everyone's part. The British navy does that to you. The British navy is something to inspire confidence in even a South Sea Islander who had never heard of the British navy.

Atherton and I did some figuring that morning. We figured we had been on the run for just about four weeks. Not quite a month. We had traveled more than two thousand miles by a lot of strange methods of transportation. We were——

But our figuring was interrupted. Someone on the *Delane* let out a bellow. Just one word. Egypt! He shouted that word. Then he pointed to the horizon dead ahead of us. Men raced to the rail with binoculars. In a few minutes we didn't need binoculars. We all could see it. Egypt! Sand! The continent of Africa! Long stretches of bright yellow sand! Alexandria! Land! Communications! The odyssey was about over now. The flight from the Germans and the Italians, the hunt for peace and some way of telling what had been happening in the Balkans was almost over. Those big white buildings must be Alexandria. One of Great Britain's greatest naval bases. The throbbing heart of the Middle East. Of the British Empire.

The pulley on the bridge squeaked. The gunners ran to their stations. The yellow flag went up. Enemy planes were approaching again. But no one paid any attention to the yellow flag this time except the gunners. The rest of us didn't even look up into the clouds. We were all staring at the skyline of Alexandria. We could float in on our backs to Alexandria and safety now, if we had to.

CHAPTER SIXTEEN

Back to Unreality

————◆◆◆————

Alexandria.

The largest ships in the harbor were French. Battleships, cruisers, destroyers. Their crews lay around the decks playing cards, reading, sleeping.

"Gentlemen sailors," growled one of the *Delane's* crew. He said it with bitterness. "Look at them! We made an agreement with them when France collapsed. The British government pays them their wages. All they have to do is not to run away. We agreed to pay them the going wage for French sailors. That was all right at the time. But that crowd in Vichy is smart. Every month or two they issue an order raising the wage scale for French sailors. Which means that we, the British, have to pay more and more each month to bloody fools like these fellows you see lying around on the decks of the interned French ships. They get more than we do. And they don't do a lick of work. Their ships are gradually going to hell. Look at them. Rusty, dirty, covered with barnacles. And we have to keep a small fleet of our own standing there watching them to be sure they don't sneak away some dark night. I wonder how much longer we're going to play cricket?"

Alexandria.

When we finally got our feet on land again Atherton and I were placed under technical arrest by the British. We might be spies. Well, this was one time we didn't blame them. And anyway, we were reconciled now to being taken for dangerous foreign agents anywhere we went.

Finally they let us go. We were free. Free to write stories and use telephones and dispatch cables to America. Except, of course, all the government offices, all the censors, were in Cairo. Better get on to Cairo they advised us.

We were tired and dirty. We wanted a bath before we did anything else. Soapsuds and warm water pouring from a shower. Yes, that must be the first thing. So we went to the Majestic Hotel. Here was Elegance with a capital E. Women in organdy and men in white linen suits. Army officers and navy officers in well-pressed dress uniforms. Limousines and sport roadsters. Elegance with a capital E all right.

We looked down at ourselves. I still had on the Serbian peasant socks that said I was a virgin. My shoes were still caked with mud and my trousers with blood. My hair was matted with dirt and salt from the sea. My typewriter case was badly battered. The knapsack over my shoulders was filthy. Atherton by comparison looked like a gentleman, but still he was pretty grimy.

"It's a damn good thing," he said, "that I got this new pair of trousers so that my tail doesn't stick out any more. I don't think Alexandria would have liked me that way."

Well, Alexandria didn't like us any way. The dark-skinned doorman at the Majestic held his hand up when we started through the entrance. He was very sorry, he said in good Oxfordian English, but he couldn't let us go in. Absolutely impossible. The hotel had its standards. This was a very expensive and exclusive hotel. What we probably wanted, he said, was a cheap hotel. He pretended to be very understanding, very helpful. We would probably find the Majestic much out of our class anyway. Why didn't we try the little hotel down the street? No, of course it wouldn't have showers or even bathrooms, but still . . .

If we'd only messed up that fellow and his smart white uniform I think we would have felt better. But instead of that we reconsidered and decided to get on to Cairo immediately so that we could send a cable to our papers before night.

The taxi to Cairo cost a dollar a mile. I think Cairo is about fifty miles. Fifty miles right across the desert. The highway, made by the British out of asphalt, is just wide enough for two cars. Four times on the way across those fifty miles of desert a double line of British army lorries bore down at us. Our Egyptian taxi driver didn't seem to know there were such things as brakes. He just kept his foot on the accelerator and raced ahead. When collision seemed inevitable he'd suddenly swerve off into the sand. The army lorries would sail by, and then Atherton and I would sit in the blistering sun while the taxi driver stood in front of his car shaking his head and jabbering to himself.

There isn't much you can do when a car gets deep in sand except use a long strip of canvas with slats of wood nailed to it. You put it on the sand under the wheels and it makes a track. It's almost as essential a piece of equipment in that part of the world as a jack or a tire pump. It converts your car temporarily into a caterpillar tank. It's about the only thing to get a car out of the sand. But our taxi didn't have one. Each time we got into trouble we had to wait for someone else to come along and lend us one. Each time we waited, the taxi driver said the dollar a mile didn't include waiting time, so our bill would be more than the fifty dollars agreed on. And then we had to shell out handfuls of money for the rental of the strips of canvas and wood. But we finally got to Cairo.

Cairo. The Great City of the East. Magical, mystical Cairo. A city of Oriental splendor, romantic glamour, ancient wonder.

But the first thing we saw when we hit the outskirts of Cairo

was a huge American-style billboard bearing in giant letters
the slogan:

KEEP UP WITH THE NEWS
KNOW WHAT'S HAPPENING
READ THE ASSOCIATED PRESS
DISPATCHES NOW APPEARING
IN YOUR CAIRO NEWSPAPERS

We found out later that Ed Kennedy, AP war correspondent
with the British forces in the Middle East, had taken time off
between covering battles and air raids and evacuations to sell
the AP service to the Egyptian press.

Coming fresh from the battlefields of Europe, we got a ter-
rific slap in the face from those signs, which we saw all over
Cairo. Reality. The world of newspapers and journalistic rivalry.
Keep Up with the News. Read the AP Dispatches.

Yes, read the AP dispatches about the bombing of Belgrade
and the Yugoslav war. Read about what happened in Sarajevo,
Cetinje, Cattaro, Corfu, Patras, Corinth, Argos, Crete. Read all
about it.

We laughed. Just try to read about it.

But those signs made us decide to get a story out over the
wires before we even took a bath or got undressed. Atherton and
I agreed to that. One story, even if we fell asleep writing it.

The Continental and Shepheard's are almost side by side on
the main street of Cairo. If you think the Waldorf-Astoria in
New York or the Drake in Chicago are swanky, you ought to
see the hotels of Cairo. Oriental slaves begin bowing to you
before your taxi even stops. From the curbing to your room
there's a line of men (you seldom see an Egyptian woman in
Egypt) bowing and scraping before you. Men in long flowing
white robes with bright-colored turbans twisted around their
heads. High priests of the Holy Order of Foreigner-Fleecers.
Men who keep alive the tradition of Oriental splendor and mys-
ticism while Ford automobiles zip around the streets and movie
houses show the latest Hollywood films and you can buy

Granger tobacco for sixty cents per ten-cent package. Leeches living on other leeches who live on you. Like the taxi-getter getter in front of the hotel, in a fine white robe, who makes a deep bow from the waist as only an Egyptian can, a bow that is almost a holy rite, and says solemnly in perfect Bond Street English: "Sir, do you desire a taxi? If so, I shall get a man to get a taxi for you."

We stumbled through the heavily draped lobby of the Continental and asked for a room. A thousand eyes were on us. We knew we were out of place. We were dirty and tired and war-weary. These people sitting in the lounge sipping delicate cocktails were fresh and crisp and clean. This might be Middle East headquarters, G.H.Q. for a British army that was fighting for the preservation of the Empire, but there was no sign here of war except that everyone had on a smart uniform. It seemed to be a tradition around the better places in Cairo that you mustn't let the sordid side of war creep in. That's probably why so many eyebrows were raised at us. We were just some of the dregs of war. Signs everywhere warned that only officers were permitted to enter these sanctums. The men who were fighting for the empire a hundred miles or so out on the desert were barred from places like this when they got their furloughs. Privates sometimes had wounds, missing arms. But wounds and men with missing arms would spoil this scene of glamorous respectability.

They gave us a room big enough for a regiment. When we protested, they said this was one of the smaller rooms. It was so big that, when Atherton sat off in one corner with his typewriter and I off in another corner with mine, we had to shout at each other when we wanted to confer on facts like the number of casualties or the day this or that happened.

Finally we got our first dispatches written. They were not the journalistic masterpieces we thought we were capable of, after having lived through so much real war. They were nothing to be proud of, but at least we finally had some of the story on paper and almost on its way to our employers. The next step, we were told, was to get a stamp of approval on each page of each dispatch from: (1) the British military censor; (2) the British naval censor; (3) the R.A.F. censor; (4) the Egyptian and British civil censors; (5) the telegraph office censor. Then, they said, our stories would be subjected to what they called a "hidden censorship" and finally would start on their way.

Atherton and I went to the building that housed the censors. It was five or six o'clock in the afternoon. Flunkies just shook their heads when we said we had some stories we wanted censored. The censors had gone. Come back tomorrow. The censors worked several hours each morning and several hours each afternoon. No dispatches could be sent at any other time. Most government offices here in Cairo worked on the same sort of a schedule. Four or five hours' work a day. War mustn't interfere with leading a normal life.

We asked where the censors might be found. We were going to track them down, even if it was contrary to custom. We had stories to send. We'd been through almost a month of hell trying to get somewhere where we could file those stories. Now, by God, we weren't going to be stymied by anything like this.

The flunky suggested the cricket grounds at Mena House. Mena House was out in the suburbs. Across the Nile. Out near the pyramids. The censors might be there playing cricket or swimming in the pool or just having cocktails. The naval censor, the flunky said, was probably at the Grezira Club. You know, THE club. The place where officers sit around drinking tall glasses of whisky and soda and chatting about things far removed from the horrors of modern war.

I had often heard the British expression about something not being cricket. I understood what cricket wasn't. But I had never had any firsthand knowledge of what cricket was. We took a taxi to Mena House. A lot of ultra-respectable British officers were out there playing cricket all right. It looked like a very dull game. Finally at one point things seemed to be getting just a bit exciting. A player had hit a ball with a strange bat that looked like a beaver's tail. He was running to a base, just as you do in baseball. Except that he was running in a very dignified manner, quite leisurely. But just then a whistle blew. I thought maybe someone had committed a foul. A man in white walked out onto the field. The umpire? No, it was a flunky, and he announced in stentorian tones:

"Gentlemen, tea is served."

And so the game was called off for a while, and the exhausted players had tea. That gave us a chance to inquire for the censor we were looking for. But he wasn't there.

Late that evening we finally did get enough stamps on our dispatches to give some hope that they might eventually get tapped out over the cable lines. But we were completely worn out by that time. We had had to chase censors all over Cairo. We found one of them in an elaborate apartment surrounded by all the luxuries of modern civilization plus a corps of bowing, scraping men servants. We found the naval censor living over again some old campaigns in the East with his cronies at the Grezira Club. We avoided the necessity of an R.A.F. stamp on each page by scrupulously scratching out every reference in our stories to airplanes—or lack of airplanes.

Atherton and I had both decided to work backwards in trying to tell what had happened during the last month. These first dispatches were simply about the completion of the evacuation from Greece and Crete. I had written that the Greek evacuation had not been another Dunkirk. No, there was no comparison between Dunkirk and Argos Bay, because Argos Bay had been so much worse. Then I had gone on to tell why. I had listed the losses. Naturally I had not included any specific information like the names of ships. I knew no censor would allow that. But I had told some of the stories I have already told you.

When my dispatch was finally approved by all the censors and was ready for the telegraph operator it stated that the Greek evacuation had not been another Dunkirk.

The sentences that followed had been eliminated. The impression that remained was that it was not another Dunkirk because it was much less of a debacle than Dunkirk. Just the opposite of what I had been trying to write.

Naturally we argued. The censor pointed out that London had just announced a total loss of three thousand men in Greece. Three thousand men killed, wounded, and captured in the land battles and drowned in the evacuation. Our twenty thousand figure was ridiculous. Three thousand it was. We argued. We showed the censor our list of ship losses. We cited the *Diamond-Wryneck* incident. One incident in which we knew nearly five thousand men had been lost at sea. We were told that we couldn't mention the incident, even without the names of the ships. (Days later the British Admiralty did finally announce the loss of the *Diamond* and *Wryneck,* but the story of what happened and the number of casualties was of course not mentioned.)

Both of us were too weary to argue for long. And it wouldn't have done any good anyway. We knew that. We were lucky to be able to send anything over our signatures. And so we filed our stories. Stories that said just the opposite of what we had originally written. Argos Bay was not another Dunkirk.

Then we went back to the Continental and pulled off our filthy clothes. It may sound foolish, but I hated to shed them. As long as I had on those grimy trousers with their caked blood, those Serbian socks, and the dirty shirt open at the neck I felt as if I belonged. As if I were one of millions of people who were going through part of the war. Reality. As if I were close to reality. As if I knew what it all meant. But then we took off those refugee clothes and had a bath. The water was hot. It was the first hot water we'd had since the night before Belgrade was bombed. The soap had a sweet, luxurious scent. The hot soapsuds felt good on tired muscles. Fresh underwear felt good too. And then we got into some new clothes that a porter bought at a shop for us. Now we were gentlemen again. Respectable. Clean. Presentable. But we both felt strangely out of touch with reality. Now we were part of Cairo. Part of this city of unreality. Now we could drink a delicate cocktail in the Continental lounge and no one would look twice at us. Now we belonged to the land of make-believe. This land where they were still trying to fight a war in the Kipling tradition.

The beds at the Continental were tremendous and the mattresses were deep. The sheets were clean and crisp. There was an electric fan over each bed. But we couldn't sleep that night in Cairo, nor any other night. Noises of war beat through our brains. All night long Stukas dived down at our heads. Little girls with shredded arms kept whimpering. Men with their guts sticking out screamed for aspirin tablets. The smells of war kept us from sleeping too. Especially the smell of cooking human flesh.

The next day a lot of things happened.

We heard that the young R.A.F. officer who had driven us from Patras part of the way to Corinth had been killed. Atherton and I remembered so vividly how he had dodged around bumps so as not to jostle Leigh White. And how we shook hands with him and said we hoped he'd get along all right. And how he had just answered "What the hell?" and shrugged his shoulders and gone tearing down the road toward Patras—and death. It hadn't been a very pleasant death. They told us that a machine-gun bullet from a plane, probably that same plane that had been following us, struck the gas tank of the lorry. The tank exploded. The young R.A.F. boy was cremated.

That afternoon Atherton and I got to work on the story of our trip down through Greece. When we came to the part about the ride in the improvised R.A.F. ambulance we told what really happened to the driver. The censor wrinkled his forehead and changed the wording of the sentence. And so the story that went to the Associated Press that day said the driver had been shot, not burned to death. I was curious about the change and asked why it was made. The censor explained patiently, as you would to a child, that we must lean backwards in trying not to make war seem horrible. Death by bullet wounds is all right. Death by cremation is not very pleasant to think about. Not very pleasant for the people back home. And for people in America. We mustn't make war seem horrible, that's all.

I wrote a rather graphic description of that day of hell in Argos. The censor did a lot of slashing when he came to that part of the story. Then we had a real knock-down argument. I tried to make my case very logical. First, all the suffering I was trying to write about was the result, principally, of the inability of the R.A.F. to drive off the Nazi dive bombers. Second, that was due to too few British planes. Third, the only place to get more planes was from the United States. Fourth, people in the United States were still buying automobiles by the hundreds of thousands. Fifth, if the American people were aware of the death and suffering going on in Europe because of the lack of British planes and if the story of what was happening could be brought home vividly enough to them, they might stop buying automobiles and let airplanes be made instead. Sixth, my story of Argos gave a grim picture of that death and suffering, and therefore the British should pin medals on it as a piece of powerful propaganda, which might get them more airplanes so that it wouldn't happen again.

When I got all finished, the censor slapped me on the back. Yes, he said, I had the idea exactly. More planes from America were just what they did want, and they realized that horror stories were one way to get them, but . . . And the censor's face dropped a mile. Modern methods of communication complicated the problem. Horror stories were all right for America, but England and the rest of the Empire must not be told how bad things were. The Empire must be told that everything was in fine shape. Horror stories for America. Back-stiffening for the Empire. But the Empire listened to the radio, and it was impossible to keep the stories for America and the stories for the Empire nicely pigeonholed. Modern communications were responsible. And so the policy was neither fish nor fowl. Neither the one extreme nor the other. Just some safe middle ground. And that was the reason, he said, that the Argos story could not be told. Not completely and truthfully, as I wanted to tell it. Sorry, but that's the policy.

That same day we met some members of the Yugoslav General Staff. They had escaped by plane with members of the Simovich government. I had two questions I wanted to ask them, now that they could take down their hair and be natural. First, why hadn't that steep mountain pass into Skoplje been dynamited to stop the Nazis from pouring across the southern tip of Yugoslavia and cutting off all contact between the Serbs and their Greek and British allies? The answer was simplicity itself. Naïve simplicity.

There wasn't a bit of dynamite within a hundred miles of that pass when the moment came to blast it, one of the Yugoslav officers told us.

We asked if he thought that that lack of preparation had been intentional fifth-column work. He just shrugged his shoulders.

The other question was whether the Serbs had set off all those elaborately wired bombs in the big airplane factory at Kraljevo before the Germans got there. We recalled so vividly how an official had said, "All we have to do is to light one match. Just as soon as we get the order. We wait for the order. Then we light the fuse. Then good-by factory. The joke will be on Hitler. He will never make airplanes in Kraljevo."

The officer shook his head sadly. He was sorry to say that planes probably were being made today for the Luftwaffe in that factory at Kraljevo, because the order to light the fuse had never been given. Why? He didn't know. Could it have been because there were traitors in high places within the Yugoslav High Command? The officer said "No," very indignantly. But still he couldn't explain why that order had never been given. Why Hitler now had intact one of the largest airplane factories in that part of the world.

We ran into Russell Hill that same day. He explained everything. When he got to Canea he had met some British war correspondents and had spent the night with them. Early the next morning they had all gone to Suda Bay and hopped a ship that later caught up with the *Delane* and got to Alexandria about the same time we did.

That afternoon Atherton and I both went to the Anglo-American Hospital and got some pictures taken of our legs. The X rays showed that we both had jagged pieces of steel buried deep against nerves and bone. But the surgeon suggested we let well enough alone and not have them removed for the moment.

Later in the day I said a reluctant good-by to Atherton. He was off to Palestine on a new assignment. Before he left he had a jeweler scratch the word *Makedonka* on a silver cigarette lighter.

"I know you won't ever forget the *Makedonka,*" he said when he gave it to me, "but whenever you look at this gadget remember that life isn't all Continental hotels and clean sheets."

Jimmy Roosevelt and an American captain of marines dropped in on Cairo that same day. They were like a breath of fresh air. They were the first Americans we had seen in a long time, except for our own kind: diplomats and newspapermen who had been out of touch with our own country for so long.

We all interviewed them and they told us how they had just landed by plane from Iraq. Only the censor wouldn't let us say they had come by plane.

"Well," Jimmy said with his boyish laugh, "just say we came thousands of miles in six hours and let your readers guess how we did it."

In the bar of Shepheard's that afternoon a young private, quite contrary to rules, sat talking to some Americans. He was a Russian prince, well known in New York, Paris, London, and all the other capitals of the world. He had joined up with the British and had been fighting out on the western desert. Now he was on a short furlough and he was telling about some of his desert experiences in a quiet voice over a glass of whisky.

An Old School Tie major at the next table suddenly wheeled around and called the soldier's attention to a sign on the wall forbidding the discussion of military matters in public.

The prince, with all his regal suavity, replied that he was not discussing unit numbers, places, time, or anything else of a military nature.

"After all," he said, "the only pleasure we soldiers get when we come in on furlough is talking about our experiences."

But a few minutes later the major turned around again and called him to task. The prince, still calm, replied: "Major, it's none of my business and I don't want to seem impertinent, but would you mind telling me how long you've been here in Cairo?"

The major hemmed and spluttered a few seconds, then blurted out: "Eighteen months. Why do you ask?"

The prince just nodded his head and said, "I thought so. That's just about since the war began, isn't it?"

The major suddenly got the point, jumped to his feet, and bellowed: "I have half a mind to have you court-martialed for insubordination."

The prince rose slowly, with great dignity.

"Major, that's all right with me. Because if I'm court-martialed and you, a major, testify against me, a private, I will of course be found guilty. But my offense is not too serious. I wouldn't be executed. They'd probably just put me in prison. Then, don't you see, Major, my chances of being killed in this war would be just about even with yours."

The major whipped out a pen and a notebook.

"I demand your name and unit number, young man!"

The prince bowed low.

"I'm sorry, Major. You have just been cautioning me against mentioning unit numbers and names and other definite military matters in public, and so you must excuse me."

Then he walked slowly to the door, dashed out and around a corner, and was gone before the major could catch his breath.

That same day I got a cable congratulating me on the "fine story you sent last week about the bombing of Belgrade." It was the first dispatch received from any of the English or American correspondents in Yugoslavia. BBC and the American radio stations had used it on the air all day. American newspapers had given it a big front-page play.

Well, there was a real mystery. I still hadn't written a line about the bombing of Belgrade. And last week I had been riding a Greek food ship, a Greek troop train, and a British destroyer, trying to get somewhere to send a story just like that. But I hadn't yet sent it. Still, you don't cable your paper and ask them to retract a message of congratulation. You just wait. The truth always comes out somehow.

I didn't have to wait long, because that same afternoon Henry Stokes, the little Australian newspaperman who worked for Reuter's, handed me a note written on sheets of toilet paper. It was from Dave Walker. Dave had gone to Cattaro, as he had planned to do. The destroyer they expected had never arrived. But the British navy did send two Sunderland flying boats for the little army of refugees huddled on the shores of Cattaro Bay. Two Sunderland flying boats capable of snatching from the clutches of Axis invaders about forty of those hundred and fifty men and women waiting on the shores of Cattaro for deliverance. Forty could be saved. The other hundred or more? Their fate would be dubious, to say the least. They would have to stay behind and be captured. Someone had to draw up a list of who should be saved and who should remain behind. High credit to that little band of Englishmen. The forty selected to go were all Czechs, Rumanians, Hungarians, Austrians, Serbs, Greeks, and people of other nationalities who had been risking their lives to help the British and who now faced execution if they were caught. In one of the flying boats there wasn't a single Englishman. In the other, just one. A man who had been seriously wounded in the bombing of Belgrade.

Walker's note said, "They showed all of us the list, but there wasn't a single protest from anyone who was being left behind."

Then the note explained the mystery of the story I had never written. Dave, up there in Cattaro, had pounded out a dispatch for Reuter's and another one for the London *Mirror*. Then, remembering his parting remark in Cetinje that whoever got out first should file a story for the other fellow, he had written a short dispatch addressed to the AP and signed it with my name. He gave all three of them to one of the Sunderland passengers with instructions to file them with the cable office in Athens.

It was Dave Walker, not I, who should have received that cable of congratulations. But poor Dave had had a tough break.

Apparently my story had gotten to New York and then over to London before his dispatches.

Dave's letter wound up like this:

"We haven't any chance, now, of getting out. The morale is good, although we're due to meet the Boche tomorrow and a lot of us will probably be led to a brick wall right away. The situation here is so unreal we can't believe it. Campbell [the British Minister] is here, but our Legation says there is no hope. They are out of touch with any Serbian government. Good luck to you and give my best to all our friends. Things are not so bright here, but you can say that the British Colony went down laughing coarsely, and none so coarsely as those who knew they were going to get the works. We had pretty good innings and a lot of better people than us have had to go before. So what the hell! Good-by and good luck."

That night a party was held in the shadow of the pyramids. The yellow light of the moon was reflected in the slow-moving waters of the Nile. It was a hot evening, but the glasses were full of ice and everyone wore crisp cool clothes. It was a party of thanksgiving. A gathering of dozens of refugees who had escaped capture up in the Balkans. There were a lot of people we knew at the party, but there were a lot of people missing.

We raised our glasses and drank toasts to luck and to British courage and to many other things. But it was a hollow party. The laughter was false. The hilarity was artificial. All of us were playing make-believe. All of us had too much in our minds to be happy and carefree.

Occasionally there would be one of those dead silences. Then someone, trying to make casual conversation, would ask: "I wonder what happened to So-and-so?" No one would answer. Everyone's thoughts would jump back. Back to Yugoslavia or Greece. Back to the last place anyone had seen So-and-so.

There were wives at that party whose husbands were back there. Wives who would hope and pray and try to be lighthearted but who might never see their husbands again. There

were a few children who might never see the parents who had
sent them on ahead to safety.

The party was not much of a success. And no one ever tried
to hold another one like it. You can't rejoice over your own luck
when you think of the others. You can't do any celebrating when
you have a letter in your pocket from your best friend that says:
"We're due to meet the Boche tomorrow and a lot of us will
probably be led to a brick wall right away."

So I went home early from the party on the banks of the Nile.
I went home and lay in an overstuffed bed thinking of Dave
Walker, who by now might have been liquidated. Of Sonia, who
must have stood on the dock at Cattaro watching those Sunderlands taking away people she knew and leaving behind so many
others who would have to take their chances with the Axis invaders when they arrived in a few hours. Of Paul Vadja, who
they now said had been captured by the Germans when the
Germans entered Skoplje. Of Pappas, the Greek, who for some
reason hadn't been given a place on either of the Sunderlands.
Of Edwards and Aroeti and Duka and the Polish playwright
with the letter from Mrs. Roosevelt, and all those other people
whose escape was cut off and who today might be in concentration camps, if they were lucky.

Frank Gervasi, of *Collier's,* saved me from going stark mad
that evening. He came in for a nightcap. When I told him why
I couldn't sleep, he said, "Let's go up on the Continental roof
garden and watch them having fun."

The roof garden was packed. Lovely women in organdy and
men in cool cotton uniforms. A jazz band playing tunes they
were also playing on roof gardens back in New York.

Dave Walker was probably dead at Cattaro. But men and
women were dancing lightheartedly on top of the Continental
under a hot Egyptian sky.

British soldiers were dying tonight out on the western desert,
their lungs full of burning red sand. But on the roof of the Continental you could forget death if you drank enough and watched
Hashmet Fatima, the Egyptian belly dancer, contorting her

lovely body up on the stage for the applause of well-fed officers who had wedged themselves into every corner of the open-air night club.

Yes, if they got their hands on Dave Walker, of course they'd shoot him.

But have another Scotch and soda. Drown out thought. There's no sense thinking. You'll go mad.

So we got drunk that night instead of going mad.

CHAPTER SEVENTEEN

Reunion with Eda

———◆———

One of the first things I did when I arrived in Cairo was to cable Eda in Istanbul to start packing. She had spent some miserable weeks in that city on the Bosporus, not knowing what had happened to the missing American correspondents. Somehow a story had gotten to Istanbul and to New York that we had set sail on the *Makedonka* and then had vanished. The implication was that we had been lost at sea. Eda knew what kind of a sailor I was, and she knew all about that swimming medal, and so she had every reason to believe the implication.

When I managed to get an Imperial Airways flying boat to agree to take us the five thousand miles down through Africa on the way home, I cabled Eda again that she had just four days to get to Cairo. She had some wild adventures of her own getting down through Anatolia, Syria, and Palestine in that record-breaking time. She had to travel by a lot of strange methods of transportation. But that's her story. Now we were together again at last. A happy reunion. Eda had made it with just a few hours to spare. She arrived in Cairo late one night. The flying boat would leave early the next morning. We spent the intervening

344

hours in strange fashion. I had lost everything but a few foolish articles in a knapsack. But Eda had a truckload of trunks and suitcases. Imperial Airways was charging a dollar and a half a pound excess baggage. We had hundreds of pounds over the maximum limit. So we dumped everything in the center of that big room Atherton and I had shared and we spent the night sitting there weighing each article by hand, by guess, to determine whether to take it with us. Like the *World Almanac* I had lugged everywhere. Eda handed it to me.

"What's your guess?"

"Two pounds."

"That means three dollars."

"It'll only cost sixty cents to buy a new one in New York."

"Then throw it into the discard."

When we got through playing that game we had a mountain of discards, but still enough excess baggage to wreck a newspaperman's bank account.

On our way south from Cairo the plane stopped at Khartoum, Kisumu, Moçambique, Lourenço Marques, and Durban. Then we went by rail to Johannesburg and finally Cape Town, South Africa.

An elderly English lady with an extremely sad, quavering voice telephoned the hotel the first day we were in Cape Town to ask if I could tell her what had happened to her sister in Belgrade. Didn't I know whether she was killed? I tried to explain that there were three hundred thousand people in Belgrade that bombing day and that I was practically a stranger in the city. But still she asked, "Please can't you try to remember? Can't you tell me something?"

The next day she telephoned again. "I forgot to tell you. My sister is English, like myself. Her husband was a retired Serbian government official. Now can't you remember? Can't you tell me, please, was she killed?"

And the day after that. "I forgot to tell you. They lived out in the Dedinje section. That ought to help you remember what happened to my sister. Now can't you tell me, was she killed?"

Every day that we stayed in Cape Town waiting for a ship to America, the almost hysterical old lady telephoned the hotel. "Please, try to remember! Please tell me what happened to my sister in Belgrade!"

It was going to be like that now wherever I went. Hundreds of people, distressed, heartsick people, wanting to know about friends and relatives over in that land of silent people. Of course they knew that Belgrade was a large city, and that there were millions of people in Yugoslavia and Greece. But you couldn't blame them for their hunger for news about friends and relatives. They hoped so much that by some slim chance we could tell them, yes, she's safe. She didn't get killed. I know she's well and that life isn't too bad for her now.

That's what I finally did tell the old lady in Cape Town. I told her I had just placed her sister. Just remembered who she was. Yes, she was safe all right.

I lied that way because I knew the agony the poor old lady was going through. She'd die, probably, before she ever found out the truth. It might be a long, long time before anyone knew what had happened to people trapped in Yugoslavia and Greece.

The day we arrived in Cape Town the local papers carried a story about several hundred natives being killed. The way the story read, it appeared that they had all suddenly dropped dead in their tracks. No cause. No explanation. When I met some of the local newspapermen I asked them what it all meant. They laughed and blamed it onto censorship. The rule was that you couldn't ever mention the weather. Not yesterday's weather, nor today's weather, nor even the forecast about tomorrow's weather. Weather is information valuable to the enemy. The natives had been drowned in a flood, but a flood is weather, and weather is information valuable to the enemy.

Yet every afternoon a certain radio station in Germany put on a special news broadcast on a beam directed to Cape Town. In that broadcast they announced the names of the British warships that had arrived in Table Bay, Cape Town, during the past twenty-four hours, where they had come from, how long they would remain in Table Bay, how many men were aboard each ship, the identifying numbers of their units, and their ultimate destination.

It was no secret how this information got from Cape Town to Berlin. The German consul in the neutral Portuguese town of Lourenço Marques, which borders on the Union of South Africa, ran up a telegraph bill of about five thousand dollars a month, they said. And he had only a handful of German nationals to look after. He wasn't spending five thousand dollars a month telegraphing about the weather or the state of health of his few German charges.

The British newspapermen in South Africa asked the same question that British newspapermen everywhere asked: "When will we base our censorship and all our other war policies on the assumption that our enemy isn't completely dumb? Why can't we be realistic?"

The day we hit Cape Town a cannon suddenly went off at noon, right in the heart of the city. After weeks of bombing and machine-gunning, that noise sent me instinctively running for shelter. People around me started shouting. I didn't realize they were shouting at me. I didn't notice at first that no one else was running. No one was even moving. The whole city seemed to have been suddenly turned to stone, as if some mysterious death ray had paralyzed all life. Through the window of a millinery shop I could see a girl who had been about to try a hat on a young woman. Now she stood with the hat in her hand, just a few inches above the woman's head, as motionless as a statue. Through a restaurant window I could see waiters who had been rustling bowls of soup to hungry British sailors. Now they were frozen in their tracks, still holding the bowls of soup in their upturned hands. All traffic had stopped. I stopped too.

After the people finished shouting at me there wasn't a sound anywhere. If someone on a boat out in the harbor had coughed, I'm sure we could have heard it in the center of the city, it was that quiet. But finally a bugle sounded off in the distance and life quickly became normal again.

Cynics in Cape Town said they had those two minutes of silence, announced by the booming of a cannon every noon, to remind the people in this British colony that there was a war going on somewhere. Actually it was a revival of the old two minutes of silence to commemorate the armistice, an idea that had had its birth in Cape Town. Today people are supposed to spend the two minutes praying for victory.

But the Union of South Africa is a divided Union. We soon found that out. Afrikanders, people of Dutch descent, make up about half the white population. And most of them are anti-British. They plot secretly about overthrowing what they call their British masters, and few of them join the volunteer army. But so far their policy had been largely one of passive resistance. Except that the Ossewabrandwag has caused a little internal bloodshed. We found out as soon as we hit the Union of South Africa what the Ossewabrandwag was. The word means ox-cart wheels, something typically Dutch or Afrikander. The organization boasts of three hundred thousand members. The more daring wear beards to advertise their opposition. Beards are also considered typically Afrikander. The beard I had worn for two years in Europe, which had been such a journalistic asset because I was so often mistaken for a diplomat instead of just a newspaperman, became in South Africa the mark of a traitor. Ossewabrandwag members sneaked up to me on the street and started discussing rebel secrets in a whisper. The pro-British shunned me or arrested me. Pro-British taxi drivers refused to haul me. Pro-British sales people refused to serve me. The reason so many people had shouted at me during that two minutes of silence, when I started to duck for shelter, was because Ossewabrandwag members often went on about their business during the brief period of prayer. Naturally, they assumed from my beard and my failure to halt that I was a rebel, too.

In Johannesburg I had to hide in my hotel room the one night we spent there because the Ossewabrandwag and the pro-British people had just gone through days of fatal rioting, all started by a man with a beard not unlike my own. Feeling, the local newspapermen warned me, was still running too high for an innocent man with a beard to walk the streets at night.

While we waited in Cape Town for a ship, wave after wave of refugees from Europe, from Palestine, from Syria, from all over that part of the world poured down there to the tip of Africa. The wife of General Simovich, the head of the Yugoslav state for such a short time, was one of them. She got quick passage to America, but hundreds of others are probably still in Cape Town waiting, for the waves kept coming, and only a dribble got out at a time. Ships go around the Cape loaded with war materials for America. Tin, rubber, and coconut oil. There isn't much room for passengers. Even Americans must wait for months. We were lucky. We had to wait only a few weeks.

CHAPTER EIGHTEEN

They'll Never Know

———————◆◆◆◆————————

NEW YORK.

A siren screams in Fifth Avenue. Probably it's only on an ambulance going to an automobile accident. But it screams just like those sirens back in the Balkans. Those sirens that announced the approach of death.

A plane roars over the Roosevelt Hotel. Probably it's only a mail plane off for Chicago. But it roars just like those Nazi planes roared over Belgrade.

A flower garden in Westchester. We sit playing with tall glasses of something cold. Women in crisp, lovely dresses talk about what happened last night at the country club dance. But the smell of flowers makes me think of Corfu, where lilacs were in bloom and olive trees were in full leaf that April day when Nazi planes rained hell down on Corfu.

New York is ablaze with lights. The lights of electric signs, and the lights of office buildings, homes, and automobiles. But back in the land of silent people millions live in perpetual darkness. Literally and figuratively.

Child's Restaurant on Madison Avenue at noon. Crowds of people, who never have known and probably never will know what hunger really is, sit around tables trying to decide whether to spend twenty-eight cents for corned beef and potatoes and rolls or twenty-nine cents for ham and eggs and rolls.

Rockefeller Plaza. Hundreds of men and women shove and push each other to get a place where they can stand for half an hour watching ten trained seals flop around the sunken pool of a swanky restaurant.

The subway at rush hour. They're all reading newspapers announcing that five million men have been killed on the eastern front. They're impressed with figures like that. Five million! It really does sound like a war, doesn't it? It must be terrible! But how about those little items at the bottom of a column that few people even bother to read? Corfu had a slight air raid today. There were a few casualties. Minor damage was done to residential buildings. No targets of military importance were hit.

They'll never know, these people who seem to me so unaware, what human tragedy is buried between the lines of those insignificant little items they don't even bother to read.

A crowd around the window of a smart shop in the Forties, reading a startling announcement:

WARNING

If you don't feed your puppy
DOGGIE WOOFIES
our special new vitamin biscuit
his hair won't be shiny and his
diet won't be balanced
HE MAY EVEN DIE

Yes, these are grave days for America, and who said America isn't conscious of it?

A lecture platform. The chairman has just one word of advice. Please remember that you're speaking after the dinner hour. Make your remarks pleasant. Don't make war seem too terrible. We don't want to disturb their digestions, you know.

Ah no! America's digestion must not be disturbed. Of course war must not be made to seem terrible.

A literary friend says, "Don't try to write a book until you've been back for a few months. You must get the feeling of America. Go to the country for a while and try to forget all you've been through. Then you can come back and write calmly, with perspective."

L'Envoi

I DIDN'T make pleasant remarks in that lecture.

I didn't go to the country to try to forget.

Maybe I don't have perspective.

But I have told you now all that I saw and heard and smelled, and just a bit of what I thought, during a few weeks of war. I have made it as honest and accurate as I could.

If there are conclusions to be drawn, you draw them. I have tried to be just a reporter.

Venice
YUGOSLAVI
Genoa
Sarajevo
Ilidže
Budva
ITALY
CORSICA
Rome
Bari
Naples
SARDINIA
AL
CORFU
Patra
SICILY
Tunis
TUNIS
MALTA
MEDITER
N
Tripoli
ITALIAN LIBYA